CONTENTS

KU-202-680

ACKNOWLEDGEMENTS

Suzanne and Tracey would like to thank Sandy, Heather, Pete and Maggie at PCCS Books for all their help in making this book happen. Particular thanks also go to Dorothea Kast, whose keen editorial skills and availability were invaluable in this process.

Suzanne wants to thank: Conal for his support and patience through the difficult times, Finbar for being himself, Tracey for being a continuous source of creative energy and life and all the contributors for their passion and commitment.

Tracey wants to personally acknowledge: Martyn, my husband and friend, who is always behind the scenes supporting and encouraging me, and my two incredible children, Jenny and Peter. Joanna for her congruence and sisterhood. My colleagues and friends at PCCS Training Partnership, Frances, Josie, Judith, Violet and Jean, all of whom have added their own idiosyncratic contribution to enable PCCS Training to have existed and held a place in the training community. To the staff at the Buzz, Rose, Tam, Pearl, Anita, Phil, Lascel, John, Lisa and Gary. Suzanne, my co-editor without whose personhood, integrity and wisdom this book would not exist and who, throughout this process, has just been a star. We seem to have managed through the collaborative experience of editing, endless discussions, phone calls and creative licence to have enhanced and strengthened our friendship. Finally to all who have contributed, supported and encouraged this process; it has indeed enriched my learning and life.

PREFACE

A few years ago we both realised how many person-centred therapists there are who, like ourselves, work with children and young people. We also realised how little we hear about their work. When we do get together, for the rare professional development opportunities focused on this work, it is clear that there is a wealth of diverse and innovative practice happening across the UK. This is how the seeds for this book were sown: a book by practitioners for practitioners. We invited some people whose practice we were familiar with to contribute chapters about their work. We then met as a group to discuss emerging themes and out of that came our foreword from Ashley on the politics of adulthood. We were very excited when Richard and Sue agreed to write a second foreword on the state of childhood today. Both forewords help not only to put the work that we do in context but more importantly to emphasise its inherently political nature.

Our motivation to publish this collection of chapters is not only to hear from workers at the coal face, and as editors we wanted to hear their voices in as unadulterated a form as possible, but also to highlight the political significance of listening to children and young people from a person-centred perspective. This work is not focused on tasks, equipment or exercises, but on relationship. The potency of listening to those who are rarely heard without judgements or assumptions cannot be underestimated.

Love, respect and time for listening to children and young people are what all contributors have in common. They do this in a multiplicity of settings including primary education (Cate, Tracey, Jo), secondary education (Nadine, Sue), further education (Suzanne), a pupil referral unit (Tracey), voluntary agencies (Lisa, Gill), adoption (Cate), hospital (Sheila), hospice (Seamus), community (Julie) and the streets (Ashley). Some focus on specific areas: Lisa on working with lesbian, gay and bisexual (LGB) young people, Seamus on loss and bereavement, Gill on self-harm and child protection, Nadine on emotional literacy in a school and Ashley on work on the streets with rent boys. Some write about using different expressive media: Nadine about psychodrama, Jo about sandplay and Cate and Tracey about play therapy training and practice. Gill and Sue have written in-depth accounts of one particular relationship and Sheila and Sue write as person-centred psychologists.

All contributors give examples of their work with particular children and young people. They all share something of how they embody person-centred theory in their work, often beyond working in a counselling room. They are all imbued with person-centred qualities, values and principles including respect, acceptance, empathy, patience, love, commitment, care, attention, humility, courage, sensitivity, awareness and self-questioning. All describe how much they have learnt from working with children and young people.

The most striking theme to emerge from all the chapters has been how vital it is to be aware of the systems that children and young people live within and to work with these both explicitly and implicitly. This is the interface where some of the most creative practice emerges. The difficulty in working with children is in knowing how to find creative fissures to get through not only the social structural systems but also the increasing rigidity in the professionalisation process. It is an edge where practitioners are at their most vulnerable and exposed, working often as lone counsellors, negotiating the grey areas of child protection, being empathic to the different systems they and their young clients are part of and knowing that most children have no power to change much about their environments. Translating theory into ethical practice in these situations often demands skills and ingenuity in the moment as well as a trusting and challenging supervisory relationships and kinship with other practitioners.

One of the most common questions from trainees on person-centred child therapy training is 'How do we do it?' followed by 'Can we do this and still be person-centred?' This collection of chapters offers a range of idiosyncratic responses to those questions with a clear message that not only do we wholeheartedly believe that this is person-centred practice but that it is person-centred practice at its cutting-edge best which deserves to be known about more widely and to be honoured. We are very glad to have brought together these chapters focused on practice and are delighted that PCCS are publishing a sister volume on person-centred working with children and young people from a more theoretical perspective and from across the world.

Suzanne Keys and Tracey Walshaw
London and Manchester
February 2008

THE PHENOMENON OF 'TOXIC CHILDHOOD' FROM A PERSON-CENTRED PERSPECTIVE

RICHARD HOUSE AND SUE PALMER

I want to talk about learning. But not the lifeless, sterile, futile, quickly forgotten stuff that is crammed in to the mind of the poor helpless individual tied into his seat by ironclad bonds of conformity!

Carl Rogers

It is a privilege to write a foreword for this important new book on how a person-centred approach, as inspired by the work of educationalist and psychologist Carl Rogers, might help counter the 'unintended side effects' of modern technological culture on children's well-being.

We write from diverse perspectives—Sue Palmer as a writer, former primary head teacher and independent literary consultant, and Richard House as a counsellor-psychotherapist, writer and Steiner Waldorf early years teacher—but also from what we share together, which is a campaigning zeal for children and their suffering in 'modernity'.

These concerns led us to compose and seek widespread authoritative endorsement for two open letters to the national press on the parlous state of modern childhood,[1] both of which were signed by hundreds of professionals and academics. The letters highlighted the many challenges and vicissitudes of being a child in a world transformed by several decades of rapid social, cultural and technological change. In galvanising and focusing 'like minds' across a wide range of professional and academic fields, they have been part of a discernible sea change in the British policy-making agenda. Children's well-being is, thank goodness, becoming a topic of increasing concern in political circles.

The first letter, published in the *Daily Telegraph* on 12th September 2006, drew attention to the increasing incidence of children's mental health problems, and propelled the terms 'toxic childhood' and 'junk culture' into the public realm. It precipitated a media 'firestorm' which quickly spread like wildfire across the globe. We were so heartened by this response that one year later we decided to repeat the exercise, this time with a slightly more focused theme—the way children's play has become seriously compromised in the modern world.

For us, this lack of respect for children's play is a particularly serious issue: 'real play'

---

1. See <http://www.telegraph.co.uk/news/main.jhtml?xml=/news/2006/09/12/njunk112.xml>; and <http://www.telegraph.co.uk/opinion/main.jhtml?xml=/opinion/2007/09/10/nosplit/dt1001.xml#head8>.

is social and intrinsically relational. It is also first-hand and loosely supervised. Such play has always been a vital part of children's development, and its rapid erosion is likely to have serious implications, not only for children but for our collective future more generally. We were again overwhelmed by the extraordinary reponse to this new open letter, signed as it was by close to 300 prominent professionals and academics from around the world. The concerns about play are clearly ones that cut across child-related professions and academic disciplines and which find resonances and responses throughout this book.

Richard's training as a counsellor and psychotherapist has had a strong Rogerian, person-centred input, so when we were asked to contribute a forewording chapter to this book, it seemed to us that there were strong links to be made between many of the concerns expressed in our two open letters and the kinds of arguments about student-centred learning that are at the core of Carl Rogers' seminal text *Freedom to Learn* (1969), and the so-called 'core conditions' of person-centred counselling. Most particularly, there is a pressing need for adults concerned with children's development to concentrate on unconditional positive regard (or *love*, broadly defined), empathy (or the mature capacity for attunement to the needs of the other), and congruence (sometimes termed 'authenticity' by such authoritive philosophers as Martin Heidegger and Lionel Trilling).

Rogers' *Freedom to Learn* also advocates the need for learners to experience proactivity in, and some volition over, their own learning, as is the case in authentic, unintruded-upon play. Rogers believed that learners should be trusted to develop their own potential, and supported to choose both the way and direction of their own learning. *Learning-centred* assumptions (as we might call them) suggest that learners should have meaningful control over what and how things are learned, which includes how learning outcomes are measured. We can call this approach 'student-centred' or 'learner-centred', or even more appropriately, *learning-centred learning*.

This important new book written by person-centred psychotherapists and psychologists working in a range of settings draws out many of the insights that Carl Rogers brought to education, learning and counselling, and thus has central relevance in addressing the many damaging effects of 'toxic childhood' that concern us, and which Sue has written about at length (Palmer, 2006, 2007).

Below we present those parts of our two open letters that we see as being especially relevant to person-centred praxis, demonstrating how Rogers' and related thinking urgently needs to be factored into culture-wide action to 'detoxify' modern childhood.

MODERN LIFE LEADS TO MORE DEPRESSION AMONG CHILDREN
Daily Telegraph, 12/09/2006

... we are deeply concerned at the escalating incidence of childhood depression and children's behavioural and developmental conditions. We believe this is largely due to a lack of understanding, on the part of both politicians and the general public, of the realities and subtleties of child development.

... [Children] ... need what developing human beings have always needed, including ... real play (as opposed to sedentary, screen-based entertainment), first-hand experience of the world they live in and regular interaction with the real-life significant adults in their lives.

They also need time. In a fast-moving hyper-competitive culture, today's children are expected to cope with an ever-earlier start to formal schoolwork and an overly academic test-driven primary curriculum. ...

Our society ... seems to have lost sight of [children's] emotional and social needs. ... [T]he mental health of an unacceptable number of children is being unnecessarily compromised, and this is almost certainly a key factor in the rise of substance abuse, violence and self-harm amongst our young people.

This is a complex socio-cultural problem to which there is no simple solution, but a sensible first step would be to encourage parents and policy-makers to start talking about ways of improving children's well-being ... .

LET OUR CHILDREN PLAY
Daily Telegraph, 10/9/2007

Since last September, when a group of professionals, academics and writers wrote to the *Daily Telegraph* expressing concern about the marked deterioration in children's mental health, research evidence supporting this case has continued to mount ... We believe that a key factor in this disturbing trend is the marked decline over the last 15 years in children's play. Play—particularly outdoor, unstructured, loosely supervised play—appears to be vital to children's all-round health and well-being.

It ... provides opportunities for the first-hand experiences that underpin their understanding of and engagement with the world; facilitates social development (making and keeping friends, dealing with problems, working collaboratively); and cultivates creativity, imagination and emotional resilience. This includes the growth of self-reliance, independence and personal strategies for dealing with and integrating challenging or traumatic experiences.

Many features of modern life seem to have eroded children's play. They include ... the aggressive marketing of over-elaborate, commercialised toys (which seem to inhibit rather than stimulate creative play); parental anxiety about 'stranger danger', meaning that children are increasingly kept indoors; a test-driven school and pre-school curriculum in which formal learning has substantially taken the place of free, unstructured play ...

[We are] calling for a wide-ranging and informed public dialogue about the intrinsic nature and value of play in children's healthy development, and how we might ensure its place at the heart of twenty-first-century childhood.

We believe that the late Carl Rogers would have shared many of these concerns, and that it would have deeply pained him to witness just what is happening to children today—whether it be the medicalisation of childhood experience bemoaned by commentators such as Sami Timimi (2005), or the way in which the high-stakes testing 'audit culture' has swamped educational experience (e.g. Mansell, 2007) and criminally deprived children of their birthright—the right to enjoy and be empowered by a developmentally appropriate learning environment (House, 2002).

Back in the optimistic days of the 1970s, Carl Rogers' educational work, encapsulated in *Freedom to Learn*, laid the foundations for a truly empowering and growth-orientated learning experience which, if faithfully implemented, would surely counter much of the 'toxicity' of modern childhood. There is, therefore, an urgent need to reaffirm Rogers' seminal progressive views—that is, towards a child- and *relationally centred* learning experience for children, and away from the anxiety-saturated *politician-centred* education system from which modern Western education systems are chronically suffering (House, 2008).

We believe that the various symptoms of distress we have labelled 'toxic childhood' should be interpreted as children's insightful commentary on just how badly we adults are doing, rather than some 'psychopathology' that needs to be medicalised and 'treated'. And again, we see such a view as entirely consistent with Carl Rogers' whole corpus of work in the fields of education and therapy, and his admirable anti-diagnostic approach in particular.

Our own view is that modern childhood is in crisis—which itself perhaps reflects a crisis of *adulthood* more generally, and the milieux (family, educational, environmental) that we are creating for our children. These crises demand urgent consideration if the toxic juggernaut is to be halted and reversed. This welcome new book shows how person-centred practice can inform this consideration, and we wish it wide readership. The issues it raises and the responses it champions will be an essential aspect of the healthier future that we all wish to forge for children the world over.

REFERENCES

House, R (2002) Loving to learn: protecting a natural impulse in a technocratic age. *Paths of Learning* (USA), *12* (Spring), 32–6.

House, R (2008, forthcoming) *The Trouble with Education: Stress, surveillance and modernity.* Montreal: Ur Publications.

Mansell, W (2007) *Education by Numbers: The tyranny of testing.* London: Politico's Publishing.

Palmer, S (2006) *Toxic Childhood: How modern life is damaging our children … and what we can do about it.* London: Orion Books.

Palmer, S (2007) *Detoxing Childhood: What parents need to know to raise happy, successful children.* London: Orion Books.

Rogers, CR (1969) *Freedom to Learn.* Columbus, OH: Charles E. Merrill.

Timimi, S (2005) *Naughty Boys: Anti-social behaviour, ADHD and the role of culture.* Basingstoke: Palgrave Macmillan.

Trilling, L (1974) *Sincerity and Authenticity* (Charles Eliot Norton Lectures). Cambridge, MA: Harvard University Press.

Zimmerman, M (1981) *Eclipse of the Self: Development of Heidegger's concept of authenticity.* Athens, OH: Ohio University Press.

THE POLITICS OF ADULTHOOD

ASHLEY FLETCHER

In March 2007, a remarkable and inspiring event happened. Ten of the contributors to this book met in Oldham with the largely technical task of drawing threads together and agreeing an editorial preamble.

Beyond this, in the course of an afternoon, the authors were able to develop a shared political understanding and perspective on their work and its limitations, the obstacles and the barriers posed by structure and a culture theoretically looking after the interests of children but primarily seen and understood from the position and interests of adults.

This level of consensus was not the product of argument, nor the subject of disagreement. It was in reality a remarkable sharing of understanding held by those who share and practise person-centred philosophy and who value the 'way of being' in relationship above the 'way of doing', which devalues intimacy.

The following, however, is neither a detailed documentation of these discussions, nor is it intended to be a 'manifesto' of any sort. It is rather one of the author's individual ruminations on the themes and moods of that discussion, although the attempt to record it in this manner was in itself an agreed outcome of our collective process.

One of the first realisations to emerge was the primacy of politics throughout this subject, on both a macro level of philosophy and social agendas and a micro level of management and the perspectives and vulnerabilities of adults working with young people.

The origins of the person-centred approach lie in the humanist and existentialist traditions, themselves an anguished exploration of the individual as isolated and alone. A view of the world where David is pitted against Goliath, often unsuccessfully and where the power of the state, its institutions and economy, grow exponentially in inverse proportion to the status and role of community and of the individual.

The value of the individual is less and less seen holistically as the sum of our parts and concepts and our capacity to grow and contribute to the growth of those around us, but rather focuses more and more on constructed value, based on our ability to conform, produce and consume, where difference is seen increasingly as dissident.

A cultural and social dislocation from community shifts our locus of evaluation, our ability to value and appreciate ourselves, ever more from our own experience and perspectives to the processes and institutions on which we are conditioned to depend:

on work, and school, on peer pressure, on cultural norms, and on virtual or detached communities whose knowledge of us is less as a key component, but more as a cog in a machine, alienated from others, and ultimately dispensable.

Against a background of the practical abolition of the experience of life in community, therapy itself can only be at best a sticking plaster on the wounds of that absence.

On a micro level, and in the context of working with young people, the experience of being human is forgotten in favour of the need to control and to manage.

Childhood itself is progressively being pathologised as a problematic condition that needs to be managed. Squeezing young minds into the requirements of adult-designed institutions creates reactions that are challenging to the politics and imperatives of adults. Adults who for the most part are far removed from any level of connection or community in the life of the young people involved.

A fundamental cause of conflict, isolation, neglect or lack of understanding is not a universal problem of being young, but the politics of adulthood. A politics itself formed by experience of childhood and its insecurities, that on the one hand forgets its own experience of childhood and loses an ability to empathise, while on the other treats it as simply an endemic pre-condition to growing up, a universal condition shared by all and confined to a largely irrelevant and slightly trivial phase preceding the real thing: the trials and struggles of the adult world. This 'adult' relationship to childhood, that sees it as something else to be managed and controlled, in turn shapes understanding, policy and practice.

In contrast, it is the quality of relationship, authenticity and intimacy that is central to the client–counsellor relationship in person-centred practice, not tools, exercises, homework, reframing or expertly directed practice. Yet, it is this relationship that is most feared by the politics of adulthood in its pathological suspicion of young people and our relationships with them.

It is paradoxical that the adult world, and its way of working with young people, should appear so unfamiliar with the experience of being young. Such mystery rarely applies to work in other disciplines or 'client' groups. Paradoxical because uniquely, childhood is the only 'state' or 'condition' that we all have in common. Rarely do we have such 'shared' experience with our clients!

That is not abstract, nor theorising. We were all children. It is something (all be it with a myriad of different experiences) we can all draw upon: a shared momentary concept of powerlessness; not being listened to; a struggle for identity and a place in the world; our first experience of the power of the judgements of others; and the surprise at what appears random and often arbitrary justice.

Yet, we seem to grow so imbued with the paranoia and imperatives of our emergence into adult society that when we look back we don't seem to see remembrance, recognition and empathy but a world of challenge and strangeness that needs either control or protection.

It's as if being young is dismissed merely as something we all just had to go through, like measles and school, as if the arrival to adulthood is simply a call to 'get over it'. Concepts of young people's rights, autonomy and integrity are much talked about (e.g. the ministerial Department for Children, Schools and Families, the Children Act and its updates, Sure Start and Every Child Matters),[1] but more often than not are just considered 'political correctness gone mad', with a counter-swing to keep young people in their place, such as curfews, ASBOs[2] and current proposals to make children retake their final year in primary schools and fine parents for letting them out of their sight.

If the past is 'another country', childhood can be seen as another planet. Yet if we reflect on our own experience of that 'other world', most of us have moments which we can draw on, where we can see the impact of empathy and relationship in our lives—that teacher, that half hour with that adult—and the difference which that made.

It is precisely this 'difference' that is progressively being ruled out. Adult relationships with children and young people are increasingly viewed with suspicion and any concept of intimacy is considered unhealthy. Such relationships are invariably viewed as, at best, unprofessional, and, at worst, abusive. Such is the experience of many of the authors in their effort for effective and authentic relationships, which have the agenda of the child as the prime concern.

A classic example given by several contributors working with young children is the impossibility of a secure and exclusive space offering privacy and security for the child as client. Working, for example, in windowed rooms, where the window must be kept clear so that what is happening inside between the therapist and the young person can be easily seen by third parties. How many of us would accept such conditions in our own consultations with therapists, doctors, or with anyone from whom we were seeking connection and help?

While some might see this as the necessary price of child protection, the uncomfortable truth remains that, overwhelmingly, the most systematic and violent abuse takes place in the home, one of the few places where popular belief is that the child or young person is at their safest.

Men, and gay men in particular, are especially vulnerable to these suspicions and paranoia, with the result that it is harder and harder to recruit men to work with young people, especially children. This potentially deprives a generation of male role models and relationships outside the family unit.

Another paradox here then is that it is widely understood by person-centred practitioners, who are attempting to build authentic and therapeutic relationships with children, that such precautions and measures, the child welfare 'protocols', 'guidelines' and good practice, have less in reality to do with child welfare than with protecting adults—and/or the institutions that employ them—from accusation and complaint.

That children can be seen in many ways as 'hard to reach' is a damning indictment of how far down this road we have already gone. We know all too well from working

1. See <www.dfes.gov.uk>.
2. Anti-Social Behaviour Orders, <www.homeoffice.gov.uk>.

with anyone, but particularly the most vulnerable, that if you don't work with your client's agenda, you will eventually stop working in any meaningful sense with that client at all. Without respect there will be no communication, without communication there can be no relationship, without relationship there can be neither honesty nor openness and without openness, there can be no empathy.

Thus authenticity and the hope of therapeutic relationship are undermined. 'Adult insecurity' in the guise of child protection imposes duties to disclose on so many different levels that the pressure to betray a child's confidentiality is standard procedure—it has become the norm, not the exception. Few adults are entitled, encouraged or allowed to model intimacy for the next generation of adults to learn and follow. The stitching of the fabric of community is left to fray as an irrelevance.

It would be wrong to conclude from this however that schools in particular are failing in their primary role. Schools were never designed to maintain community or to genuinely facilitate personal development. Popular education is a recent phenomenon and has very clear objectives. Learning is secondary to the role of 'schooling' itself.

At its origins lies the need to organise and get the displaced urchins of the industrial revolution off the streets. This was in order to learn the values and requirements of a 'new' social order, to learn time-keeping for the factories, to learn reading for indoctrination, to follow instructions, to gain the discipline to be effective producers, and to set goals for success. In short, the aim was to create the next generation of effective workers and effective consumers.

Prioritising the needs of the students has always been the liberal educators' dream, but it has been an alien concept to the state's agenda. Schooling is about behaviour management and has helped breed the generations of adults that continue to view school and, in many respects, child services in this way—albeit often filtered through a genuine belief that this is all in the child's or young person's best interest. The 'it never did me any harm' refrain has some parallels to 'only obeying orders'.

Thirty years ago children simply didn't have needs outside of cleanliness, discipline and nutrition. The Victorian hangover persisted, echoed in the cultural mantra 'seen and not heard'. Today in many ways it is simply a variation on that theme, with colourful words about commitment giving rise to avoidance on a grander scale.

A running frustration emerging from the discussion amongst contributors to this book was the erratic rhythm of interest in child welfare. In reality it was felt that most child service resourcing is essentially tokenistic, with little money, few staff, and driven 'reactively' by events. A recent government white paper entitled 'Every Child Matters' (2004),[3] for example, while billed as a 'public services agenda for the whole child', was a political response to the tragic abuse and death of Victoria Clombie, and was more of a series of statements of laudable principle than a concrete change of approach and values. All too often, it was felt, money comes in following a tragedy, dribbles away over five years, and awaits the next tragic event to gain a new temporary lease of life.

---

3. See <www.dfes.gov.uk>.

Even when money does come in, the avoidance continues as one expensive needs assessment follows another before ending up as an understaffed, underfunded project, burdened with paperwork and monitoring for the short duration of its funded life. The agenda of the 'state as manager' is always impersonal; its quick fix, goal-centred, soulless on-budget number crunching part of the politics of adulthood.

A common theme amongst practitioners working with children and young people is to feel undervalued and undersupported. It has always been the case, most certainly writ large by the creation of 'internal' markets and latterly commissioning, that whilst providers have a complex and detailed concept of provision, commissioners have a simplistic one based on funding and politics which is not driven by a passionate desire to deliver appropriately, but to deliver 'economically'.

These concepts make the most uncomfortable bedfellows. Practitioners are left with the tension of trying to get the money with one hand, and deliver well with the other despite more often than not engaging in practice contradicting funders' expectations.

As I discuss in my chapter, those who funded, or with whom we had to cooperate to effectively work with 'rent boys', believed our key goal was to 'get them off the streets' and stop them having sex, rather than our reality, which was working effectively with our clients' agendas, helping them have the sex they wanted (which they were doing anyway) and helping them to have it more safely. This wasn't just the experience of my project, but the shared dilemma of my colleagues around the country. Who did whom more good is best evidenced by the UK's enviable and deserved reputation at limiting the AIDS epidemic here.

I have no doubt that many will find the thoughts and observations I advance in this forward challenging if not plain wrong. I am unashamedly partisan and political as well as passionate on the benefits of the person-centred approach.

It was a strongly held view of the contributors during the discussions, that much of the contents that follow amount to a practice-based evidence of the potency and effectiveness of this approach, particularly applied to our work over a generation with children and young people. Evidence-based practice, the commissioners' current buzz word, is not about relationship but rather about controlled environment and abstracted study. Whilst this has a value of its own, it is academic based rather than client or practitioner focused and crucially has its 'eye on the buck'. Quality is seldom about value for money in the real world.

The contents of this book speak for themselves. The credence and value given to it will, I believe, largely depend on the political eye of the beholder. Central is our confidence in the ability and integrity of young people and their enormous capacity to navigate the consequences of their world, which is dominated by the rights of adults.

A contribution from one of the authors in the discussions that led to this foreword powerfully summed it up for me: 'past traumas or future traumas, I am always impressed how they [young people] always manage to hang on to a sense of self'. We should perhaps trust less in the 'we know what to do' approach and more in children and young people's innate resilience.

CHAPTER 1

CREATIVE DISCERNMENT

THE KEY TO THE
TRAINING AND PRACTICE OF
PERSON-CENTRED PLAY THERAPISTS

TRACEY WALSHAW

As I was thinking about what would be most useful and informative to a reader, I felt the place to begin was to tell you a little about my own journey as a trainer and a person-centred child counsellor. This seemed fundamental, as it is in my experiences that I have developed and grounded the provision of my training courses for practitioners working with this client group, and in particular the provision of person-centred training.

I have been developing and running counsellor education programmes for more than fifteen years, and have become increasingly interested in working with counsellors who, like me, have felt drawn to working with children and young people. For the last fifteen years I have been a co-director of PCCS Training Partnership in Manchester and have also run a private practice for client and supervision work. PCCS Training Partnership would define itself as a 'classical person-centred training organisation' providing courses such as the Diploma in Person-Centred Counselling, Diploma in Client-Centred Play Therapy and the Advanced Certificate in Therapeutic Play. Our aim at PCCS Training Partnership is for our students to be theoretically sound in their understanding of their core theoretical and philosophical model; to encourage healthy challenge and criticism about 'what's out there' in terms of the counselling culture and systems they find themselves in; to have a sense of their own internal ethical and moral codes; and, above all, to prize the relationship they have not only with their clients but with themselves. I became a trainer because I wanted to be part of the individual practitioner's journey to be the best, most creative counsellor they could be. Although I struggle with the word 'trainer', which conveys a more directive approach to facilitating learning than I aspire to or practise, my intention is to convey the depth and breadth of educational and learning interventions that can contribute to facilitating the process of actualising individuals. I will therefore use this word throughout the chapter.

MY OWN JOURNEY

I began over thirty years ago, with what I refer to as 'my continual on-the-job training'. After completing a degree in psychology, I joined the National Health Service (NHS) where I trained and worked as a Registered Mental Nurse (RMN), a professional qualification whose wording evokes great mirth to some of my friends! I was continually perplexed in my work in the NHS by my repeated encounters with the same patients on admission. I began wondering whether there might be another way of helping clients to achieve a better emotional quality of life. My questioning brought me to counsellor training and through this into my huge journey of reflective practice, creativity and ultimately to the point where I began to challenge the systems I worked within.

As a qualified counsellor I initially continued to work within the NHS as an RMN carrying a small counselling caseload. It was here I began to notice, particularly in my work with voice hearers (those carrying the medical label 'schizophrenia'), that an expressive medium was useful in enabling me to enter into the world of my clients. Working with people who do not use language in standard ways and have thoughts that do not fit the more usual ways of expression, I found that an expressive medium enabled us to co-create a therapeutic language. At the same time, I began to struggle more and more with the medical model and beliefs about the right form of treatment for these clients and, in particular, the lack of autonomy and self-direction that this model implies. The increasing incongruence between my person-centred values and the values of the organisation within which I worked became more and more challenging and I began looking for opportunities to co-create a different kind of practice, one that was structurally person-centred. PCCS Training Partnership offered that opportunity, and my relationships with my business partner, training colleagues and students have been fundamental in helping me to develop training which is person-centred, creative, realistic, responsive, moral and intimate.

My experience working with clients for whom just talking did not seem to be particularly helpful, together with the subsequent dilemma of how I could respond differently to these clients whilst still working within a person-centred practice, highlighted questions for me about my core theoretical model and practice. I felt grounded in person-centred theory and was not convinced that I needed to abandon this to more expert-led techniques and approaches. I was sure that there had to be a way of interfacing expressive media and person-centred practice and training. Initially this search took me into Person-Centred Expressive Training developed by Natalie Rogers. This training focuses on the authentic creativity each individual brings, and incorporates expressive media in expanding the individual's understanding of their process through creativity. Whilst some aspects of this training did not directly fit with my own practice (it is broadly person-centred in its approach but has a more structured facilitation style), nevertheless, this programme stimulated a hunger to develop an expressive and creative training that still honoured the actualising tendency and put the student at the centre of their learning.

I wanted to engage with the creative process yet not make it a technique or have any particular attachment to specific media, holding the relationship as central. It was fascinating to be open to expressive media as a means of dialogue with my clients and students. With my developing enthusiasm for using creative media in my work, it was perhaps inevitable that I would be drawn to working with children and play where this is the most natural medium of expression. My first young clients were referred to my private practice. As I became more interested, I sought out work as a primary school counsellor.

When I initially came up with the idea of developing child practitioner training at PCCS Training Partnership, the challenge was how I could develop a training that was person-centred in its delivery and incorporated creative media; that supported my creativity as a facilitator, and facilitated each individual student in becoming the best child counsellor they could be.

My experience throughout all our training indicated that personal development is key in this work. Some years earlier in PCCS Training Partnership's course selection procedure we realised that whilst training can enhance skills and theoretical understanding, it is the student's ripeness and ability to engage with their own reflective process that has been the soundest criterion for selection. This felt crucial in developing a course facilitating counsellors to work with children. Training for me involves engaging people with their humanity, helping them to develop their own internal moral and ethical codes, to question rules and recognise when these rules need to be upheld or challenged. Developing trainees to be articulate self-reflective practitioners in supervision, peer work and personal work is what, for me, maintains the safety in this work. I firmly believe that sound and creative reflectors make good therapists.

The training therefore involves experiential work, lots of reflective process, having your work examined and discussed not just with the trainer but with your peer group, intimacy in training. The trainer's practice as well as the students being open to scrutiny is what I mean by intimacy. Good training to me is about transparency in that nobody, myself included, has anywhere to hide on the course (and no need to!). I strongly feel that if we are in the business of relationship therapy then we are in the business of relationship training. Fundamentally necessary in developing a course that is about working with this vulnerable client group is one which is co-created and responsive to the current and ever-changing needs of the student, evolving as a consequence of their work and reflective practice about their clients. I believe that it is this format and not an abundance of technical information, exercises, health and safety instructions and a tightly constrained model of what a child counselling relationship should be like, that keeps clients safe.

The structure and format of the course is fundamental to providing a secure and challenging environment for the students. Having a syllabus, which can be flexible in its delivery, is crucial. Having supervision groups happening within the course is important for students to uncover all the nuances that seem to exist with child work. The sharing of recorded work with clients for reflection and feedback from peers and trainers, often using clay, miniatures, paint, etc. to communicate their practice and personal processes are crucial. I wanted the course to encourage students to experiment with their own creativity within the therapeutic relationship and to be able to reflect on this in a way that is both supportive and challenging and grounded in theory.

It became apparent that often students who had been trained in the person-centred approach had not been exposed to the original writings of key thinkers in the field and their theoretical frameworks were not always grounded in clear philosophical principles. The delight of students as they became aware of the wide literature available to them in their own discipline, of writers such as Natiello, Bozarth, Keys, Wyatt, Proctor, Warner,

Schlien and Schmid was evidence of the gifts that a strong theoretical understanding can give to day-to-day practice. The development of this understanding was therefore central to the course and we used expressive media to make the theory even more exciting and vibrant. Dolls' houses, clay, paint, glitter and a whole range of materials were used to explore theoretical and professional concepts. Personal learning statements, which were developed in the learning community, were also crucial to feedback. My intention was to design a course that gave an abundance of feedback and ample opportunities for reflective practice, with all assignments being peer and trainer assessed. For me the play therapy courses have been some of the most stretching, rewarding, challenging, difficult and exhilarating courses I have been involved with at PCCS Training Partnership.

THE ROLE OF CREATIVE DISCERNMENT

I have found that frequently play therapy students come with constraining mantras about what is and what is not person-centred. They seem, at times, to arrive at PCCS Training Partnership having internalised rigid conditions of worth about being person-centred which puts them into a straitjacket that limits creativity. These are highly creative people yet not only do they often carry childhood rejections about creativity (about being able to paint or draw correctly), they have subsequently acquired more introjected rules from their person-centred training and communities. I can empathise with this experience, as I recognise my own internalised 'person-centred thought police' along with the professional litigious snipers occupying my frontal lobe. As I write this, I am reminded of Colin Feltham's 2007 article in the British Association for Counselling and Psychotherapy journal on 'ethical agonising' which speaks volumes to me as a child therapist. A particular challenge in working with this vulnerable client group is how to balance received wisdom on ethical practice against the risk of stepping fully into a creative and therapeutic relational space with this client group.

I feel the biggest asset I bring to the relationship as a person-centred practitioner is my ability to co-create relationships, engaging my spontaneity and creativity. The learning I encounter again and again in my personal, professional and creative life is that of trying to invalidate myself to validate others (or in more jargon-free language, making myself smaller in order to make someone else bigger). I have learned to recognise that this is not only disrespectful but is also not effective. My aim is to meet people in my potency with all my creativity present as a person, a counsellor, a supervisor and trainer, and to help them to step fully into their power, meeting me as an equal.

In a recent group a friend of mine talked about the idea of 'discerned stretching' in terms of understanding emotional responses as information. She invited students to test their initial internal responses to a new possibility to see whether the discomfort represented a stretch—something that might feel uncomfortable and a little risky but was worth it for the benefits that they were likely to achieve—or whether the discomfort represented a stress—something that was providing appropriate protection and should be honoured and respected. Sometimes we resist novelty out of habit rather than because there is actually much current and real risk. You exercise discernment when you listen to the information, test it and make an informed choice. In counselling, a discerning practitioner may choose to hold a boundary because it is an ethical choice, not because it is a rule or familiar pattern. The internalisation, development and ownership of your own personal, ethical and moral codes are fundamental and crucial. Developing as a child practitioner seems to me to require a high level of discernment. Can spontaneity be open to discernment? Yes, if it is underpinned by a strong theoretical and philosophical understanding of the person-centred approach.

DISCERNMENT CHALLENGES FOR CLIENT-CENTRED PLAY THERAPISTS

ASKING QUESTIONS IS NOT PERSON-CENTRED

Well, I guess nailing your client to the mast with questions is not. Expressing interest and curiosity in what the child is doing whilst playing is not only useful it's crucial. The social context of children involves seeking information; it feels pointless as an adult not to enter their social context as well as their internal emotional frame of reference.

BEING IN THE CLIENT'S PLAY WORK IS NOT PERSON-CENTRED

This one takes great undoing. Students come in with such statements as 'I'm not there to play, that's the client's job' and 'I'll facilitate their process by observing and commenting'. This rigid approach can be paralysing for the relationship with a child. Most of us who work with children experience that they want us to participate, just as we want them to participate in the therapeutic relationship. So the risk here is if the child leads the play, you do not know where it will take you, but this is also true in the talking relationship. When students realise that it is the relationship that is fundamental not the medium then they become freer to explore with the child in play.

THE WORK HAS TO LOOK A PARTICULAR WAY AND BE IN A PARTICULAR PLACE

A creative process could be working with a child on a bench in the sunshine, having a tea party, being involved in playing differing roles the child wants you to play, not to observe from a distance. Trusting your intuition in the relationship with the support of a sound theoretical underpinning of person-centred principles opens up the child's world in play therapy. We do children a disservice by being uncreative and professionally reserved. It is the therapist who carries the structure internally. If you know what counselling is and what it is not, the place you meet is pretty incidental.

YOU NEVER GIVE A CLIENT INFORMATION OR ADVICE

As adults we sometimes have information that would serve our young clients well. One student was concerned about bringing a piece of work to the course. She felt it was not person-centred because she had made a suggestion. She was working with a child who was going to court and this frightened the client. The therapist suggested they set the court scene up using the miniatures as a way to explore the fears the young person had about each of the stages. The therapist had the information about the system the child did not. The offering and facilitation of this upheld person-centred principles. The therapist had information and offered it to the client, having made a judgement that it might be in the best interest of her anxious client, as opposed to letting her be exposed to the system and then retrospectively processing it. Whether or not this is true to person-centred philosophy is detectable in the manner in which the counsellor's expertise and knowledge is offered, not the fact of it being offered. The therapist here was not bidding for power. In effect the therapist is saying 'here is some potential information that may or may not help; do you want to play with this?'

IF WE ALL REMEMBER WHAT IT IS LIKE TO BE A CHILD THEN WE CAN HELP THEM BETTER

Rubbish! What is important is that for the therapist working with children remembers that they are remembering from an adult perspective. This sounds so basic, but I have noticed that sometimes students arrive with the notion that as we have all been children we know what it's like or we can imagine it. We are all adults yet we don't presume to understand an adult client's world. We recognise the complex range of factors that make each of us and our experiences unique. Even taking into account the huge social and cultural changes that have occurred since my childhood, I cannot know fully what is best for my child clients. The world has seen dramatic changes since the years of Axline and Rogers. It does trainee child therapists a disservice not to respond to these changes in their work.

I NEED TO COMPLY WITH ALL RULES HOWEVER RIDICULOUS BECAUSE THEY ARE IN THE BEST INTEREST OF THE CLIENT

Let us not confuse the task of keeping adults safe from litigious process with activities which are in the best interest of the child or young person. Today's therapists have to balance their spontaneity and responsiveness with their fear of litigious process and of negotiating health and safety hazards. Some questions have already started. One student was instructed by her line manager to ask me how I sterilize the sand, and whether we should wash all the equipment after each session? Bemused, my reply was 'Well personally if it's a small sand tray I turn it around three times then blow on it, any other suggestions?' Soon we will be filling in check forms to see if children are allergic to paint, glue, the therapist's wool fleece and indeed the air. How we facilitate students to find their own way through the sometimes ridiculous protocols is a chapter in itself. I constantly feel privileged to work with these trainees who despite all this red tape are still passionately driven to work with children in an enthused and creative way.

I NEED A SPECIAL EXPENSIVE ALL-INCLUSIVE PLAY KIT

No. All the counsellor needs is some imagination and creativity to utilise the resources they have in the environment around them. Use your common sense, have a small menu of creative media for the young person to choose from, which can range from crayons, glitter, paper, clay, stones, the furniture in the room, to specialized kit like sand and miniatures. It never fails to amuse me that play therapists would be better named 'bag people' as inevitably if there is not a purpose-provided playroom we carry our resources around with us. In my experience over the life of the course students will learn to exercise discernment about what they take; they start with a lot and then eventually size it down to a much neater kit. Mustakas (1973) suggests that the range of toys available is less important than the opportunity for each child to use material as he or she chooses. It is the choices clients make in pursuing whichever part of the process they want to which is important, and not us deciding 'Oh, I think it's important to focus on … '.

I REALLY LIKE A PARTICULAR MEDIUM AND FEEL GUILTY FOR NOT PROVIDING THE ONES I DON'T LIKE

We all make choices about our comfort zones. I particularly don't like black paint after a client once flung it about the room. I think it put me off paint. But I do like other messy media like sand, glitter and clay. This still boils down to me. It is not about the medium, but how the relationship is co-created and facilitated. Children let me know what they want to use, so I follow their lead.

I GET UPSET WHEN THE CLIENT USES ALL THE GLITTER, I DON'T LIKE SAYING NO

This is a discernment call too. A very wise supervisor once told me that just because you can do something doesn't mean that you should. Saying no, negotiating the boundaries and quantities of your resources with your client seems perfectly reasonable to me, and more importantly the dialogue and the transparency you have with this.

I SHOULD NOT LET THE CLIENT TAKE HOME ANY OF THE EQUIPMENT BECAUSE SOMEONE ELSE MIGHT WANT IT

It depends! Sometimes you know that a particular miniature, doll or whatever may be useful for the client to look after for a while. It could cause you to have to dialogue with other clients if that equipment is not there for them, but you make a judgement call.

MY CLIENTS SHOULDN'T GIVE ME A GIFT AND IF THEY DO I SHOULDN'T ACCEPT IT

I think this should read: I should not expect gifts, but if a child brings along a gift I will take it in the spirit in which it is given. How untherapeutic it would be to say to a child 'No, I couldn't accept this because it might contaminate the relationship'. However, if I sense that a child feels the need to buy my affection and regard with gifts, then we need to have a conversation about this. Discernment is needed here.

CONCLUSION

This is a summary of what I think is key to being a person-centred child practitioner:

- Go back to the basic principles of the person-centred approach, read the theory, explore it creatively, check it against your own ongoing experience and practice and challenge it!
- Experience each child as unique and resourceful and trust in the healing power of real, robust, vital relationship.
- Explore your own creativity—learn to play with creative media until you become fluent in their use.
- Be prepared to stretch into new places—with discernment.

To be a client-centred child therapist is to relinquish the safety of the expert role, exercises, and a clear task orientation, and instead to facilitate the presence of the core conditions, to uphold principled non-directiveness (Grant, 1990) and to explore relationship. To do what is in the best interest of our child clients may mean that we, as therapists, are the most vulnerable of practitioners. In this vulnerability we are also the major interface and sometimes spokespeople for one of the most vulnerable client groups. Never more than now are our ethical creativity and discernment needed, otherwise we, as professional adults, will also be in danger of abandoning our child clients.

To be writing this chapter at this time seems to be both a poignant and reflective task for me. By the time this book goes to print PCCS Training Partnership will be in our last year of providing Professional Counsellor Diploma training for a number of reasons. The main reason being a discerned choice about the constraining impact on counsellor training of state regulation. What I would advocate for would be a range of approaches and training offering healthy alternatives allowing for the discerning choices of practitioners. I have had the privilege to work and grow with practitioners of great passion, skill, ethicality, reflectiveness and wisdom, developing creativity within their practice, challenging their person-centredness, working within the social context and cultures of child work, working in and with organisations, working with and for their clients. These practitioners have the courage to continually question the 'why' as opposed to the 'must' of some of the professional rules, and indeed myths, around working with this client group. To all those discerning and creative practitioners I give my thanks. They are inspirational and their creativity will be what forges the route forward for the provision of child therapy, which holds the values and principles of the person-centred approach in our troubled world. Maybe I am now talking about *principled person-centred creative discernment!*

REFERENCES

Axline, V (1947) *Play Therapy*. Boston: Houghton Mifflin.

Axline, V (1964) *Dibs: In search of self*. Harmondsworth: Penguin.

Bozarth, J (1998) *Person-Centered Therapy: A revolutionary paradigm*. Ross-on-Wye: PCCS Books.

Feltham, C (2007) Ethical agonizing. *Therapy Today, 18* (7), 4–6.

Grant, B (1990) Principled and instrumental nondirectiveness in person-centered and client-centered therapy. *Person-Centered Review, 5* (1), 77–88. Reprinted in DJ Cain, (Ed) (2002) *Classics in the Person-Centered Approach* (pp. 371–7). Ross-on-Wye: PCCS Books.

Keys, S (2003) *Idiosyncratic Person-Centred Therapy: From the personal to the universal*. Ross-on-Wye: PCCS Books.

Mustakas, C (1973) *Children in Play Therapy*. New York: Aronson.

Natiello, P (2001) *The Person-Centred Approach: A passionate presence*. Ross-on-Wye: PCCS Books.

Proctor, G (2002) *The Dynamics of Power in Counselling and Psychotherapy: Ethics, politics and practice*. Ross-on-Wye: PCCS Books.

Rogers, CR (1957) The necessary and sufficient conditions of therapeutic personality change. *Journal of Consulting Psychology, 21*, 95–103.

Rogers, CR (1959) A theory of therapy, personality and interpersonal relationships, as developed in the client-centered framework. In S Koch (Ed) *Psychology: A study of a science. Vol 3: Formulations of the person and the social context* (pp. 184–256). New York: McGraw-Hill.

Rogers, CR (1961) *On Becoming a Person*. Boston: Houghton Mifflin.

Shlien J (2003) *To Lead an Honorable Life: Invitations to think about client-centered therapy and the person-centered approach* (Ed: P Sanders) Ross-on-Wye: PCCS Books.

Schmid, PF (1996) 'Probably the most potentent social invention of the century.' Person-centered therapy is fundamentally group therapy. In R Hutterer, G Pawlowsky, PF Schmid & R Stipsits (Eds) *Client-Centered and Experiential Psychotherapy: A paradigm in motion* (pp. 611–25). Frankfurt am Main: Peter Lang.

Wyatt, G (series Ed) (2001) *Rogers' Therapeutic Conditions: Evolution, theory and practice Vols 1–4*. Ross-on-Wye: PCCS Books.

CHAPTER 2

'THIS IS NO ORDINARY THERAPY'
THE INFLUENCE OF TRAINING ON DEVELOPING
THE PLAY THERAPY RELATIONSHIP

CATE KELLY

INTRODUCTION

Between March 2006 and March 2007 I participated in training to obtain a Diploma in Client-Centred Play Therapy. In October 2006, starting my school placement working with children, I arrived with a balanced level of confidence in my ability as counsellor. I had worked for almost ten years with adults and felt that seven months intense preparation on my course had put me in a good starting place. Reading, thinking, self-awareness, learning from our tutor as well as from the diploma community group all seemed to be enough grounding to make a start. First sessions with three children that morning of October 31, 2006 made me realise that nothing had primed me for the enormous difference I would feel between working with adults and working with children. I ranged from a sense that I didn't know whether what I was doing was therapeutic to a feeling of magic encounter and the facilitation of client process. My awareness of difference has run parallel with a consciousness of similarities: transferable skills. Still I hold a deep sense that play therapy with children is not *ordinary*. It feels special and different.

The title for this chapter comes from the recent advertisements for Marks and Spencer's food. 'This is no ordinary potato salad', says the tempting, sultry voice, indicating a sense of something 'other', something 'magic', '… this is hand-picked baby new potatoes from rich organic Italian soil with lavishly prepared luxury mayonnaise …'. The way I trained and learned to practise as a play therapist and continue to do so certainly feels like *no ordinary therapy*.

In this chapter I want to reflect on some of the 'learnings' I made during the course and to present my understanding of the application of the person-centred approach to working with children with particular emphasis on the issue of how and why I feel that the relationship is different. This will include what both child and therapist bring with them into the relationship; how my training has contributed to my capacity to expand the range of what I have to offer as a therapist in this setting; the power of expressive media and the potency of the play and joining-in aspects of this therapeutic approach; how I experience a different feeling about boundaries; how my sense of the child's childhood state contributes to my sense of difference; how a child experiences a sense of difference from other relationships; the difference in the referral process; the difference in involving a third party (a parent figure); and whether or not talking is an essential part of the therapy.

I would like to acknowledge the contributions to my thinking from all my interactions, past and present, personal and professional, with our diploma community and how learning from other people's experience and thoughts stimulates enormous learning and reflections for me. I believe that although it cannot be formally referenced, this source of wisdom is of equal importance in my development to the absorption of knowledge from person-centred writings. I have found surprisingly little written on working with children from the person-centred perspective. I have, however, been influenced positively by the work of two play therapists who worked in the USA in the 1940s and 1950s (Virginia Axline and Elaine Dorfman) and I quote from their writings in this chapter.

THE PERSON-CENTRED APPROACH TO WORKING WITH CHILDREN

When working with children I have observed the child's actualising tendency, their striving to be the best they can be, whatever their circumstances. The person-centred approach (PCA) trusts that because of this tendency a child will be able to take from the therapist and from the relationship what he needs: the healing is in the relationship. It is this kind of relationship I have had the privilege of experiencing with some children. Through my practice experience with children I believe that the core conditions are necessary and sufficient and that expressive media are complementary to the way in which a therapeutic relationship can be forged with a child. I have also observed the equal relevance to children's work of a non-directive approach and valuing of the child as his/her[1] own expert. Virginia Axline, the renowned pioneer of play therapy with children, describes it this way: 'When the nondirective therapist says that the therapy is client-centered, he really means it, because, to him, the client is the source of living power that directs the growth from within himself' (Axline, 1947: 22).

WHAT THE CHILD BRINGS TO THE THERAPEUTIC RELATIONSHIP

Although Rogers did not develop client-centred therapy until the 1950s, and therefore could not apply his new approach to children, in his 1939 book *The Clinical Treatment of the Problem Child*, he was developing his ideas in this area. In his second book *Counseling and Psychotherapy* (1942: 4–6) he wrote about 'child guidance' — the term used to describe child work at that time. It was significant that in his 1951 book *Client-Centered Therapy*, he included a chapter on play therapy by Elaine Dorfman (1951: 235–77).

Rogers' theory on the development of the personality (1959: 225) describes the growth of the child's self-concept as being founded on his learned need for love. Rogers

---

1. I will use the non-gender-specific 'he' to denote all clients.

refers here to the child's relationship with his mother. Despite the semantics (I believe that if this writing was current he would probably refer to a parent, parent figure or care-giver rather than a mother), I read it as Rogers' view of the importance of how first and subsequent caring relationships influence the way infants come to consider themselves and are able to form relationships.

> The infant learns to need love. Love is very satisfying, but to know whether he [sic] is receiving it or not he must observe his mother's [sic] face, gestures, and other ambiguous signs. He develops a total gestalt as to the way he is regarded by his mother and each new experience of love or rejection tends to alter the whole gestalt. Consequently each behavior on his mother's part such as a specific disapproval of a specific behavior tends to be experienced as disapproval in general. So important is this to the infant that he comes to be guided in his behavior not by the degree to which an experience maintains or enhances the organism, but by the likelihood of receiving maternal love.
>
> Soon he learns to view himself in much the same way, liking or disliking himself as a total configuration. He tends, quite independently of his mother or others, to view himself and his behavior in the same way they have. (Rogers, 1959: 225)

Rogers took the view that beginning, growing, developing and maintaining behaviours which could be described as attachment behaviours, is an interactional business, based on relationships (this topic is also covered in Chapter 10, p. 85). It was also his belief that relationship was the key to the healing facilitation of process through a therapeutic encounter between client and counsellor.

If a healthy emotional relationship is to develop between an infant and his mother (parent figure) the two must be in psychological contact. The adult must have an empathic understanding of the child's needs and be highly focused on responding to and meeting those needs. The child must perceive the adult as genuine in their response. The adult must feel and demonstrate an unconditional acceptance of the child, a belief in the child's desire and capacity to reach their full potential (actualising tendency) and the adult must be fully engaged in the relationship in a way in which the infant feels he is loved and valued by a person who is real in their responses. The extent to which this has or has not been present for the child shapes not only their personality development, but also their perception and expectation of relationships. Furthermore, the child's ongoing experience with others (relatives, friends, teachers, etc.) will influence his view of himself as well as his understanding of his world, both small and large. The child brings these perceptions with him into the therapeutic encounter.

As well as the child having internalised conditions of worth, he will also bring with him to the therapy room his experience of the social context and culture of his life. This also embraces his experience of power, his own power as well as the way adults have used their power in relationships with him. A child may come into the therapy room with an expectation, based on past relationships, that I (another adult) will automatically exert power over him. I believe that in a therapeutic encounter, power is not located in the person of the therapist but rather in the dynamic of the encounter. The healing power is what happens between us in our relationship. My awareness and acknowledgement of the power which I as an adult hold in the relationship with the child, coupled with the offering of the core conditions, will communicate to the child that this is not power *over* him, rather that something powerful, something dynamic happens *between* us. My openness in acknowledging the difference between the therapeutic space and his experience of other relationships becomes an expression of the mutuality of our relationship.

DIFFERENCES IN WHAT I MIGHT BRING TO THE RELATIONSHIP AND THE INFLUENCE OF TRAINING

In Wyatt's volume on congruence, Greenberg and Geller (2001) remind the reader of the fundamental importance for a person-centred counsellor to maintain an ongoing commitment to continued learning about themselves. Through this self-knowledge or 'psychological maturity' the counsellor can be more fully present within the relationship. Greenberg and Geller argue that 'the therapist needs to be fully *present* in the therapeutic encounter in order for congruence to be therapeutic' (2001: 142). Wyatt quotes Rogers as follows: 'the more psychologically mature and integrated the therapist, the more helpful is the relationship that he or she provides. This puts a heavy demand on the therapist as a person' (Wyatt, 2001: 84).

In our diploma community I had the 'luxury' of engaging in essential learning about myself. Through this I gained a new sense of the way in which aspects of my professional and personal development are being inextricably interwoven so that I can be more fluid within therapeutic encounters whilst continuing to work within a professional boundary. I have always striven to be fully present in my relationships with my clients but it feels as if this particular form of training has enabled me to bring more of me into my awareness so that 'more of me' is present in the therapeutic encounter. I have grown and accessed learnings previously denied to my awareness. Expressive therapy through music, dance, painting and writing poetry, sand tray work, the use of miniatures and the unexpected learning through puppets and dolls' houses have all evoked a variety of deep emotions. Other ways of expanding my self-awareness come from continued journal writing and the creativity of sewing and quilt-making. Formerly I saw quilt-making as the creation of different patterns with a variety of fabrics. Now the patchwork represents the details of my own therapeutic process. My greater knowledge of myself and my openness to new experiences are available to me to be drawn on during therapeutic encounters.

In thinking about what feels different in me before and after play therapy diploma training I focus particularly on the therapeutic value and influence of our group process and the way this paralleled relationships when working with children. Quickly we established, in the training environment, a co-collaborative trust which enabled me to feel safe to explore any issues as they came into awareness during the use of expressive media. I was able to challenge my established self-concept as a counsellor for adults and to feel the power of my being able to offer greater fluidity in my work. For instance, from having started the course and my first placement with a car full of play media and equipment (what I had understood to be the essential tools if I was going to do this therapy properly) gradually I came to really believe that the therapeutic ingredient is what I bring of *myself* into the relationship rather than the range of toys I may carry round with me. I came to understand that the relationship was about process not the product I may be able to provide. I also realised that there is an interplay between the relationship the child has with the media and the relationship he has with me.

I have found that there is a different kind of facilitation of client process when building a relationship through sharing in an activity. This echoes my experience on the play therapy course residential weekend, when we cooperated in different creative activities. Because I can trust my own experience that the healing is in the relationship I have gained confidence in the view that offering a choice of activities is consistent with the PCA. This feels new, as previously I had worried about whether giving such a choice was being directive. A child coming into a playroom with a person-centred counsellor may be overwhelmed by the apparent level of freedom he has in choosing what he might want to do, because the choice can be so huge. Indeed it could feel like an alien world compared to the classroom or his family where he is probably used to having a lot of direction or rules about what he is allowed to do. It could be argued that it is not offering the core conditions to place a child in this space without helping him to understand the choices that are available to him. Furthermore, I am aware of the impact on me of the child's desire for me to join in and play with him: the potency of the child's invitation to 'join in' engenders a feeling of humility as well as excitement and challenge to be therapeutic … to make a difference through our relationship. All my clients have wanted my involvement in this way. It is my experience that the trust engendered in this co-collaboration on an activity is facilitative.

I know that I feel differently about responsibility and boundaries when I am working with a child. I believe that, whilst fully honouring the child's actualising tendency and the fact that he is his own expert, I feel a different kind of accountability. Partly because of the developmental and the power status of the child I sense that I charge myself with a higher level of responsibility than I do when working with adults. In day-to-day life, at home and in school, children have less power than adults. This leads to their greater vulnerability and means that they may be at greater risk of abuse within a counselling relationship than an adult might be. In the playroom I sense that my awareness of this means that I assume a special level of commitment to guard against any possible abuse of power and to ensure that the child feels safe enough to trust me in our relationship. Furthermore I sense that with children I have a different negotiation of boundaries than I do with adults. While maintaining safe boundaries for and with a child, I am able to be more adaptable in my expressive work with children because of the play element of the relationship. Although I always work in a way which provides psychological and emotional safety for a child I also want to ensure that my professionalism does not get in the way of the humanity of the encounter. Without a therapeutic relationship which embodies the humanity of the core conditions, the space, boundaried or not, will be sterile, empty: effective as a place in which to enjoy play but not a space in which to experience play as part of a therapeutic relationship. I feel I am more flexible about taking the risk of getting something wrong with children, because they have different cultural and developmental expectations of what is allowed in counselling. It is my experience that a child will respond in quite a straightforward way when telling me I have not properly understood what he said and that this can deepen rather than impede our relationship.

I also take with me into the relationship with a child my own introjected values, both personal and professional. My own experiences of early and subsequent attachment relationships have informed my self-concept. Thirty-four years as an adoption worker and ten years as a counsellor influence the emergence of my self-concept as a children's therapist. I know that I have changed, that I am, like the child Axline describes: 'growing—growing—growing—growing in experience, growing in understanding of himself and of his world' (Axline, 1947: 11).

OTHER ASPECTS OF DIFFERENCE IN PLAY THERAPY RELATIONSHIPS

THE CHILD'S REALISATION THAT SOMETHING DIFFERENT HAPPENS IN THE PLAYROOM

In my practice with children I sense this as being the embodiment of the sixth condition, namely that the child perceives and receives from me the core conditions and, through the establishment of psychological contact in our relationship, he experiences that something is *different* from other interactions. Seven-year-old D told me that this was his perception of what happens in our playroom: our shared space, so much so that he wondered 'Can I come and live in this room?' During his third session six-year-old K said, 'Every time I come here it gets more better. It's weird but nice weird.' This is also documented by two play therapists: Virginia Axline (1947) and Elaine Dorfman (1951). The latter describes a conversation between two children where one explains to the other how it is different: 'You can do what you want ... You don't have to be polite ... there are very few rules' (Dorfman, 1951: 255).

SEEING IS BELIEVING: THE POWER OF 3-D WORK

In the training environment, before I started working with children, I had several personal experiences of the power of expressive media. In college we were able to use miniatures and to express our 'world' in a sand tray. A doll's house workshop made a particularly powerful impact on all of those who participated. Seeing really was believing. I saw this for myself as well as seeing and hearing it from all other members of our diploma community. This workshop made me realise that the potency of seeing a world in miniature could have an enormous impression on a client. It told me that, in my practice, I must not underestimate the impact of a child 'seeing' something, which had formerly been denied into awareness. Moreover, what I offer of myself in the relationship with a child can facilitate his awareness of and understanding of what he sees. Clearly, this adds a different dimension to the therapeutic encounter from one in which the primary facilitation of process is verbal. This happened in a session when a seven-year-old boy, B, was drawn to the Duplo house and wanted to know whether I had made it myself. He commented he wished he had been there to help me, to which I reflected that he could make his own house if he wished. My client started to make his own house, telling me that it looked lonely. Gradually he added more and more furniture, people and miniatures, rearranging the different spaces as he went along. Several times I reflected that he looked pleased with his house and that it no longer looked lonely. Finally my client surrounded his house with all the large soft puppets in the room. B did not want to talk to me about this world he had built. However, there was a big visual impact on me and, although I cannot 'know' what the impact was on him, I can remember my feelings as he built his world and my transparency in reflecting to him the pleasure I saw in his face in what he had done. I felt that through the trust in our relationship it was enough for him that I had witnessed what he showed me without either the need for him to offer explanations or for me to pass comments.

HOW THE REFERRAL PROCESS INFLUENCES THE RELATIONSHIP

Adults make their own decision about whether they wish to seek counselling help. To me this feels pivotal in the building of a relationship. In the school where I worked children did not self-refer. Understandably, this creates something of an agenda, in that the school has given me details about a child, details that I would not have if an adult were coming to me for counselling. I am aware that there is a power imbalance in my having information which has not been disclosed to me by my client but by a third party. I was able to talk to one parent of each of the children I worked with, and some of the experiences reinforced this sense of unease, as there seemed to be a divergence between the reason for the referral as stated by my link person at the school and the understanding expressed by the child's parent. Such a referral system strikes me as sitting uneasily with the PCA.

In each of the initial sessions with the children I found myself wondering: does the child know why he is here? Despite my contracting I was left with an uneasy feeling about the initial lack of openness. During the following weeks I had a very strong sense that this in particular seemed to set work with children in a different context from work with adults. At first I wondered if some of the difference was about use of language and that an adult client will elect to see a counsellor. It has often been my experience that in our first session together many clients have told me with great trust why they have chosen to seek counselling. I have not found this to be the case with children. Whilst language may be relevant, it is likely to make a difference if a child can openly elect to come to the playroom because he thinks that I may be able to help with something that is bothering him. I note that Axline's view is that it is not necessary for a child to feel that he has a problem in order to benefit from therapy (Axline, 1947: 21).

INVOLVING A PARENT IN THE RELATIONSHIP

In relation to the referral process I had a completely different experience in meeting the mother of six-year-old K. She was my only source of information. I felt as if she and I connected immediately. I sensed that she felt she could trust me and she was very frank in telling me her concerns about her child in school and the differences in the school's and the family's perceptions. I felt I was able to put her at her ease so that she did not feel threatened or judged by me (Rogers, 1951: 517, Proposition 17). We then went to the child's classroom and brought him into the playroom to talk to us both together. I explained to K what play therapy was about. K seemed comfortable with his mum being present and that she knew what was going on. As a result of this transparency I felt that in my first session with K the agenda as well as the starting point for the relationship were more open and that this set a helpful context for our following twelve sessions together. A couple of times K referred to the initial meeting in positive terms.

On another occasion I involved the parent figure of eight-year-old D in one of the therapy sessions. I feel sure that it was my increased self-knowledge and growth as a therapist which led me to take this risk. During our sessions I had come to realise that there were things about his background to which D wanted answers but he was not sure how to ask, and also that he wanted to see some significant photographs from his past. I negotiated with D that we would ask J (his elder brother and parent figure) to join us in one session. It worked really well. After initial reluctance D was soon freely asking questions to which J gave poignantly phrased answers. It was an incredibly moving twenty minutes during which I witnessed the relationship between D and J. Indeed we all saw the range of relationship between each of us. It seemed to expand the therapeutic encounter between D and myself in that the following week he proudly brought in the significant photographs, which facilitated new disclosures.

CAN THE RELATIONSHIP BE FACILITATIVE WITHOUT TALKING?

We had many discussions in our diploma community about whether, in order to be deemed facilitative, the child has to tell the therapist what is going on for him. I am left wondering about this. Can it be that the relationship can do its work, can heal without my client specifically telling me what is going on? I am aware that in all my counselling relationships with adults, talking is a major ingredient in facilitating client process, but I wonder whether the same thing can be said about my counselling relationships with children?

In the session with seven-year-old B described earlier, I/we could see in the doll's house that he had created a space which was no longer lonely. This was visible. Although I did not know what it meant to him I did *see* and reflect to him the look of intense pleasure on his face at what he was creating. Although at that moment B did not want to tell me what it meant to him I cannot dispute the realness of what I saw. Dorfman concludes:

> Perhaps it is this neutralisation of fears through their concrete physical representation that is a basic aspect of play therapy. It may help to understand the apparent successes when there is little evidence of insight or verbalised attitude change. (Dorfman, 1951: 244)

Although I have increased in my assuredness about offering an invitation to a child to help me understand their world as a way of building our relationship (and I know I ask more questions than I would with adult clients), my practice tells me that it is an important and carefully balanced judgement to decide when to pursue something with a child. This has happened with two boys, both of whom let me know when they would allow me to go a bit further or (by their words or their silence) when they wanted me to stop.

The first example is seven-year-old B, in session three, when he was constructing a track for a train set, then playing with the train. He concentrated intently for about twenty-five minutes and made it clear he needed to be in his own world. I was sitting beside him on the floor, making reflections on what he was doing, inviting him to share what he was thinking and feeling. B did not speak at all and at one point turned his back to me to reinforce his 'leave me alone' message. By respecting this request and staying silent I stayed in B's frame of reference, offering him empathic understanding in accepting what he was asking of me.

In session five with D he let me know when I was allowed to seek more information from him and when he needed me not to take the issue further. He responded to a couple of my reflections which I felt were almost 'pushy' yet still acceptable to him. He then moved to a different activity and I accurately responded to his cue not to continue. I am comfortable with following the child's lead—they talk or they don't talk at different points in sessions. I feel the connection of our shared psychological contact and our growing relationship. Trust is present. It feels that many reflections are a fine line between congruence, i.e. my being fully present, and a balanced judgement about when to invite a child to share more with me and when to wait until he may, or may not, indicate that *he* wishes to do so.

SUMMARY

My ending is the same as my starting point: non-directive, client-centred play therapy with children is not ordinary. I conclude that my sensing of a different kind of relationship springs from a number of sources, including the impact of psychological maturity as a result of the particular training I received which enabled me to *feel* the potency of the use of expressive media. I believe that I have a heightened sense of responsibility because of the child's developmental status and that because of their greater vulnerability to abuse, relative powerlessness and restricted range of choices, the therapeutic relationship feels to me to be more intense and, maybe, more precious. It is my experience that children in therapy both expect and require a higher degree of flexibility of approach. I attribute this to the different understanding present in childhood culture regarding what therapy is supposed to be like and how I am supposed to behave. I have described two occasions where the involvement of a parent, prior to or during therapy, has enhanced rather than detracted from a healing relationship. I remain open-minded about whether or not it is necessary for there to be talking in order for the relationship to be facilitative.

Despite this exploration, I am left with a feeling that I have not really captured why I have such a deep sense of difference. However I can trust my feelings of awe that I am allowed entry into the world of a child and that through the building of a therapeutic relationship I can, in some small way, make a difference.

REFERENCES

Axline, VM (1947) *Play Therapy.* London: Churchill Livingstone.

Dorfman, E (1951) Play therapy. In CR Rogers *Client-Centered Therapy* (pp. 235–77). London: Constable.

Greenberg, L & Geller, S (2001) Congruence and therapeutic presence. In G Wyatt (Ed) *Rogers' Therapeutic Conditions: Evolution, theory and practice. Vol 1: Congruence* (pp. 131–49). Ross-on-Wye: PCCS Books.

Raskin, NJ (2005) The nondirective attitude. In BE Levitt (Ed) *Embracing Non-directivity: Reassessing person-centered theory and practice in the 21st century* (pp. 329–47). Ross-on-Wye: PCCS Books.

Rogers, CR (1939) *The Clinical Treatment of the Problem Child.* Boston: Houghton Mifflin.

Roger, CR (1942) *Counseling and Psychotherapy: Newer concepts in practice.* Boston: Houghton Mifflin.

Rogers, CR (1951) A theory of personality and behavior. In *Client-Centered Therapy* (pp. 481–533). London: Constable.

Rogers, CR (1957/1990) The necessary and sufficient conditions of therapeutic personality change. In H Kirschenbaum & V Henderson (Eds) (1990) *The Carl Rogers Reader* (pp. 219–35). London: Constable.

Rogers, CR (1959) A theory of therapy, personality and interpersonal relationships, as developed in the client-centered framework. In S Koch (Ed) *Psychology: A study of science. Vol 3: Formulations of the person and the social context* (pp. 184–256). New York: McGraw-Hill.

Rogers, CR (1961) *On Becoming a Person: A therapist's view of psychotherapy.* London: Constable.

Wyatt, G (2001) The multifaceted nature of congruence. In G Wyatt (Ed) *Rogers' Therapeutic Conditions: Evolution, theory and practice. Vol 1: Congruence* (pp. 79–95). Ross-on-Wye: PCCS Books.

CHAPTER 3

THREE YEARS AS A PERSON-CENTRED COUNSELLOR IN A PRIMARY SCHOOL

TRACEY WALSHAW

Three years ago I entered the world of a primary school counsellor. I was new to this context but fundamentally grounded as a person-centred expressive therapist and experienced in working with children as clients in my private practice.

> Inequalities in society are set up such that those at the bottom have to submit to the authority of those above them. This inequality is always present in the therapy relationship due to the roles of the therapist and client but it is exacerbated when the therapist has more power than the client due to other aspects of their identity as well. (Proctor, 2006: 75)

When I read this it consolidated some of the thoughts and challenges that working with primary school children raised for me. Age discrimination seems to be a potent discrimination that is far from addressed. Nowhere do I experience such powerlessness and the potential for having 'power over' than I do with this child client group. Primary school is one of the first organized agencies for social control and the potential for abuse of power by adults is frightening. This abuse of power is often not from any malign intent but due to economic and time pressures. I have yet to meet a teacher who intends to deliberately exert their power over a child in a negative way. However, this is one of the first places where professionals begin to label clients and respond to them accordingly. It is heartbreaking to hear a child who has come to me for therapeutic help saying 'I'm here because I'm a naughty boy'. Yet this has been a frequent event. And as I hear them, I am asking myself whether this child is really being naughty or whether they are trying to make sense of their sometimes deprived social, economic and emotional environments in the best way they can? This group of children cannot even vote with their feet. Running away is not an option for many.

Working as a therapist in primary school raised for me a whole new aspect of oppression, including how I might oppress my therapeutic relationships by under-involvement in the context in which my clients were living, by professional containment and by my own political naïvety. I have emerged from this work with more questions than answers. A key question is how I engage with systems to aid growth and change for my clients. Working in isolation with this client group does not feel enough and thus developing therapeutic relationships with those that have power in these situations seems fundamental in any model for change.

BEING POWERFUL

When therapists ignore the links between social inequalities and psychological distress, they serve the interests of privileged social groups rather than those of their clients. (Proctor, 2006: 71)

In counselling we talk about the importance of boundaries and confidentiality but not much about how extending boundaries can aid our young clients who can be oppressed in many different ways. This insight came to me as I began to recognise how often the focus of my work with these children was in helping them develop mechanisms to exist in systems that seem damaging; systems in which they had no power to effect change. Unlike adults, they do not have the power to affect economic, social or even in some cases emotional changes from their carers. Therapy seems at best a space to understand their situation and their responses to it. In an ideal world children would be fully nurtured by their families and the wider society and it would be easier to identify the source of 'naughty' behaviour. In reality however a lot of children are doing the best they can with the poor hand life has dealt them. What follows is a taster of what brought me to these conclusions.

It is my first week in this school and I am sitting in my counselling room, which is a multi-space, which means in reality an unloved, communal space. I am wondering what I can do to make this an inviting space for children, when I hear the loud voice of a supply teacher issuing instructions that seem to manifest as commands that must unquestionably be obeyed. As I sit there, having all my stereotypical judgements about teachers reinforced, I am not surprised that I have a client list as long as my arm. Thus begins the most fundamental necessary learning within the context of this organisation. My smugness soon leaves me the following week when the Head asks me to go into a class of 28 nine year olds who are having a lot of difficulties with their relationships with each other. So off I go with my plastic animals and the fragile confidence that I tell myself comes from extensive experience of being in large community groups. Within ten minutes, I find myself shouting and out of my mouth leaps such person-centred blasphemies as: 'Put my plastic squid down now!' 'Take that snake from around Johnny's neck this instant!' and 'NO you can't have a balloon now, it's too late!' I come home, put my head on the kitchen table and wail that I am a terrible therapist. The response from my daughter, with her infinite and consistent ability to see things for what they are, is: 'Oh get a grip mum!'

So I did get a grip, with my fundamental theoretical underpinning. What I had not engaged with in that situation was the first condition of psychological contact, not only with the children but also with myself! My craft as a therapist had been specifically within the ring-fenced arena of one-to-one therapy, couples counselling and person-centred community groups.

This was also the beginnings of my encounter with institutional power, the experience of power-over and how easily I had been seduced into responding to what the organisation wanted without consulting with the children. So, the context had been established. Here in school the challenge was providing therapeutic support within the context of the organisation and family structures, whilst recognising the position of low power children have within these systems. I recognised that this work was going to challenge the way I approached and experienced counselling relationships and I had a sense that this was not going to be pain-free learning.

BEING VISIBLE

I had inherited the counselling practice at the school from a therapist who had been there for six months, and whose approach was different from my own. Previously, the therapist had selected her clients. What I wanted was for the staff to feel included so I asked them to suggest clients. They were concerned and honest enough to acknowledge that, if this was their choice, then I would be sent the naughtiest children in the school. That seemed fine by me. I also inherited a dinnertime drop-in during which my predecessor had seen four clients, each for 15 minutes. I naïvely thought it would be a good way to access self-referrals. I quickly learned the folly of this when in the second week I had thirty self-referrals, ranging from 'trouble with life' to 'me mum hates me'. How to choose? Well I couldn't, but it jump-started me into thinking about the value of children accessing me and my visibility within the school. So I had to find a way to negotiate a compromise. I began with an hour drop-in session at dinner for children who may have been identified as upset or struggling by the teacher, parents and themselves. This cut down the numbers. Throughout my life, and relationship with the school, and by this I mean the children, staff, parents and other organisations that had input to struggling children, I have endeavoured to develop flexibility in my work, to be responsive rather than reactive. I came to this by thinking about having a shape that was movable, fluid and flexible as opposed to rigid and brittle. I consistently ask fundamental questions about how I can respond to my clients and significant others in a way that is respectful and not dismissive, and ultimately is in the best interest of my clients.

I was reminded about the person-centred principles that underpin community groups and this concretized my thinking of the school as a community, working together for the children. Pretty soon I identified the importance of being in relationship with both clients and the significant adults in their lives in a way that did not breach my clients' confidentiality. This arose as I saw primary school children as having very little power and I recognised I had some creative thinking to do. For example, the teachers at this school were exceptionally good-hearted towards the children, and genuinely interested in their progress. There were real benefits to be achieved from including them in the therapeutic work and it felt detrimental to exclude them. I was very aware of the information they could use to change the environment and systems in ways that would help the children. This was probably where thinking about integrating the system into the client work as opposed to the client into the system became clearer.

I remembered how theory gives me support so I began to talk to the staff about some client processes in terms of theory without breaking confidentiality. How could I facilitate this? I knew two things from my own experience. The first was the potency of receiving the core conditions in groups and how therapeutic relationships had changed me as a person. The second was that theory has always been my ballast in stormy times. I find it dynamic, creative and comforting. I noticed that teachers and support workers asked me what I was doing with the children when they gave me reports on the children. I realized that there was value about my accessibility and visibility in the school not just with my client group but also with the staff.

Initially, I was concerned with fears that the children would see me as 'one of the staff'. Then there was the challenge of holding confidentiality as teachers clearly wanted to give me information about my clients, their children. Once I'd stopped reacting to this and thought about the roles teachers played, it made sense that they wanted to share information that they thought would be helpful to me in my work. I quickly recognised that this was not an attempt to sabotage my relationships with my clients, but that the staff were trying to be helpful. I have always been accessible to the staff, and I have found them to be respectful of boundaries once they understand what they are and why they are important. I identified that I wanted to be a part of the school community and not reside in a clinical ivory tower. This obviously took me to questioning how this would be with the children, so I tried to be very explicit in my contracting, explaining how this might look, that they would see me talking to teachers but that I was clear I would not be breaking their confidentiality unless we had discussed this first, i.e., issues around self-harm and others hurting them. I remembered hearing Tony Merry at a conference suggesting that we should show our clients how we work.

Being visible invites people in and worried parents began to approach me in the corridor. I would tell the children and make it explicit to parents that I would not be telling them about the content of their child's work with me. I was concerned about what the impact might be of trying to brush off the approaches and worries of parents and took my lead from my experience in couples counselling where it is possible to validate different people and processes at the same time. My son had therapy quite a few years ago and I remembered how vulnerable I felt and how important it was that I had a sense of the therapist to whom I was entrusting my child. In private practice I contract with my child client's parent or the family member that brings them as there is then clarity about what needs to happen for me to provide a safe space for their child. So, at school, I began to invite the parents to the first session to explain how I would work. Frequently parents did not come but I always held the possibility that they might turn up later on.

BEING CHALLENGED

Whilst my theoretical background had helped me significantly in establishing my school practice, I experienced a number of challenges that I had not read about.[1]

---

1. Details have been changed to protect the confidentiality of the children talked about in this chapter.

THE POWER OF THE PARENT IN THE PLAYGROUND

I worked with one child, having first negotiated the confidentiality of our work with her mother. The child's behaviour improved but six months on the parent wanted information about what we had been doing in the sessions. I reminded her of what we had negotiated when I initially started working with her child concerning the boundaries of the confidentiality. I held the confidentiality and this frustrated mother had a lot to say about me in the playground, so that, for a while, other mothers were reluctant to let their child come to see me. I talked to the class teacher about how I could address this. She told me (in her own words) that there were other dynamics at play and that basically I had to trust that other parents had had a positive experience and that this would eventually balance out one parent's perceived negative experience. It was ironic that another professional was telling me to trust the process! Which I did. On reflection I think at this point I had the potential of responding to my internalised interjects about unfairness and wanting to defend myself. I left it and after a while the referrals came in, helped I am sure by the teacher's understanding of what the playground politics at that time were about, which still remain a mystery to me!

A ROOM WITH A WINDOW

When I eventually got a very nice room I had to have a window so that people could see into the room that I was working in with the child. This, I was assured, was for my protection as well as the child's because the window would ensure that people would know if anything untoward was happening. This reminded me of the old movies where actors could only kiss in a bedroom scene providing they kept one foot on the floor, because we all know you can't have sex if one foot is on the floor! But for me there was also the challenge of how a window impacted on the confidentiality of my clients' work, and my ability to create a secure space for their work. Other children, knowing there was a room full toys were highly likely to peer through the window whilst we were working, as could passing adults—staff and parents alike. The conflict between the institution's need to guarantee the safety of the child and my need to create a private place where they could work secure in the knowledge that they would not be seen and judged was irreconcilable. Whilst recognising and endorsing the need for vulnerable children to be protected from preying adults, the reality that a window might fulfil this function seemed absurd so that it felt neither valuable as a safety device nor therapeutic. So, we negotiated a window with frosted glass.

NOT ALIENATING THE STAFF WITH THE EXPRESSIVE EQUIPMENT

As I began to equip the therapy space, I realised that some of the staff were viewing all this equipment in the playroom as mysterious, and therefore with some apprehension. I had found sandplay using a sand tray and small objects or miniatures to be a facilitative medium with my child clients and became aware that some of them talked with their teachers about what they had been doing when they returned to the classroom. We had been able to purchase some expensive sandplay equipment and this raised a lot of curiosity amongst the staff about how this would be used to change children's behaviour. I saw this as a creative opportunity to dispel the myths about what I might and might not do in sandplay work. I began looking for a way in which I could give a taste of how expressive work may help. One member of staff expressed a particular interest so I explained that sometimes seeing things manifested in the physical world gives us different information. I invited her to think about something that she was concerned about in one of her relationships, and then to pick miniatures to symbolize this. Her response was immediate and as she selected and placed her miniatures in the sand tray, it was apparent that she was able to crystallize something that she had been struggling with. Later that day, I went into my room to find this member of staff with some of her colleagues 'having a go' in the sand tray. This spontaneous and human interaction did more for understanding about what I might be doing than my theoretical descriptions.

SOME NUISANCES WITH GROUPS IN PRIMARY SCHOOLS

I was running a group with six girls who were continually falling out with each other. On one particular occasion, one of the girls felt 'got at' by the group and subsequently, outside of the group time, she argued with two group members in the playground, and in some distress, told her mother what had happened. Her mother, concerned to protect her child, withdrew her permission for her daughter to attend the group. By the following week, the argument and distress had blown over and when the group met, this girl came along and wanted to stay with her friends—these same girls that she had felt angry with last week. However, in view of her mother's intervention, I had to explain that she could not be in the group as we no longer had her mother's permission to work with her. She refused to leave and momentarily I was at a loss. With adults this is not a dilemma. With children it can be, as I cannot go against the parent's wishes. The child physically refused to leave the group and I felt anxious about her just being in the same room as the group as I was fearful about how this could be interpreted by her mother. After a brief panic, I surrendered the dilemma to the other group members and one of the girls said she really wanted the group to run and took the initiative to seek out the Deputy Head, who had the power to move the reluctant participant. How strange it feels, to forcibly remove a client from a therapy group! I once more learned that in counselling children I must maintain an acute awareness of the adults in their life, and that this sometimes blocks the immediacy, spontaneity and flexibility of my work around family systems. For myself, I feel there is a direct correlation between my spontaneity and flexibility, and my anxiety levels about how my work will be interpreted; between my theoretical underpinnings and philosophical model and the process of professional accountability.

BEING CREATIVE

Allowing myself to be creative and to challenge some of the perceived rigid concepts or mantras around in the person-centred approach proved to be some of the most facilitative work I developed within the school setting. Being authentic in my relationships with the children often meant trusting their process more than the discomfort created by my introjected values and conditions of worth around my role as children's counsellor within an organisational setting. Spontaneity and responsiveness are key learning edges. For example, received wisdom, with which I had previously agreed, was that counselling should occur in a specialised room with just the therapist and the child. One of my clients was doing some deep work about the loss of her grandmother and in the moment it became vital for her to find some information on the internet about the place where her grandmother had lived and was buried. My room was next to the Information Technology room so off we trotted and I was not only amazed at the competence of my young client on the computer but also how deeply important it was for her to be given this freedom. We were in the room with other children, curious about what she was doing. My immediate concern was to protect her and to maintain the confidentiality of her therapeutic work. My client however was more robust than I had credited her and fielded questions in a very matter of fact and confident way.

One of the most memorable pieces of work I did was with Wendy, a young girl whose mother had died and whose father was now living with a new partner. Wendy disclosed that she could not have any pictures of her mother up at home and how upsetting this was for her. We explored in our session whether and how she could access any pictures of her mother and she decided to ask her aunt. Her aunt duly sent her a picture, which Wendy then brought to our session. She decided that she wanted to make a memory box about her mother and placed the photograph in the box, which she left with me in the counselling room. It had become apparent how important it was for Wendy to be able to have contact with her memories of her mother and how significant this photograph was for her in this process. I decided to take a risk and had the picture enlarged and laminated and put copies around the walls in the playroom when she next came. Her expression as she came into the room is still imprinted on my heart. In a voice choked with emotion, she said, 'There is so much of my Mum in here!' This was a significant breakthrough for this little girl and she decided that she wanted to take the pictures home and stick them onto her bedroom door. I braced myself for a potential visit from an angry stepmother. None came. Instead, I learned the next week that Wendy had talked to her father for the first time about missing her mother and that they were now planning a visit to her grave. I followed my intuition with this client, despite the risks and although I have questioned my intent, I am happy with risking spontaneity.

One of the clients I had the most learning from about the power of trusting the actualising tendency was Sadie. She was referred because her behaviour was seen to be out of control in class, culminating in her throwing a chair across the classroom. She was frequently seen sitting in the corridor outside her classroom, excluded for bad behaviour. I was beginning to think the only thing she was learning was just how many coat pegs were on the opposite wall and how many tiles there were on the corridor floor. When we began to work together, it became clear that her issue was her grief about her grandmother dying three years previously. She had not felt able to talk about her feelings at home as the adults would get upset. So instead of the work on anger management suggested by the educational psychologist, we spent a lot of time together talking through play and making things about her grandmother. And of course, without needing recourse to any anger management programme or coping strategies, her behaviour outside the therapy room improved, so much so that she was awarded 'pupil of the week' on several occasions.

On one occasion after I had just emerged from my room at the end of a session with another client, I found Sadie distraught outside the Headmistress's office. I invited her into my room to see if I could help. She was upset because she felt she had been misjudged by one of the teaching assistants, had protested but was ignored, and in her frustration she had thrown a pencil, though not at the teacher, she hastened to say, as she would have done in the past. In her own words she spoke of feeling judged because she used to react in a certain way and identified how unfair this was as she had now changed. We talked about how we can get labelled and when we change how difficult it is for others not to refer back to how it had been in the past. I asked her what she wanted to do and she said she wanted to apologise to the teaching assistant but also that she wanted my help to explain that she had changed, 'because she'll believe you, you're an adult' (a comment I found deeply wise and just as distressing). So we invited the teaching assistant in and Sadie apologised and in lay terms I explained the person-centred theory of change, of self-concept and about how we judge people. The teaching assistant understood immediately and began to talk with Sadie about what had just happened. My sense was that when the teaching assistant understood and took responsibility for judging Sadie, a potentially better relationship emerged.

I think this is the work that helped me to acknowledge that I need to engage with the wider system to help my clients to change their self-concept within a friendly environment. In real time I see each of my child clients for an hour a week and the rest of their time they are steeped in the presence of significant others such as teachers, peers and families. If the work done by clients to effect change is not to be sabotaged by these systems, then I have found it necessary to get involved with them, to help them to understand the change process, and at times to intervene on behalf of my clients, with their permission. This is what I have come to understand as not being 'under-involved' with my clients' environment.

As another example of direct intervention with a client: we were in the playroom and she was talking about how the other children teased her and called her dirty and smelly. It was at this point that I noticed a small army of head lice marching across her forehead. I decided to comment on this as it felt ridiculous to ignore them. I considered what I thought to be in the best interest of this client, to talk about head lice with an awareness that her mother had been sent several letters by the school about this problem but had ignored them, or to take direct action and eradicate the ones I saw. I asked her what she wanted me to do, and her response was unequivocal—she wanted me to kill them as her mother ignored the letters and she would be teased. So we talked as I deloused her hair. Again, I am aware that this could be seen as risky as I clearly stepped beyond the boundaries of a normal counsellor–client relationship and into the ethical minefield that is child protection policy. This is a dilemma that faces all adults working with children—teachers, teaching assistants and youth workers—where the attempts to protect children with legislation leads to bizarre and apparently uncaring behaviours.

A clear example of this presented itself one day when a reception child came to the staff room with a splinter sticking out of her very small finger. I was just about to pull it out when I was told I was not allowed to do this, as under the school's health and safety policy the correct procedure was to call her mother or to take the child to the hospital. So consequently we had to sit there until her mother came, coaxing the crying and distressed child to keep her hand still. This seems both ridiculous and inhumane and I am ever watchful for the potential of such behaviours creeping into increasingly regulated counselling relationships. My experience is that relationships fuelled by fear are unlikely to fulfil their full healing potential. I see counselling relationships without fundamental and basic humanity as both scary and impotent.

In conclusion, being a person-centred children's counsellor in an institutional setting is both potentially hugely potent and also absolutely crazy and a very risky business within the current climate. Will I jump ship? No! Although I acknowledge the need to develop some crazy and creative fluidity if I am to co-habit with organisational structures.

REFERENCE

Proctor, G (2006) Therapy: Opium of the masses or help for those who least need it? In G Proctor, M Cooper, P Sanders & B Malcolm (Eds) *Politicizing the Person-Centred Approach: An agenda for social change* (pp. 66–79). Ross-on-Wye: PCCS Books.

CHAPTER 4

SANDPLAY
'GROWING GROUND' IN PERSON-CENTRED PLAY THERAPY

JO WOODHOUSE

Jane spells out 'W-A-T-E-R'. 'You want to put it in the sand?' I ask. She nods. I get water in a jug and she tips it in, wetting the sand. The water swirls round, Jane's eyes sparkle. I say, 'You love the way the water goes into the sand'. She nods and starts heaping the wet, muddy sand, patting it down, building a tall mound. I feel her total concentration and notice the way she uses her whole body as she's working. Carefully, Jane buries two horses she's picked out—a little one and then a much bigger one. She adds more water around the sand heap, then takes a tiny spade and a figure of a girl and digs for the horses, eventually uncovering the big horse. The horse gambols round in the muddy sand and water, making horse neighing sounds, and then the small horse joins in. Jane lies the big horse down in the water then it rolls around in the mud, over and over. She laughs out loud, delightedly, as she rolls the horse about. Catching her feeling, I laugh with her. She briefly looks up at me, meets my eyes (something she rarely does) and smiles. I realise in the midst of all this that I have forgotten that she never speaks (in school); I am so caught up in what she is saying.

Andrew carefully buries two white skeletons (they are two brothers) in the sand, making sure the strings on top of their heads are just sticking out. Two other green skeletons (also brothers) are relaxing on the 'beach' but they don't realise they are in danger, he says. The brothers on the beach talk to each other; they are having a good time on their holiday. But there is a lurking sense of danger, which I can feel. I reflect on it to Andrew. He nods, continuing with the story. After a few minutes, the brothers lie down to sleep. At this point, Andrew picks one of the strings out of the sand and the white skeleton slowly rises out of the ground, roaring and shaking. Then the second one also rises up. There follows a fierce fight where the two green brothers are attacked and bricks are thrown at them and their heads are knocked in by the bricks. Andrew describes this in detail as he goes along. The bricks are hurled, bodies are kicked down and eventually the green skeletons are dead. Andrew buries them in the sand, but soon they will have revenge: 'because they are already skeletons, they can't be killed as they are already dead'.

INTRODUCTION

The opening sequences are from recent sandplays (within play therapy sessions) with two children, Jane and Andrew. They illustrate not only the vivid nature of sandplay but also the physical and sensory aspects of working with sand as a material. The strong storytelling possibilities of sandplay are also reflected in these opening pieces and explored further in this chapter. Within a person-centred therapy relationship, all these aspects of sandplay interrelate and can allow children access to their experience on levels they may not otherwise be able to speak about.

Most of the people I work with are children, and I usually work with them in school. In writing this piece, I felt how important it was to talk to each person whose sand work I wanted to include. Once we began talking, it became clear the concern with all of the children was largely about respecting the ways each person wished to appear. This means that all children chose with me which pieces of their stories to share.

The growing interest in sandplay, with both adults and children, speaks of the value of this expressive way of working. Traditional sandplay therapy is based in Jungian psychodynamic theory. Most writing and research on sandplay comes from this approach and is linked to the family therapy tradition (Rabone, 2003; Boik & Goodwin, 2000; Kalff, 1991). Although working with a sand tray has been part of play therapy since its earliest beginnings (Dorfman, 1951; Axline, 1974), there is little written about sandplay within other approaches, including person-centred therapy. This lack of theory or literature on sandplay from a person-centred perspective made my own sandplay practice initially daunting, but this chapter explores how I have developed my work within the person-centred approach.

The focus of Jungian sandplay—on the technique of sandplay, the knowledge and expertise of the therapist with this technique and the way they use it to 'treat' the client or patient—places most of the power in the hands of the therapist. Although accompanying the client during sandplay and 'witnessing' the process in the sand is important, the intent behind this is for the therapist to interpret and place meaning on the client's material and process. Often this is done through preconceived meanings for images, symbols or metaphors used by the client. This differs fundamentally from how I see working with sandplay within a person-centred relationship; here the value of sandplay is based implicitly on trust in the client's process. My commitment is to travel beside the client—not to do anything to them—and to listen for, and try to understand, the client's own meanings, free from preconceived interpretations.

Sandplay is offered within person-centred play therapy sessions as one possibility from a range of experiential work. Children choose when and how they engage with sandplay and many return over and over to work in the sand. I usually work with two trays of sand so that one can be kept dry, which some people prefer. Objects, figures, animals and various structures can be put in the sand; sand can be moulded and sculpted to create landscapes and features. Water can be added to wet sand to create pools and mud. Containers holding water can be sunk into the sand to create pools or lakes. The wide range of materials and objects that can be used allow rich possibilities of expression (Kalff, 2003; Weinrib, 2004).

Sometimes children make pictures, designs or scenes that are static. More often, they tell stories, with the sand as the ground or landscape within which the tale unfolds. Some children like to use the sand to play games that involve burying things or 'hide and seek'. Some of the most moving times for me have been with young people using the sand (often with water) in physical, sensory-based ways, experiencing the touch and feel of being in contact with the sand and being in the moment. This can provide precious times of calm and relaxation in an otherwise hurried and pressured existence.

Working to be in relationship with children engaged in sandplay means being open to the many ways they may speak through this expressive way of working. Listening needs to be with the whole of myself—all my senses and intuition. My intent is to grow a relationship where the child is free to be themselves and where they will be accompanied on their journey. In sandplay, the challenge is in listening to and hearing the unique voice of each child, and communicating my understanding of what I'm hearing. I feel these challenges especially in working with children because of the child's lack of power and the trust they often give me.

Rogers argued that change occurs when people experience themselves more fully (Rogers, 1980). The qualities of sandplay, including its non-verbal nature, facilitate this, especially in work with children. When offered in the context of a person-centred relationship, sandplay offers children a less intimidating means of communication that may allow them a fuller experience of themselves than would happen otherwise in therapy. Trusting children to do what they need to do, I see them return again and again to work in the sand tray, leading me to believe they are getting something important for themselves at that time.

GROWING RELATIONSHIP

Alice (aged twelve) used animal figures, including lions, to tell a story of a family, with different-sized figures to show the daughter lion growing up and the pattern of family relationships. Her work was often around conflict and difficult relationships within her family. In her second sandplay, Alice poured herself into a lively story which seemed to tell more about relationships in her family than she had ever been able to say in previous sessions when we'd talked together. Alice showed how it was for the young daughter lion, including feelings she and other lions had for each other. This work felt powerful as Alice moved through such a lot of her world that had been so hard to talk about. During the story I heard the conflict between 'people' and what it meant. Much of the empathy was about sensing the energy and movement going into the sand during the story because it seemed to reflect how intensely some characters were feeling. Alice worked strongly and freely, putting a lot of energy into physical contact with the sand—shaping it, creating places for different characters and moving it about. She seemed able to relax and go into her process and my sense was she was feeling safe with the sand as well as with me.

This work seemed to release something in Alice so that she was then free to move into expressing directly (for the first time) how angry she was feeling with one person in her family. Later she talked of her frustration and upset in being caught in the middle of the conflict between people who she wanted to care about her. Following her sandplay, Alice was able to talk more freely about what was currently happening in her family and the difficult feelings she had about it. Later, she moved even further, considering possibilities for change, perhaps through a meeting with family members. She seemed to be feeling more power and experiencing herself as a separate person with her own feelings and needs. She was thinking about choice—something she had previously not felt was possible.

This sandplay, offered within the relationship we had grown together, allowed Alice to experience and move through part of her world that she had previously been unable to describe. In person-centred terms, the sandplay helped Alice to experience herself more fully and freed her to look at aspects of her life she found very difficult. She was even able to think about how she might now manage things differently than in the past.

Being able to meet a child in this way through sandplay can allow them to clarify aspects of their lives that cannot be directly spoken about. Alice had previously been unable to think about how it might be to meet with her family members. The non-verbal processing which sandplay allows becomes especially important when working with children as it allows the child or young person to choose to work at a level that feels safe for them. This is why it is important to stay within the story the child is telling (Axline, 1974) and not interrupt the process by trying to identify characters as real people in children's lives. The nature of sandplay means that children may often be working with material outside or on the edge of their awareness. In empathic understanding, such meanings are sometimes revealed and reflection by the therapist may help the child to become aware of feelings that were previously unclear. But the story must be allowed to unfold in its own time.

It is often clear to me that I am working with several aspects or 'parts' of a child during sandplay. My experience suggests this is very much a process of working with 'configurations of Self' (Mearns, 1999) that are often revealed during storytelling (as characters, for example). In this process, it is important to work where the child is (i.e. remain in the story) and to listen 'as openly as is possible to all the different parts and meanings and conflicts gradually unveiled by the client' (Mearns, 1999: 125).

Empathy during sandplay facilitates the child's awareness of themselves. When the therapist is able to meet the client, this may be understood as the client letting the therapist into the 'inner dialogue' they have with themselves (Mearns, 1999). Sandplay facilitates this meeting in work with children, often powerfully. Unconditional positive regard (UPR) is communicated through accepting the child's world as it unfolds in the sandplay, including the characters, along with their actions and feelings. As the child pours their process into the sand, they make a vivid picture of their inner dialogue and ways of seeing the world (as did Alice with her family situation). Sims (1989/2002) uses the idea of 'indwelling' (a term first used by the philosopher Michael Polanyi (1958)) to describe our full experience and knowing, through directly meeting the world. In person-centred terms, the therapist's role is to indwell the client—enter into their world—and in this way help the client experience themselves. This seems to happen through empathy and the prizing of the client's experience (McMillan, 2004). Sandplay facilitates the possibility of indwelling the client at a level that may not be possible simply through dialogue, particularly when working with children. This is because through sandplay children can safely encounter and experience people, and work through feelings they may not be able to speak about directly.

COMMUNICATING IN SANDPLAY: SPEAKING AND BEING HEARD

The children with learning disabilities that I work with often do not 'fit in' to their worlds and the labels they have been given can profoundly get in the way of them being heard or seen. In working with both Jane and Michael, where verbal communication is very difficult, sandplay has helped us in growing our relationship. It allows the children to communicate their ways of seeing the world and facilitates them in finding their own unique ways to 'speak' and be heard. It also allows me to meet them—to see and 'hear' how they see the world and communicate my intent to be with them and to allow them to be where they are. This work helps me understand how children can use sandplay to relax in ways that allow them to be in relationship whilst staying safe. The sensory nature of sandplay allows children to find ways to get in touch with their process and to feel safe enough to communicate within the relationship.

Jane, aged six, (whose sandplay opens this chapter) spoke little at home and not at all in school. Believing this is how she needed to be, I wanted to meet and accept her where she was, seeing beyond her silence and the problem this is perceived as by others. This was not easy for either of us. Working in the sand allowed Jane to 'speak' without talking—she could communicate in our relationship at a level that I trusted felt comfortable for her at the time. At times I experienced her as 'speaking' intensely—the sandplay helped me hear her and understand what she was experiencing and feeling. There were times of relaxation, such as in the opening sequence. In other moments, I experienced myself as clumsy and stumbling, trying to understand where Jane was and communicate to her what I heard. I worked to try to meet her in her silent world and hear whatever she was able to 'say'. The sand helped us both in this process; it allowed a lot of communication without talking and let me into Jane's world when she felt ready to do this, in ways she chose. Jane was in control of the process—how much she said and how she said it. This was important. I believe that through it, she felt more secure in the relationship. Somehow, in contact with the sand, she could relax enough to communicate something to me, sometimes a nod or shake of her head. She began occasionally to say one or two words and look at me.

Jane has now begun speaking in school, in a gradual process she's deciding for herself. This has followed many months of work, trusting Jane and myself in our process together, alongside significant support within school. At Jane's request, we worked with her mother in many of the sessions. This has helped Jane to speak and become more confident. Jane often used the sand tray during this time, talking to her mother, and gradually, to me, about what she was doing. It seemed to me the sand was a familiar place for her during this time when a lot was changing. I had a sense of it as some sort of 'solid ground', holding the mysterious process we were all in, which seemed to me an incredible transition. Jane's mother often joined in the sandplays and gradually we began to relax together.

As Jane spoke more to me within the sessions, she was working almost wholly in the sand and I found myself with her in places which were at the same time, very familiar and also incredibly changed, through us now being able to speak together. These were such different experiences for me, to witness Jane's world and hear her words. I can now understand things that I had only been able to guess at previously. We both of us share delight in discovering and communicating our understanding.

Jane seems to have found ways of using the sandplay to feel safe. As she moved into our changing relationship, finding her own way, she has talked as much or as little as she wanted. She began to make some eye contact and this is increasing. Recently, I've become aware of subtle differences emerging in Jane's speaking; for example, during her sandplay, she may say clearly to me what is happening; or she may talk quietly, almost to herself, or sing to herself; at other times, the 'people' or animals in the sand tray are talking to each other. In this I hear different voices, different qualities and ways of speaking which Jane is exploring. The sandplay is facilitating, as she can move easily between various sorts of speaking whilst being in relationship in new ways and moving at her own pace with all of this. As she is becoming more confident, she has been in contact and dialogue for more of the time in sessions. I experience her closely, feeling our meeting in moments of intimacy that seem incredibly powerful and very precious. Our work begins to feel relaxed and easy and is often full of humour, as Jane enjoys this increasingly within our relationship.

Michael (aged six) finds people difficult to understand and too much contact can be overwhelming. I trust him to know what he needs—for me this is about him having control and power in what happens when he is with me, something that is very difficult in other parts of his world. Michael moves in and out of contact during his sandplay time, sometimes talking with me, other times going into himself, often through strong, sensory contact with the sand, talking to himself, singing or humming softly. After a quiet patch, he begins to say what's happening in the tray again. Michael clearly loves the sand—he uses it freely and is visibly relaxed after a few minutes working in it. I felt from the beginning how important it is that he can be himself, regulate his process and have time without the pressures to conform that are found outside. I feel his way of being with himself in the sand as marvellously creative—he has found ways to be in a relationship that feel safe for him. In this the sand has helped us both in our work together.

The sandplay means Michael can 'speak' and communicate something of what his world is like. He makes pictures of his ways of seeing the world, picking out what is important—often particular collections of objects or figures. His worlds can seem disjointed—full of scattered items and people. At times I am only able to reflect each part separately, not understanding if, or how, they link together. More recently, Michael has begun telling stories which have a thread that I can follow for at least part of the time. This seems to be a real change. His stories are now much more about people, relationships and feelings. I experience this as a change in him.

STORYTELLING

Andrew (aged eight, also from the opening sequence) did not use the sand until later sessions of his play therapy. He was initially very unsure of it. In early sessions he was also intensely careful and watchful, playing warily, watching me to see my reaction to things he did. He seemed to be watching for something to go 'wrong', which he said was how he felt. I tried to let him know that he could be as he was during the sessions with me and I would be OK with however he wanted to be.

Andrew began telling a story in the sand tray that he developed over the next eight weeks. At the beginning, the story involved rival animals in battles where one character won and was 'the king'. The stories were full of conflict, elaborate, fierce fighting, anger, violence, horrible deaths and destruction. My sense was Andrew was very much part of the story, and from the start I felt him inviting me into a world which was uniquely his own. Andrew related the story carefully, occasionally checking I was following. I worked to be with him to hear and understand the feelings of the characters and meaning of events for them. This was not difficult as the story was powerful and vivid.

Despite the violence and fighting, Andrew played all this out largely in silence. In the third sandplay, when one character had destroyed a lot of others violently, but in silence, I shared my observation with Andrew. It seemed this character also needed to be silent. Andrew nodded at my comment, but didn't say anything or look up, concentrating on the sand and the characters.

In the following sessions, Andrew seemed to relax and played more and more freely. After a while the characters began to be much noisier. He was also using the sand much more freely—often shaping it and moving it about. His play now centred around two pairs of skeletons (brothers), describing a world where danger lurked everywhere, even when things seemed safe. Andrew seemed to need to develop more and more dangerous situations for the brothers, building up an intense sense of peril. The action described in the opening sequence of this chapter was part of a session where I shared with him my sense of how nothing seemed safe in the brothers' world, even though things looked OK. At the time I felt strongly that this was how he saw the world—he seemed to be saying (through his characters) over and over: the world isn't safe, danger is all around; things are not as they seem; I must be on my guard; to survive I must attack; if I am hurt I must have revenge. Over several weeks, I was able to reflect what the characters in the story seemed to be saying. As we went along and I shared what I was seeing, Andrew said some more about the brothers' world and what he thought about them. He told me the brothers were brave and loyal because they kept defending each other and fighting when things went wrong. They didn't give up. But they kept getting into trouble because they could never tell where the danger was, so they kept getting caught out and hurt, and then had to seek revenge. This confirmed for me the intense struggle I was feeling in Andrew's stories about the brothers. It also seemed that our relationship had become closer and more trusting through sharing the sandplay stories, so that Andrew could now say something more about how he saw his world.

In the following weeks, Andrew's story gradually changed; although there was conflict and opposition, gradually the danger and violence seemed to fade away. Humour began to creep in, the characters were having fun and there were stories of cats and dogs. Andrew's sandplay was much less violent and seemed much less angry. None of the scuffles were very intense, everyone seemed to be having fun and nobody got very hurt. Eventually they ended up in a family. At this point Andrew asked to finish his play therapy. In his last session, he told a moving story where cats and lions struggle and find a home; he built several sand bridges, which the different animals crossed to reach their home together. By this session, he was freely shaping the sand landscape and spent time at the end smoothing the sand in a soothing, calming movement that seemed to reflect the peaceful place he had found.

Andrew's process during his sandplay felt very powerful to me and it clearly led somewhere for him, although I was unaware of how it related to his life outside. The work with Andrew reminds me of the need to trust the process in person-centred work. What was important was being with Andrew in his process. There was no need for directing or imposing an interpretation (as in traditional sandplay therapy), nor for me to understand how Andrew's sandplay related to his current life. Andrew went where he needed to go. Over eight weeks he had moved to a different place within himself. Trust in the child's actualising tendency is fundamental in working in this way. As this work shows, being with a child in this way during sandplay can facilitate movement over a relatively short period of time.

It is rare that I get to know whether the work has changed things for children, even when they have clearly moved during the therapy process. However with Andrew, I did have some feedback from his teacher, some weeks later. He told me that Andrew seemed much calmer and more able to manage strong feelings when they came up. This was precious for me, to know that Andrew was having an easier time in school. It also clarified and confirmed my sense of the more settled place I sensed he had found within himself.

Verbal storytelling is now accepted as an important part of the therapeutic process in counselling and play therapy (Nicholls, 2000; McLeod, 2000). Sandplay's non-verbal, physical playing out of stories and the relationships within them makes the storytelling process immediate, vivid and powerful. Within the story, children play out what is going on for them (Wilson, Kendrick & Ryan, 1992; Bradway, 1999), making it safe for them to work through difficulties that cannot be described verbally. Importantly, children often repeat and extend stories over a number of sessions, as Andrew did. This seems a natural part of sandplay, which lends itself to children developing stories at a pace that is theirs. Retelling and replaying stories in this way seems to help children to work through things safely and clarify the meaning of their experiences.

Each story and person is individual in each storytelling process (Nicholls, 2000; Zipes, 1995). There is growing understanding of the ways that storytelling helps people work through and settle difficult experiences, a process that depends on the relationship between client and therapist (McLeod, 2000). As Andrew's process illustrates, in person-centred sandplay work this can happen without the difficult experiences ever being named or spoken about directly. My sense was that in his sandplay Andrew was able to trust both the relationship with me and, after a while, his relationship with the sand—we could both hold and witness his story. This freed him gradually so that he could do what he needed to do.

CONCLUSION

Offering sandplay in a person-centred therapy relationship opens many possibilities for enriching the relationship between child and therapist, thereby facilitating the child's process. The vivid visual and physical nature of sandplay means there are very many ways in which children can share their personal stories and experiences. Sandplay, as 'growing ground', creates opportunities for child and therapist to relate in ways that may not happen in therapy based simply on talking. The relationship gains more dimensions. This is especially true when working with children, where sandplay allows non-verbal communication. Sandplay dissolves the differences between child and adult in their ability to use language, empowering children to 'speak'. This makes it more possible for me to 'feel and understand' the child's world.

All of this brings not only the chance of greater intimacy in the relationship, but also enables the child to draw on their own power in choosing how to play and what to share. For me sandplay is about being alongside people and working to step into the worlds they are sharing. When children share their sandplay with me I feel their trust in our relationship—often very powerfully—because of the depth of feelings, hopes and difficulties disclosed. I feel this as a gift each time: the chance to share more of their journey. The sand helps us by providing ground, a means of communication and ways for the children to do the work they need to do safely, at a level they choose, and that is right for them.

REFERENCES

Axline, V (1974) *Play Therapy*. New York: Ballantine Books.

Boik, BL & Goodwin, EA (2000) *Sandplay Therapy: A step-by-step manual for psychotherapists of diverse orientations*. London: WW Norton and Co.

Bradway, K (1999) Sandplay with children. *Journal of Sandplay Therapy 8* (2), 1–2.

Dorfman, E (1951) Play therapy. In CR Rogers *Client-Centered Therapy* (pp. 235–77). London: Constable.

Kalff, DM (1991) Introduction to sandplay therapy. *Journal of Sandplay Therapy 1* (1), 1–4.

Kalff, DM (2003) *Sandplay: A psychotherapeutic approach to the psyche*. Cloverdale, CA: Temenos Press.

McLeod, J (2000) Narrative processes in experiential therapy: Stories as openings. Presentation at the BACP Annual Research Conference, University of Manchester, 20th May 2000, <http://shs.tay.ac.uk/shtjm/BAC2000narrative.html>.

McMillan, M (2004) *The Person-Centred Approach to Therapeutic Change*. London: Sage Publications.

Mearns, D (1999) Person-centred therapy with configurations of self. *Counselling, 10* (2), 125–30.

Nicholls, L (2000) Storymaking and storytelling in counselling. In T Merry (Ed) *The BAPCA Reader* (pp. 87–96). Ross-on-Wye: PCCS Books.

Polanyi, M (1958) *Personal Knowledge*. Chicago: University of Chicago Press.

Rabone, K (2003) The silent therapy. *Counselling and Psychotherapy Journal, 14* (7), 10–13.

Rogers, CR (1980) *A Way of Being*. Boston: Houghton Mifflin.

Sims, J (1989/2002) Client-centered therapy: The art of knowing. *Person-Centered Review, 4* (1). Reprinted in D Cain (Ed) (2002*), Classics in the Person-Centered Approach* (pp. 171–9). Ross-on-Wye: PCCS Books.

Weinrib, EL (2004) *Images of the Self: The sandplay therapy process*. Boston: Sigo Press.

West, J (1996) *Child-Centred Play Therapy* (2nd edn). London: Arnold.

Wilson, K, Kendrick, P & Ryan, V (1992) *Play Therapy: A non-directive approach for children and adolescents*. London: Baillière Tindall.

Zipes, J (1995) *Creative Storytelling*. London: Routledge.

CHAPTER 5

THE RISKS AND COSTS OF LEARNING TO TRUST THE CLIENT'S PROCESS WHEN WORKING WITH VULNERABLE YOUNG PEOPLE

GILL CLARKE

In this chapter I will explore a particular counselling relationship which took place over several years in order to illustrate the power and effectiveness of working in the person-centred approach with children and young people. I want to look at what can happen when you take the risk to reach out and enter into a relationship with a vulnerable young person. Although the written word cannot by any stretch show all the nuances that are inherent in a client–counsellor relationship I hope that my exploration in terms of my own and my client's process will go a long way towards the understanding of the therapeutic relationship and the achievements made by young people who have been valued, respected and given the opportunity to make their own choices about their own lives. The person-centred approach enables barriers to come down, and self-learning, for both client and counsellor, to take place.

My counselling work is split between outreach work in schools and after-school appointments at my office. Sally[1] was a young teenage girl when she was initially referred for counselling by the pastoral care team in school. They felt that she was struggling to settle into senior school life because she was being bullied. Sally was a reluctant client with a strong sense that I was yet another adult in her life who was going to tell her what to do. She had not chosen to attend this particular school and harboured an anger that seemed as yet unexplored. In our first meeting I sat looking at this angry young girl wondering what I could do to help. I was quite new in post and felt the weight of expectation on me to achieve 'results'. I felt a tremendous pressure to do something amazing and send Sally out 'fixed'. The problem was I did not know what the magic solution was.

Our first session covered the usual contracting about the boundaries of the counselling relationship and I felt it got stuck from that point. Taking time to reflect on the first session, there was the realisation that I felt compromised by the three aspects of the relationship. There was my client's process, my own process and the issues of the school. I was under the umbrella of all three and needed to find a way of not being pulled out of shape by my sense of other people's expectations that weighed heavily during that first session. I was not really sure what the school was expecting me to achieve in my relationship with Sally and perhaps with hindsight I should have talked

---

1. The anonymity and confidentiality of the client has been respected in the writing of this chapter. Sally is not the client's name. Full consent to write about our relationship was obtained.

this through with them as it may have eased my anxieties. The pastoral care team certainly had Sally's best interests at heart and offered me details of what was happening for Sally. All this well-meaning information was adding to the block that I felt in my relationship with Sally. Our first session comprised me trying to be available for my client, the school and myself, resulting in me not being fully present for Sally. I was distracted by what others thought and what I thought they may want from me. I had been unable to empathise fully with Sally and had failed to be congruent during the session about how I was experiencing our relationship. I felt helpless and confused.

My continuing reflection brought the recognition that the answer was in the relationship that Sally and I shared. Sally would actualise given the right conditions, which was a relationship characterised by empathy, unconditional positive regard and congruence. I needed to focus on Sally's process and work with that. She knew what the answers were and, together, we could embark on a journey of self-learning and discovery.

I met Sally for the second session in quite a different state of mind; ready to experience her as a person in that moment and time with the expectations of others firmly outside the door. I had made the first step onto what would turn out to be a long and rocky yet rewarding road. In that second session I made the commitment to accept Sally for who she was and not who I had been told she was. It felt risky to be me after the previous week when I had not been my real self. It felt a bit like having a bath in public. By being my true self and not feeling pressured to be something I was not, I experienced Sally in that moment and the barriers began to break down. In that second session I was able to relinquish my desire to control the session for a 'successful' outcome. I left this session with a sense of pride that I was now back on track and could offer this young person the unique experience of a person-centred relationship. I had no idea at that stage how long our relationship would last and what a privilege it would be to be part of Sally's journey.

It was clear from the first two meetings that Sally had a lot of issues to work through and that we would probably need time in which to do this. Sally needed to trust me and I needed to trust Sally. Experience has shown me that it is seldom the young person who seeks to speak to someone about their feelings and that even when they are in a counselling relationship there is not a spontaneous outburst of emotions. This was certainly the case for Sally. I strongly believe that counselling young people is not about intervening and offering up the answers, questioning and probing but rather it is about trusting that the client is the expert in their own life and will provide their own answers when the time is right. This does not always sit well with school ideas. It has been hard to trust Sally's process as some of her choices have had the potential to put her in danger but experience has shown me that I can. This proved a pivotal point in my learning and has enhanced my work with children and young people.

Sally clearly found this to be a novel situation, initially giving her a sense of distrust in me because I was not behaving in the way she was accustomed to when interacting with adults. I think that this was as frightening for me as it was for her because the relationship was taking a turn into unchartered territory where I was needing to really learn to trust the process, as was Sally. Yet, I believe that in that moment of getting back to the basics of simply offering the core conditions to Sally I had provided the 'soil' that she needed to grow.

My sense was that Sally needed time to experience the counselling space and to take stock of her situation. It was not until about week eight that she disclosed that her mum was terminally ill. Sally knew that her mother would die but in her own mind it was well into the future, when she would be settled and with a family of her own. Sally felt it was such a long way off that she did not need to think about this now. I felt an intense sense of panic as my gut instinct was that it was months away and not years. What should I do?

I felt it was important that Sally understood the truth of the situation but did not know whether or not to share this with her. I felt real anxiety and confusion. I took this issue to supervision seeking clarity about what was happening inside of me. Why did I have a desperate urge to tell her outright that her mother was close to death? Searching deep inside myself I realised it was because I had not had the chance to say goodbye to my dad, who had died suddenly. I never got to say all those things that I wish I'd said when he was alive. This has left a huge ache inside of me that has never diminished despite many years having passed. Hearing Sally talk about her mum had tapped into the part of me that will always hold regret. I wanted to protect Sally from that same painful ache and to give her the chance to make the most of the time that was left with her mum.

I realised that this was my agenda and this created another struggle within me. Could I trust the process if this meant that my client would not realise until it was too late? To complicate it further her parents were clearly not telling her the truth, which presented me with a dilemma. If her parents did not want her to know then what right did I have to go against their decision? On top of that I felt real anger towards them for not being honest with their child and allowing her to have the information she needed to make informed choices about what she would like to do. I was struggling, to say the least, with feeling overwhelmed by my own emotions yet wanting to be fully present for Sally.

Supervision was my lifeline and was a safe space to be open to myself and explore what was happening within the relationship between Sally and myself. Supervision reinforced what I already knew about accepting and respecting her need to go at her own pace. I was also able to decide that I would not collude with the false information that she was being given, so when questions were asked I would be honest. This was a hard battle for me because I just wanted to tell her what was happening and there were times during those weekly sessions when I felt I was quiet because it was safer. I feared I would at times blurt it out as she was so close to understanding, yet so far away. There were times during those weeks that followed where I felt breathless in my desire for her to see the real picture as it became more and more apparent that her mum was losing her fight with life.

It was around our sixteenth session that she came to the realisation that her mum would soon die. I still see her face etched with pain and confusion, but I knew in that moment that she was able to hear the truth because she was now open to it. It was in that instant I appreciated how much damage I could have done if I had followed my impulse to just tell her. She would not have been able to hear it nor understand it and I could have ruined our relationship, which might have left her alone and vulnerable. This way we could go through it together sharing the pain and anguish.

I felt such a sense of relief that she now had full awareness of the limited time that was left for her mother, but I feel that at times I was guilty of nudging her towards spending time with her mother. I wanted her to have what I had been cheated out of by the swiftness of my father's death. Slowly we worked through this. I learnt to take my foot off the pedal and allow Sally to take control and make her own decisions. Together we were able to explore the pain, sadness, anger and fear that she was experiencing. She was also able to talk freely about her difficulty in visiting her mum as she became aware that her mum no longer felt like her mum, as though she had already died.

Sally's mum died at the beginning of the school holidays and thankfully I had offered sessions at my office during the break. Despite spending a lot of time talking about how it would be when her mum died and her sense of being ready, she crumbled, and I was heartbroken to see a young teenage girl in such distress. I cried with her. I cried for her pain and for my own pain that had been awoken by the grief of Sally. She turned in on herself with her grief and barely spoke during our sessions. I stayed with this respecting that Sally was showing me she wanted some distance in a bid to deal with what was happening around her. I was willing to walk alongside her in her grief.

I feel that over the next few weeks I took on the mothering role, offering her the comfort and support that she was not getting elsewhere. I was overwhelmed with wanting to hug her and show her some warmth and love. Initially I was thwarted because of fear of the child protection protocol. Physical contact with a young person is not allowed. I struggled with this because all I saw in front of me was a young person who needed comfort and I sensed that I could give something to her that would help. I felt angry at the legislation and angry that it made me question what felt right within this relationship. I took the plunge and gave Sally a hug and she hugged me back. It felt right that I had taken the risk and responded to myself and to her; I had responded with congruence. I became anxious that I was becoming over-involved and that perhaps my professional boundaries were being pulled out of shape. So I used supervision to help me understand what was happening. I knew that in no way was I trying to replace her mother but I was giving her the tactile comfort that she wanted in those initial weeks to cope with the pain she was experiencing. I trusted the core conditions would keep me safe within our relationship and would inform me when it was time to step back into a less tactile role.

It was during this time that Sally began to self-harm. I did not know this until some twelve months later. She concealed it well and I believe she used it as a way to cope with the pain she was experiencing in her grief. Sally finally found the courage to share her self-harming with me and I remember the sense of shock that I felt, praying that it did not show on my face. It felt important that she did not know what was really happening inside of me as I feared this would silence her, and I wanted to understand what was happening for her. I felt a gamut of emotions. I berated myself for not being good enough. How on earth had I not noticed? My old introject of fearing failure and not feeling good enough came back to haunt me. I felt with a sense of panic that I should not be working with Sally. I felt like I had let her down by not realising that she was self-harming. The logical part of me could see that she had chosen to conceal her actions and that without her telling me I would never have known. It was her secret that would only be shared when she was ready. Through my offering the core conditions Sally had felt safe enough to reveal her secret to me.

Her arms were a mass of lacerations in various states of healing. I understood the risk that she took in revealing this to me as our contract talks about the need to break confidentiality when self-harming is taking place. It was in that moment I took the decision to maintain our confidentiality as the cuts appeared not to be life-threatening. My heart was in my mouth when I simply advised her to keep the cuts clean. This felt like it was in the best interest of Sally as I felt that breaking confidentiality by talking to the child protection officer at this time would have been damaging to her. This did not stop my sense of panic: What was I thinking? My God, what if it got out that I knew about this? Would I lose the respect of the professionals around me? Would I be judged as not being fit to practise?

I knew that the self-harming was continuing and I expressed my concern for her. This was our secret and one I felt was important to hold. By this point in our relationship she was reaching rock bottom and was struggling to stay afloat. It felt risky holding this information but she had expressed how much it helped her to cope and I had to respect her choice of coping mechanism. I was not sure from one week to the next if she would make it for our session. I relied on my gut instinct, which was that she would be safe and that our relationship was strong enough to see us through this stage of her journey. I was making myself available to Sally and she knew this. This was a pivotal point in our relationship as I feel that Sally felt truly accepted and trusted.

I was never sure how safe she was as she combined her self-harming with heavy drinking but I hung in there and trusted the process that Sally was following. I had a real sense that she would be safe but I am not sure that the other professionals in school working with Sally would have shared my belief and trust in the process. All I knew was that we were talking about it and making decisions together about how we chose to proceed. I have found to my cost that the mention of suicide or self-harm can raise hysteria in those working with young people and that the information is tossed like a hot potato onto someone else, often with a lack of respect for the young person involved. It is a frightening thing for all of us when someone so young expresses the desire to kill themselves but if we do not offer a space to talk about it in confidence I believe that we are putting young people at even greater risk. Litigation springs into my mind momentarily, but my relationship with the young person informs me of the road I need to follow. This case was different. In Sally's case, whilst it felt risky to maintain confidentiality there was something intuitive within me that told me it was right. I am well aware that in other instances this will not be the case and that it can be in the best interest of the client to break confidentiality. Counselling a young person is not a one-size-fits-all. Each decision needs to be based on that individual relationship and what is right within the relationship that you share. This is not always an easy choice to make and can produce a fraught week whilst waiting for the next session.

Sally was to prove my faith in her when she hit rock bottom and she talked to me about feeling the only way she could cope with it all would be to try to take her own life. I was saddened that someone so young felt that this was the only choice she had left. We talked and talked and at the end of that session she said, 'I don't want to do it, please help me'. As soon as I got permission from Sally I got the child protection officer involved. At this point I knew that her actualising tendency was struggling to survive but was hanging in there and driving her to seek help. She had asked for help and I wanted to facilitate what Sally felt was right for her. My biggest fear was the safety of the information that I was about to share. Once it was outside of the room I had no control. Despite this, I felt relief as the burden of knowledge was now shared. Together we drew up a plan that would support Sally through this difficult time. This included not immediately telling her dad, but giving her the space to become empowered and to talk to him herself about how she really felt. By affording her the luxury of time she found her voice. It was difficult for Sally to talk to her dad but he heard her. He tried to support her in the best way he knew how, which was to contact the Child Mental Health Team. I was shocked by this news and I felt hurt because I heard it as if I was not being seen as good enough. With time I could see that he was a father who was trying to do his best to support his daughter, whilst grieving for the loss of his wife.

Her first meeting with the psychiatrist brought a prescription for antidepressants. Anger reared its head within me—this felt wrong. Were we not masking the problem? Was she not too young to get on this merry-go-round? I questioned in that moment if our relationship was enough to enable Sally to cope. I was beginning to feel pushed out of the relationship and was not sure how Sally felt. This was a difficult thing to carry into the relationship but as ever Sally gave me the answers. She felt so much better being on the medication and felt she needed it to see her through. Who was I to judge that this was wrong when she felt it was right for her? I was able to put aside my own views on medication and work with Sally and her antidepressants.

Over those weeks I struggled to work with the fact that there was not just me and Sally in the relationship anymore. There were three of us, one who I did not know. The psychiatrist may not have been physically present in the room but his presence was felt. I found this to be difficult and at times felt that it prevented me from being fully present. I was anxious that in some way I would be judged and that perhaps my professionalism would be questioned. Sally would talk about her time with the psychiatrist and it was very evident, that like myself, she was struggling with the different approach the psychiatrist used. Regardless of this, she kept her appointments with the psychiatrist and with me. I wondered if he was feeling the same and questioning the approach being used by me. Despite all this, just using my eyes I could see the positive physical changes in Sally and this was enough for me to accept the ongoing threesome until a time came when Sally would decide what was best for her. A point was reached when Sally felt that enough was enough and opted out of therapy altogether. She stopped seeing the psychiatrist and she stopped seeing me.

This left me with a deep sense of regret and fear. I was alarmed that she was not getting support from anyone knowing how fragile her process was. I understood in that moment how powerful I was because I was an adult. I could so easily have pulled her in to see me when in school. I did not do this, even though I was tempted. Instead I kept a low profile quietly checking her attendance from time to time to make sure she was still alive. I wanted reassurance that she was OK. What I wanted to do was to respect her choice to opt out. I wanted to respect her decision to have some space for herself. I went along with it, being reassured that I had made myself available for her and I knew that our relationship was strong.

Sally had always dipped in and out of counselling, which initially was very unsettling because I felt scared that something would happen to her. It also triggered my familiar sense of not being good enough. This subsided over time as I realised it was just her way and that she needed space to try it on her own, but although it never stopped the anxiety and uncertainty that I felt, I trusted that when Sally wanted my help she would find me. Nor did it stop the feeling of frustration that the moment it felt like we were getting it right and were ready to move forward she would fall off the radar.

It was several months before her head appeared round my door. I was delighted but knew I was in for a rocky ride. I knew, however, that our relationship was established and could handle it. We are still working together.

CONCLUSION

Sally reinforced my belief and understanding that counselling is a two-way process. We learn from each other, we are companions on a shared journey. I realised the importance of just being me in the relationship. It may not always be appropriate to explicitly share everything that is going on inside me but there are times when self-disclosure is appropriate to the relationship and is vital in facilitating the client's process. For example, I disclosed to Sally that my dad had died and the feelings that I had experienced in relation to that. This felt like an appropriate disclosure that came several weeks after her mother had died. Telling Sally about my sister who had recently died of cancer at the age of thirty-four felt inappropriate and like it would block Sally's process. I kept this information to myself.

Being real and spontaneous in the moment with young people is vital in helping them to understand their own process. What I discovered during this relationship, for example, is that I used humour a lot in my work with her. It is an integral part of my personality and it is impossible to leave it outside of the counselling room door, so it comes in with me. I struggled with this at first being constrained by the 'thought police'. Counsellors are not funny, or so I thought, but working with Sally enabled me to risk that part of myself within our relationship and to see how it is as essential as joy, sadness, anger and depression. Risking it with Sally enabled me to take it into other client relationships.

Client relationships are about having a commitment to being transparent and this can only be achieved if we are committed to being congruent within our relationships. The relationship is about offering something to the client that is truly different. This is what I feel I offered to Sally: a professional adult relationship that was different from any other that she has experienced. I feel that together we built a relationship that had relational depth to it. Sally could access the depths of her emotions because she felt safe in the relationship. I feel that our relationship was facilitative because I could access those parts of me that had the same flavour as Sally's. I have experience of the pain of intense loss and self-hatred and it is the deepness of these feelings that enabled me to enter into that part of Sally's process. I know I am a survivor and trust that my clients are too. In valuing and respecting Sally she was able to value and respect herself. By learning to value herself, Sally was able to stop self-harming and trust herself.

I hope that I have been able to share with you, the reader, that taking risks within a relationship is not a spur-of-the-moment decision, but is a well-thought-out process underpinned by theoretical perspective and a professional code of conduct. Taking a risk is not easy but it is often very rewarding and enables the client to move towards actualisation. Risk is not just in relation to the suicidal or the self-harming client, it is about working on the edge and doing things that are outside of the conventional.

I want to be a successful counsellor and work hopefully with my clients to help them create their own successes. Sally showed me that measuring outcomes is not about prescribed criteria. Outcomes are personal and successes are individual. I hang onto this with new clients that come through my door and I try to offer them a space to be themselves, to work together to create their own individual successes.

Working with Sally I had to learn not to be in a hurry. We were like the tortoise from the 'Hare and Tortoise' story. What Sally wanted was to go at her own pace and I respected that. It is in the being not the doing. I learned to trust the process and respect the time that this can take for each individual client. Sally is due to leave school and with that comes the end of our relationship after nearly four years. Sally will move onto another stage of her personal journey, which will not involve me. I am not sure how I feel or rather I am too afraid to acknowledge the sense of loss that I feel in the ending of my relationship with Sally. She has been a huge part of my personal and professional journey and has enriched my life in ways she will never know. I want the best for Sally and hope she gets what she has worked so hard to achieve.

What feels even harder than the ending of this client relationship is the possibility that next year could see the end of this service. Our funding is at an end and as yet we have not been able to secure further funding. Should I wish to build an adventure playground then funding would be free flowing. I cannot make sense of the logic to cut an established and successful service specifically targeting vulnerable young people in favour of an adventure playground. I am filled with a great anger and sadness. This project works with approximately one hundred young people every year and has done so for the past four years. If this service is cut there will be no support for such vulnerable young people. What message are we sending young people when we offer a service that they value and gain support from and then cut it because there is no more money available?

I hope that through this chapter I have shared with you my unwavering belief in the person-centred approach and how this can be a liberating and positive force in the lives of children and young people. A parent said to me the other day, 'You have worked your magic' and I think she is right. There is a kind of magic that is created by the coming together of two people in this rich encounter. What a privilege to be part of such an amazing process.

46

CHAPTER 6

WORKING AT RELATIONAL DEPTH WITH ADOLESCENTS IN SCHOOLS

A PERSON-CENTRED PSYCHOLOGIST'S PERSPECTIVE

SUE HAWKINS

This chapter is an exploration of the relationship qualities that create optimal healing for young people. This theme is explored through a relationship between the author and a fifteen year-old female client.

The person-centred approach is predicated on the belief that human beings are relational. When Rogers (1957) outlined his theory of the necessary and sufficient conditions of a therapeutic relationship, he examined the interaction between the individual actualising tendency, which he believed to be innate in human beings, and the environmental conditions required for this innate tendency to grow. Although primarily writing about the relationship between therapist and client, Rogers' theory applies equally to all human relationships. Rogers' paper is important because it asserts that the therapist's ability to create the core conditions for therapeutic growth is sufficient in itself and that no further techniques, tools, methods or 'diagnoses' are needed. Healing is facilitated by the therapist's qualities as experienced by the client rather than the therapist's expertise. Research post-Rogers supports the idea that irrespective of the approach to psychotherapy, it is the relationship between therapist and client that most determines positive outcomes (American Psychological Association Steering Committee, 2002; Bohart et al., 2002).

Our sense of self is formed through our relationships with others, initially our parents or caregivers. Bowlby (1969) documented the importance of early attachments, primarily the relationship between mother and child in determining a child's early emotional development. Attachments and separation are part of our earliest experiences and how these are handled by our primary caregivers form the template for attachments throughout our life. According to Bowlby, 'There is a strong causal relationship between an individual's experiences with his parents and his later capacity to make affectional bonds' (Bowlby, 1977: 63).

For example, if our carers are empathic and sensitive to our needs, we are likely to generalise this to all relationships and therefore are likely to attract others who are similarly empathic and sensitive. Conversely, if our carers are unempathic and unresponsive to our basic needs, we are likely to attract similar relationships in later life or may avoid close attachments altogether for fear of experiencing disappointment or rejection. This is not to say that our future relationships are entirely predetermined by how well we were parented in early life. Our self-concepts are in a constant state of evolution as we accommodate and assimilate experiences, new and old.

Rogers believed that we are likely to choose experiences that fit with our self-concept. For example, if we have internalised a condition of worth such as 'Others will only like me if I am undemanding', it is likely that we will be undemanding in relationships but may then feel disappointed or resentful that we do not get our needs met.

I work as an educational psychologist with young people in schools and offer counselling as part of that role. I trained as a person-centred counsellor several years before training as a psychologist and it has taken time for me to integrate the two different roles and cultures and to find a way of working as a person-centred psychologist with a much broader role than that of therapist. What struck me most during my training as a psychologist, and subsequently working in education, is the lack of explicit understanding that children learn and grow, both personally and academically, according to the extent to which they can form nurturing relationships with significant others.

There was a time in Rogers' life when he describes feeling quite alienated from the behaviourist practices of his psychology colleagues (Rogers, 1961). I too have felt a similar sense in a profession where there is a strong belief that to be a 'good psychologist' it is primarily a wide knowledge base, a 'toolkit' that is important rather than one's qualities as a human being. I remember during my psychology training approximately ten minutes was devoted to discussing the importance of 'rapport' with clients and how to build it. It was implied that the purpose of building rapport was so that clients would be more likely to allow the psychologist to 'do things to them'. I had been practising as a counsellor for approximately nine years at this point and the development of the core conditions was very much a work in progress!

If schools were more able to offer those who work and learn in them the core conditions, the need for therapy would be greatly reduced. British education has been dominated by behavioural approaches that ironically became popular at approximately the same time as Rogers was putting forward his theories of the core conditions for therapeutic growth.

More recently, the emotional literacy/intelligence agenda has been introduced to education. However, most emotional literacy programmes do not place enough emphasis on the need for emotionally available and self-aware adult role models to facilitate children's personal development. Indeed many imply that emotional literacy can be taught just like any other subject: a set of skills that can be developed, rather like mathematical skills.

Many children remain unaffected by behavioural programmes since communicating their distress is a much greater motivation than earning positive regard or rewards for 'good' behaviour. Many of the young people with whom I have worked have learnt to elicit negative responses for 'negative' behaviours. Brazier (1993) suggests that the fundamental human drive may not be to receive positive regard or approval as Rogers asserted, but for engagement and contact with others. In other words, children would rather be disapproved of than ignored. This certainly explains the behaviour of some young people in schools. Such behaviour is often not understood by professionals and can be dismissively labelled 'antisocial', 'provocative' or 'attention-seeking'. Children's behaviour is best understood as their way of coping with the problem rather than the problem itself, or as Rogers puts it in Proposition 5 of his 19 Propositions: 'Behaviour is basically the goal-directed attempt of the organism to satisfy its needs as experienced, in the field as perceived' (Rogers, 1951: 491).

Building relationships with children who are often referred for 'problems' with attendance or behaviour has its difficulties. Barwick describes how counselling in schools can often be a 'precarious shelter at the last stop before exclusion' (2000: 2). Furthermore, with youngsters who have been designated the label of having 'Behavioural, Emotional and Social Difficulties', it is often difficult to ascertain who is the client, as it is commonly school staff or parents who experience the child's behaviour as 'problematic'. Moreover, schools, with their pressures of satisfying government inspectorates, frequently want rapid and quantifiable change. Whilst therapy occasionally provides this, I have found the most enduring change in terms of a young person's behaviour has come about through a change in their self-concept, facilitated through an accepting and trusting relationship that often takes time to develop.

So what does it mean to work at relational depth with young people and how might this be achieved? Mearns (1994) coined the term 'relational depth' and Mearns and Cooper (2005) define it as relating both to specific moments of psychological contact within a relationship as well as the overall quality of a relationship. Of course, the latter is perhaps preferable to the former but that does not make even brief moments of relational depth any less significant. Indeed, brief moments of deep psychological contact may be more than many relationships, therapeutic or otherwise, ever achieve. It is those brief moments where an individual allows themselves to let down their defences enough to be truly seen that become, at least initially, pivotal moments in terms of the development of a therapeutic relationship. This is especially true for youngsters who have been damaged by other significant relationships but is also true to some extent for most adolescents, as adolescent 'culture' in itself has its own conditions of worth that govern patterns of relating. For example, adolescents often feel that adults do not understand them and therefore assume that it would be counter-productive to open themselves up to an adult who is likely to adopt the parental role of thinking they know best, telling them what to do or judging them. Erikson (1968) argues that adolescents naturally fear intimacy as their individual identities are not sufficiently solid not to fear losing themselves in a relationship.

Furthermore, to survive amongst peers and within the school environment, young people build up elaborate defences of appearing to be 'tough' and invulnerable. Added to that are other cultural affiliations with their own patterns of relating and conditions of worth. For example, in many contexts it would be inappropriate, if not foolish, for boys to show feelings of vulnerability within their peer group. Indeed in male working-class culture in particular it is often the ability to hide vulnerability that is highly valued. Attention therefore needs to be given to the many social contexts in which a young person operates with the aim that they can begin to extend their repertoire of relating and have more awareness about the choices they make.

Children are naturally intuitive and insightful but this type of 'knowing' is frequently overlooked by both themselves and others in favour of adults' expertise or understanding. This can hinder the process of self-actualisation as children themselves begin to favour the sometimes misguided frame of reference of significant adults—parents, teachers etc. over their own intuitive sensing of what is right for them. My client, who I have called Laura, refers to this in an interview when she says: 'Children—they don't know anything—that's what people think. I know more things than most of the people in my family.'[1]

When I ask young people what helped them in terms of our work together they frequently report that being believed and trusted was the most important factor. This is often followed by a list of adults who haven't believed or trusted them in the past.

I have worked with Laura for sixteen months. I experienced her as being very uncomfortable at times, particularly at the beginning of our relationship. Initially the source of Laura's discomfort was a feeling of being 'too visible' or 'exposed' and she sometimes found it difficult to be in the counselling room. On these occasions, Laura requests that I sit next to her rather than opposite as she prefers not to make eye contact. She sometimes feels safer being invisible although paradoxically there is also part of her that wants to be noticed, heard and acknowledged.

The counselling takes place in school usually for an hour a week. Laura has experienced counselling on three separate occasions before working with me.

The following is an extract from an interview with Laura in which I ask her about the counselling relationship. Talking this intimately has not always been easy for her— as she says in the interview, she has not had many close relationships in her life. For example, Laura uses the pronoun 'they' to refer to 'therapists' generally rather than directly addressing me in the second person. Whilst I have talked to Laura about our relationship on several occasions, the intimacy of talking about my relationship with a client can still feel a little uncomfortable at times in the sense that I can also feel exposed and vulnerable. Here Laura talks about the qualities of the therapist she views as helpful:

> Laura: *It helps if they—you know—that you think they're not judging you ... And sometimes if they've not even done anything to make you feel like that, sometimes you think they are.*
> Sue: *Can you remember what judgements you feared when we first started working together?*
> Laura: *Yeah—that they'd think that you were just attention-seeking or making stuff up. Then they might not trust you—that sort of thing.*
> Sue: *Have people said that to you in the past—that you're just attention-seeking?*
> Laura: *Once that woman said that to me—you know.*
> Sue: *I think I know. Was it another counsellor you worked with?*
> Laura: *Yes. And other people think it.*
> Sue: *And I guess that would mean that you're not real—that you're putting it on.*
> Laura: *Yeah—it's really bad when people think that ... And other stuff, do you know what I mean?—Things happen on TV and they think you've been watching too much TV and that's why you see it ... That's the worst reason why people wouldn't trust you and that's the worst thing they could do.*

---

1. Permission to use this material has been granted by the client.

Sue: *So the worst thing would've been if you'd have told me about your life and I'd have thought that you were making it up or something just to get attention.*
Laura: *Yeah.*
Sue: *I can see how that would be pretty awful.*

Laura's fear of being judged and disbelieved was confirmed by a previous relationship with a counsellor but I also suspect that other adults have labelled her behaviour 'attention-seeking'. If 'attention-seeking' were a neutral term that led to an enquiry about why an individual might want attention or to what they might be trying to draw attention, then it could be useful, but my experience in schools is that it is used as a condition of worth that suggests an individual should neither want nor seek attention. Herrick and Sharp (2000) suggest that such behaviour is better described as 'attention-needing' behaviour, since it usually results from a lack of positive attention in the child's formative years.

Rogers (1951) argues that most clients come to therapy with expectations based on other relationships and are generally fearful. At first Laura found it difficult to openly talk about herself and was fearful of my response. She still finds this difficult at times, especially when we touch on material where she feels self-critical. However, she has become much more comfortable and more open over time. In the interview I ask her what facilitated that change:

Laura: *I think it was that you believed what I was saying—that I knew you weren't judging me … I think when you first start getting counselling, it makes you feel worse because you keep thinking that there might be something wrong with you. And after a while when you know that they really trust you, you get better.*
Sue: *Mm. I remember at the start you saying that your big fear was that I might think that you were mad or that other people might think that you were mad—is that what you mean?*
Laura: *Yeah. I don't have that any more 'cos I know you don't think bad stuff if I tell you those things—I tell you most things now.*

When Laura and I began working together, she judged a lot of her behaviour as 'mad' and felt certain that I would think the same. She reinforced her self-concept by acting in a 'bizarre' manner in school, consequently some people responded to her as though she were a little odd. Through my continued acceptance of her she has challenged her beliefs about herself to the extent that she no longer appears to think she is 'mad' and therefore no longer has need for the corresponding behaviours. It has not been necessary to focus on her behaviour specifically or strive to change it.

Laura's conditions of worth about being perceived as 'mad' are fairly typical of those expressed by young people with whom I have worked. In forming a trusting relationship with a young person, I believe it is crucial to avoid pathologising behaviours that are the person's best way of coping with their situation. If the individual accepts the label placed on them by a powerful adult, it can become a defining part of their identity.

Therapists acknowledge there is often a synchronicity in terms of the clients they attract and their personal learning needs. It is no surprise therefore that I met Laura at a time when I was still formulating my ideas about the kind of relationships I wanted to create with young people. Laura has taught me that there is no template for a therapeutic relationship and that if I can intuitively trust myself without judging my behaviour as a counsellor 'right' or 'wrong' by some external standards, then a relationship will develop that will be 'right' for the two people involved. This has been difficult and, at times, I have questioned the boundaries of our relationship, often experiencing a conflict between what felt right for me and some introjected external boundaries. Furthermore, I have felt vulnerable at times as Laura has drawn out parts of me that I might previously have been reluctant to share in my relationships with young clients.

I have noticed how being 'the adult' in a relationship with a young person can carry with it a set of expectations and conditions of its own. For example, I feel more vulnerable disclosing personal information with young clients because I have my own conditions of worth about being 'strong' and 'together' and 'professional'. The 'strong' and 'together' conditions of worth stem in part from a cultural view of how a parental figure should be—the giver of support and wisdom who puts their own vulnerabilities to one side to support their children, but they also form part of my self-concept from my personal conditioning. I realised that in responding to these internalised messages, I was leaving parts of myself out of the relationship with my young clients and creating relationships that did little to address the imbalance of power that already inherently exists. This theme is discussed with Laura in the following extract when she asks me what I think made a difference in terms of developing a close relationship:

> Sue: *Well, I can remember right at the start you used to ask me loads of questions about my life—you still do that sometimes—but do you remember?*
> Laura: *That's it!—See—I knew you knew.*
> Sue: *(Laughs) Yeah, but I don't want to impose my view on you, you know?*
> Laura: *Yeah—but that is right.*
> Sue: *And do you remember one session I said, 'We've not done much work today'?*
> Laura: *Yes.*
> Sue: *And you said, 'Oh—you don't see it as work when we talk about you'.*
> Laura: *Yeah. That is part of the work I think. I think it helps 'cos then you know that they are a person too, that they have experiences. 'Cos if you just say stuff, you'd think that you were talking to a robot. Do you know what I mean?*
> Sue: *Is it like you're saying that you need to know you're talking to a real person who has a real life?*
> Laura: *Yeah 'cos you wouldn't—if it's their job, it's different.*
> Sue: *Mm. In what way is it different if it's just a job?*
> Laura: *Cos they know everything that they're gonna say—they've practised it. If they just talk about other stuff then you know that they actually care because they're sharing their stuff with you and you're telling them your stuff ... They could be anything—but you'd rather know that. You can't have a friend that you don't know anything about, can you?*

Sue: *No. What I think is interesting is that you know you said you took a bit more risk—that was my own experience as well—'cos it felt quite risky sometimes when you were asking me some personal questions.*
Laura: *I think it's better to be honest though, do you not?*
Sue: *I think so, but I realise that not everyone sees it the way we see it. But what I think is interesting is that you said you gradually started to trust me and take more risks and I'm saying the same—that I gradually trusted you and took more risks too.*

Here Laura appears to be saying that it was crucial to our relationship that she knew me and that there was a mutual sharing of ourselves. My experience is that this seems more important in relationships with young people than with adults. Later in the interview Laura contrasts this with her previous experience of counsellors who 'just ask you questions and don't talk about themselves'. Some of the questions Laura asked me felt difficult as they could potentially have been professionally compromising; however, in the context of this particular therapeutic relationship, I chose to share personal material that felt risky.

At times I have questioned my positive feelings for Laura. However, as Rogers states, too often professionals are afraid of freely experiencing positive feelings towards clients for fear they may be:

> ... trapped by them. They may lead to demands on us or we may be disappointed in our trust, and these outcomes we fear. So as a reaction we tend to build up distance between ourselves and others—aloofness, a 'professional' attitude, an impersonal relationship. I feel quite strongly that one of the important reasons for the professionalization of every field is that it helps to keep this distance. (1961: 52)

For many counsellors a professional distance is seen as important. Ommanney and Symes argue that in working with children, counsellors:

> ... must pay steadfast attention to the dual qualities of intimacy and distance. Intimacy, most clearly communicated through empathic connection, congruence and unconditional positive regard is matched with an attitude of distance. This distance not only safeguards the client from the counsellor being overwhelmed and/or swept away in a flood of their own needs ... (Ommanney & Symes, 2000: 50)

While I would agree that boundaries are important in any relationship, I do not view them as synonymous with distance. On the contrary, I believe that distance can be detrimental to a therapeutic relationship as there is a danger of becoming another emotionally unavailable or withholding adult in the child's life, thus repeating a familiar pattern. Furthermore, distance can be a way of holding onto power and control in a relationship where there is already an inherent power imbalance. The challenge in my work with young people has been in finding a comfortable reciprocity and I am careful to monitor the degree to which my sharing of personal information is helpful to the young person rather than simply meeting my own needs. Inevitably this is different in every relationship. Many of the counselling textbooks refer to the therapist's use of 'appropriate self-disclosure' which implies that some personal material needs to be ring-fenced as 'inappropriate' to share with a client. However, it is important to stress that the appropriateness of disclosing any personal material is contextual and relational rather than anything inherent in the material itself.

Laura has asked factual details about my life as well as my beliefs, philosophy and intimate details about my relationships, feelings and personal history. However, moments of close psychological contact have often involved an unspoken connection or 'presence' (Thorne, 1991). Mearns (1994: 8) describes this quality as a 'stillness', 'unselfconsciousness' on the part of the therapist where she feels no need to establish 'separateness' from the client. My own experience has been that moments of close psychological contact have involved a feeling of being connected to the basic humanity of another, a feeling of being mutually transparent and I believe it is most likely to happen in relationships where the therapist has modelled transparency and vulnerability. The effect for both parties is that they no longer feel alone or 'pathologised' by their difficulties but see these as part of a universal human struggle.

Although these qualities are obviously related to congruence, I believe it is possible for a counsellor to be congruent about their experiencing of the client without disclosing much personal information.

Rogers (1951) refers to a memorandum sent by a colleague, Oliver Bown, to staff members at the University of Chicago Counseling Center. In it, Bown describes his personal growth as a therapist in terms of moving from a position where he deemed it inappropriate to become too emotionally involved with clients, partly because he was influenced by contemporary thought in psychotherapy and partly because he viewed clients as poor potential satisfiers of his needs, to a position where he recognises that it is safe and beneficial to the client for him to be emotionally involved and to feel love for a client. In the memorandum Bown describes how acknowledging all of his feelings towards a client liberated both parties to explore areas of their experience without becoming defensive.

Rogers believes this intimate connection happens when he is closest to his 'inner, intuitive self' (Thorne, 1992: 137). Kilborn summarises this idea: 'Intimacy, then, involves knowing oneself and being able to be present for another person. This would seem to be an excellent description of the therapist's role' (Kilborn, 2000: 163).

Bown argues against the view that in satisfying one's own needs in a relationship, the therapist inevitably misuses the client's vulnerability:

> I certainly feel that this can happen, but responding to this possibility by withholding any emotion which is feared may get out of hand, is for me an inadequate and castrating way of dealing with the same emotionality which I feel lies at the very heart of the best interpersonal relationships. (Bown, in Rogers, 1951: 163)

For me some of the moments of close psychological contact with Laura have been when we have shared humour. In the interview I ask her what helped to develop our relationship:

> Laura: *Erm—when we started laughing about stuff and it wasn't so serious … it's more like a friendship if you have a laugh with the other person.*

It is interesting that Laura describes our relationship as being 'like a friendship' and I think she means this in the sense of reciprocity. Laughter appears to have many functions in our relationship. Initially, I think it helped to take away some of the intensity for Laura so that she could relax. More recently, it has become one of the ways we express closeness and mutuality.

Later in the interview I discuss with Laura what I consider to be other pivotal moments in our relationship and we talk about occasions where Laura would attempt to deface things in the counselling room and one occasion in particular when I became angry about this and shouted at her to stop. The motivation for Laura's behaviour seemed to be twofold: Firstly, she wanted to see my anger so that she knew I was a 'real person'. Secondly, she was playing out patterns from previous relationships whereby she believed people who were angry with her would reject her. I remember her looking quite astounded when I told her that although I had felt angry at her behaviour, I still liked and valued her. This supports Bown's view that:

> The client establishes the same kind of relationship with his therapist that he forms with other people in his environment. It contains the same inhibitions, ambivalences, conflicts, needs, values, goals and so on; and when the therapist can perceive these elements in operation in the immediate present in therapy, he taps one of the most valuable sources of deeply understanding his client.
> (Bown, in Rogers, 1951: 165)

Although reciprocity appears to create a more therapeutic climate, I do not think it is necessary for therapeutic movement to occur. In the interview, Laura describes a relationship with a previous therapist:

> Laura: *One of them helped and I didn't even have a relationship with her though. Actually maybe we didn't need to have a close relationship 'cos anyone'd do 'cos I didn't have any friends maybe. Do you know what I mean? I probably just needed someone to talk to 'cos I never talked any time to anyone. So maybe that was just talking time.*
> Sue: *So she gave you the space to talk about what was bothering you.*
> Laura: *Yeah—that's probably what some people need and then I've changed now. Mind you, I remember her saying something about how she'd found a frog or something so she must've said little things about her life so maybe that did help.*
> Sue: *Maybe like you say people need different things at different times and at that time it was what you wanted—someone to talk to and you weren't so bothered about having a*

close relationship with them.
Laura: *Yeah.*

I agree with Laura's view that the level of emotional contact that a client needs varies. Intimacy is something that gradually evolves in a relationship and cannot be striven for. Different levels of intimacy suit different clients at different times.

A concern within some models of counselling and psychotherapy is that emotional involvement with a client can lead to dependency and I have sometimes worried when a client has seemed to feel dependent on me. For example, I am aware that Laura finds it difficult to form intimate fulfilling relationships, and that our relationship is important to her:

> Laura: *I only have one good relationship and that's with M [a friend]. And you—and I'm not just saying that 'cos you're here.*

I have learnt to trust that through greater self-acceptance, Laura will eventually form more rewarding relationships. I also trust that she will stop coming for counselling when she no longer needs it. There have been breaks in our work where we haven't seen each other for several weeks, during which I have still felt in 'psychological contact' with Laura. In the interview, she describes something similar:

> Laura: *Whenever I don't see you for a while, I always think that I'm going to see you again. Do you not think that or do you sometimes think we'll finish? Like when we didn't see each other for a while.*
> Sue: *No I didn't think that, I knew I'd see you again at some point. My impression has always been that there's more work for us to do together.*
> Laura: *Yeah, there is.*
> Sue: *But I've also thought that I've not wanted to hang on because I would miss you if I didn't see you. I want it to be for genuine reasons.*
> Laura: *Yeah. It is for genuine reasons.*
> Sue: *I agree with you but I guess if you have a close relationship like this, it feels difficult to end it.*
> Laura: *Yeah.*

The 'genuine reasons' referred to here signify my internal conflict between wanting to trust in Laura's actualising tendency and an internalised judgement that I might be creating 'dependency' or 'co-dependency' and that this is somehow 'wrong'. However, I believe if a dependency exists at times in counselling relationships, it can be a necessary but temporary stage on the journey towards independence. In summary, I believe that optimal therapeutic healing and growth can only occur in a relationship and, in that sense, we are all dependent on others. This idea is beautifully articulated by a client who Rogers calls Miss Cam:

I felt much more myself in your company than I would have felt by myself. But it's not dependent in the derogatory sense—I suppose it's what has been called 'freedom of dependence.' If you can say a fish is dependent on water, then you can say my personality, my self is dependent on association, relationship with other selves for life and growth and freedom to move around. (Rogers, 1951: 113–14)

Through my relationship with Laura and the other young people with whom I have worked, I have learnt that reciprocity and transparency are key ingredients in promoting mutual growth and freedom.

REFERENCES

American Psychological Association Steering Committee (2002) Empirically supported therapy relationships: Conclusions and recommendations on the Division 29 task force. In JC Norcross (Ed) *Psychotherapy Relationships that Work: Therapist contributions and responsiveness to patients* (pp. 441–3). Oxford: Oxford University Press.

Barwick, N (Ed) (2000) *Clinical Counselling in Schools.* London: Routledge.

Bohart, AC, Elliot, R, Greenberg, LS and Watson, JC (2002) Empathy. In C Norcross (Ed) *Psychotherapy Relationships that Work: Therapist contributions and responsiveness to patients* (pp. 89–108). Oxford: Oxford University Press.

Bowlby, J (1969) *Attachment and Loss. Vol 1: Attachment.* London: Penguin.

Bowlby, J (1977) The making and breaking of affectional bonds. In D Batty (Ed) *Working with Children: Practice papers* (pp. 56–86). London: British Agencies for Adoption and Fostering.

Brazier, D (1993) The necessary condition is love: Going beyond self in the person-centred approach. In D Brazier (Ed) *Beyond Carl Rogers* (pp. 72–91). London: Constable.

Erikson, EH (1968) *Identity: Youth and crisis.* New York: Norton.

Herrick, E & Sharp, P (2000) Anger management groups. In N Barwick (Ed) *Clinical Counselling in Schools* (pp. 124–41). London: Routledge.

Kilborn, M (2000) Too close for comfort: Levels of intimacy in the counselling relationship. In T Merry (Ed) *The BAPCA Reader* (pp. 163–8). Ross-on-Wye: PCCS Books.

Mearns, D (1994) *Developing Person-Centred Counselling.* London: Sage.

Mearns, D & Cooper, M (2005) *Working at Relational Depth in Counselling and Psychotherapy.* London: Sage.

Ommanney, M & Symes, J (2000) Working with students with disabilities. In N Barwick (Ed) *Clinical Counselling in Schools* (pp. 37–51). London: Routledge.

Rogers, CR (1951) *Client-Centered Therapy.* London: Constable.

Rogers, CR (1957) The necessary and sufficient conditions of therapeutic personality change. *Journal of Consulting Psychology, 21* (2), 95–103.

Rogers, CR (1961) *On Becoming a Person: A therapist's view of psychotherapy.* Boston: Houghton Mifflin.

Thorne, B (1991) *Person-Centred Counselling: Therapeutic and spiritual dimensions.* London: Whurr.

Thorne, B (1992) *Carl Rogers.* London: Sage.

CHAPTER 7

SEAL'D RESPECT

AN EMOTIONAL LITERACY GROUP IN
A SECONDARY SCHOOL

NADINE LITTLEDALE

'Seal'd Respect' is the name chosen by ten students, aged twelve to thirteen years, for their emotional literacy group at school. This group formed the basis of the qualitative and collaborative research that I undertook for an MA at Manchester Metropolitan University. The group chose this name, representing as it did an amalgamation of most, though not all, of our individual initials (first names) with the addition of 'respect', the concept of which came to be seen as an integral part of the group's sense of its own identity and process. This chapter is about my work with these students focusing on one particular session we had together. Through an analysis of this process I want to explore ways of developing a 'space' that enables young people to express and make sense of their emotional landscape. This chapter is based on session seven—of fourteen— that formed the life of the group and I shall address some of the content of that session, process it from a person-centred and psychodramatic perspective, and incorporate my understanding of the development of the student's emotional literacy. I shall not be discussing my overall MA findings as these were based on the whole project and this chapter is based on one session alone.

First, I want to look at what emotional literacy means and then elaborate on how I work as a person-centred psychodramatist.

EMOTIONAL LITERACY

As a psychotherapist working within a National Health Service Trust I saw many children and young people access our services who I believe, had they been given assistance earlier on, may not have needed referral into the mental health system. I have felt for some time that if we could reach young people at an early age and assist them to find a language to express their feelings, and provide them with the opportunity to develop skills in using that language and managing their feelings, they would be less likely to feel alienated in their personal and social world.

Antidote (2003: 5), the campaign for emotional literacy in schools, describes emotional literacy as 'the practice of thinking individually and collectively about how emotions shape our actions, and of using emotional understanding to enrich our thinking'. The development of emotional literacy can affect behaviour, self-esteem, and the development of communication skills. But where, and how, could emotional literacy be 'taught'? We find a clue in Rogers' assertion that the goal of education needs to be based on the 'facilitation of change and learning' (Kirschenbaum & Henderson, 1990: 304). Education, then, does not have a narrow remit. Whilst the educational system in the UK, and in the West generally, places greatest value on academic success, there have been recent developments that emphasise the importance of young people's emotional development in school (see for instance *Healthy Minds*, Office for Standards in Education, 2004).

PERSON-CENTRED PSYCHODRAMA

I work from a person-centred perspective, which encourages clients to be 'experts' on their feelings, and so, I believe, provides the potential for constructive change. The person-centred perspective is a way of being in relation to the client which encourages partnership (Natiello, 2001: 62) and a sharing of power. The person-centred approach puts trust in the actualising tendency of each individual and strives to provide the conditions for the communication of fundamental interpersonal attitudes, which may thus provide a climate for growth.

I chose psychodrama as the basis for creative expression within the emotional literacy group. The use of symbolism within the arts enables difficult material to be addressed in safe ways (Bannister, 2002: 27). The natural medium of communication for children is play and activity. By engaging in the process of play children learn to live in a world of symbolic meaning whilst exploring and learning in their own way. I believe the arts, including psychodrama and play therapy, may provide a non-verbal language, a medium to explore, express and enact their inner worlds. Having worked with children who have experienced profound difficulties during their development I have learnt something of the healing potential of the arts in working therapeutically. As a person-centred practitioner I have come to combine psychodrama with aspects of play therapy. It is psychodrama's ability to be playful and dynamic that can enable young people to use their spontaneous creativity and imaginative expression to express what is most difficult for them.

I believe that psychodrama can be practised using person-centred tenets and while this is a contentious issue (how can a director, for instance, be non-directive?) I agree with Paul Wilkins (1994: 47) that whilst a person-centred director/facilitator uses 'techniques' the emphasis is on the *relationship* between the director and the protagonist and with the group as a whole. 'Person-centred psychodrama has at its core a belief in the actualising tendency and the transformative power of the core conditions' (ibid.). This is reiterated by Jenny Biancardi, person-centred psychodramatist (and my trainer from 1991 to 1996): 'Only they [clients] know where they want to go—I may have ways to help them get there' (2003: 149). For me the question is not—are the core conditions enough? But more—what medium of expression may enable my working within a person-centred perspective? What may be helpful to this person, people, group? For a child it may be play, for an adult, words, for some it may be both. If play is a child's form of communication, maybe as adults we lose an important aspect of our creative expression if we rely only on words and see the arts as intrusive 'techniques' not suited to the person-centred approach.

Rather than insisting on a rigid structure of set exercises, the intention of the project was to follow the students' process. Rogers writes of the pitfalls of planning or setting 'exercises':

> To me nothing is a 'gimmick' if it occurs with real spontaneity. Thus one may use role playing, bodily contact, psychodrama ... And various other procedures when they seem to express what one is actually feeling at the time. (Rogers, 1970: 57)

As a person-centred psychotherapist I may communicate using words, play, the arts and through aspects of psychodrama. Nevertheless it remains a challenge to me to find a way to accommodate my adherence to both the person-centred approach and the psychodramatic approach. If I trust my intuitive 'felt sense' of a relationship, within the context of a person-centred experience, I believe I can be effective and facilitating. For me both approaches are potentially hugely powerful and affecting.

THE EMOTIONAL LITERACY GROUP PROJECT

I consulted with a Deputy Head at a local school in East Yorkshire, having chosen that school partly because I had already developed contacts there through my National Health Service work and partly because it had a track record for attempting to develop effective pastoral services. Issues of bullying, coping with life transitions, and peer relationships were cited as some of the reasons they were interested in developing the emotional literacy of their students. We agreed group membership would be voluntary and self-selecting, so I was invited to lead discussions on the meaning of 'emotional literacy' in all eight classes in Year 8. Interested students left their names with the teacher who acted as co-facilitator and school link for the group. These 'names' later became the participants of the group.

This was a time-limited group that met for fourteen hourly sessions from February to July 2005 on a weekly basis. It consisted of between four to ten twelve- to thirteen-year-olds, two co-facilitators and a classroom support assistant. The classroom support assistant is employed by the school to support children with special needs, in this case a student with epilepsy. We used the psychodramatic structure of 'warm-up, enactment and sharing'. We would usually start with a creative warm-up, an activity to facilitate creative expression such as storytelling, artwork, the use of puppets. From this the 'drama' or 'enactment' itself would usually emerge in which the story or image was enacted. Finally the group shared their experiences from role, followed by a discussion of their thoughts or feelings in relation to what had occurred, making the learning explicit if they wished to. I asked people to share from role because such sharing enables those who have been in role to be explicit about how they felt; this is particularly important if they haven't stated this during the enactment. It also allows the participants to de-role by talking *about* the character they were playing rather than talking *as* the character. Such reflection is important for the development of emotional literacy, enabling the articulation of emotions hitherto unacknowledged or unaddressed.

The group is co-facilitated by the teacher and I and in the moments of direct action I, as a qualified psychodramatist, facilitate this action. The director or facilitator is the person who facilitates the protagonist through the use of psychodrama, as well as facilitating the group process. The protagonist, in this context, is the person whose story is told and is normally the subject of the psychodrama. However because the students are not specifically using their own personal material the protagonist in this context is more ambiguous and all the members of the group can become central to the story being enacted.

The co-facilitator developed her role in our discussions together as well as within the group. Having a co-facilitator meant there was another adult in the group able to observe the action and student responses. We are co-facilitators here with different roles. We both 'hold' the group structure in the living moment, share ideas, provide input into the group, make observations and comments. However, as I have the experience of training as a psychodrama facilitator I lead in terms of the psychodramatic parameters. This led to an initial power imbalance, rather like student/tutor, that changed over time as she became more confident and assertive as a facilitator. She also remained the significant school liaison link to the rest of the teaching staff maintaining that central role during the group's existence.

I have chosen one particular session to illustrate the project partly because I thoroughly enjoyed the process of facilitating it, partly because it shows the participants engaging in a spontaneous and creative manner, but also because the participants have begun to develop a sense of group identity.

Contracting and ground rules took place in an earlier session, as a group exercise, providing participants with ownership of the process. The structure of psychodrama was also explained at the beginning of the group so the participants understood something of the method, as well as giving permission for it to be the subject of my research. Confidentiality (with the usual proviso of concerns around child safety) was ensured, as was anonymity.

OUTLINE OF THE GROUP SESSION

There were six students present at this session. Three students didn't turn up including two boys who had attended previously and one girl who had apparently left the group due to an argument between some of the girls. I learned later that one of the boys had been suspended and the other didn't want to attend without his 'mate'.

The students gathered around forming a circle. The only boy in the group sat next to me, as he often did. Each group member chose, at my co-facilitator's suggestion, a 'soft toy'. They discussed its 'story' with a partner and then fed back to the group. They introduced their characters with a brief description of the character's 'story'. These characters included:

- A pink monkey in a pink tree wearing pink beads.
- A duck called 'Boots' who can kick and dance. She has a red nose and likes to dye her mother's head red.
- Leo the lion who lives in a circus.
- A crocodile that lives in a river.
- A little piggy who has been adopted and who people tend to treat by her 'cover' (appearance).
- A stripy parrot, which flies through the jungle.
- Sylvia, a yellow creature who wears sunglasses and who can see at night.

One girl excitedly said she wanted to do the story of the pink monkey and the others, perhaps caught up in her enthusiasm, agreed to this. Two pupils, including the one boy, chose to observe with the classroom support assistant.

The setting was a field with flowers. One of the girls was a beautiful pink tree. Graffiti had been carved into her trunk with a sharp stone and she felt hurt by this. Three girls stood on chairs to be in the tree. They were Ra Ra, a female lion; Leo, a male lion; and Pinkney, a female monkey. Leo had escaped from the circus and explained he had no roar. The teacher played Sylvia, a friend, who stood nearby.

I asked people in role to think of three characteristics to enable them to *become* their character. The girl whose story was chosen helped with this process. The tree mentioned a beautiful snail at the bottom of its trunk and I asked the two observing group members if they wished to take on the role of snail. One shook her head but the male pupil, with encouragement from the other group members, joined in the scene as the snail. Although he was initially reticent, he was smiling and looking pleased with himself, so I imagined he was enjoying being a beautiful snail lying at the bottom of the tree. Throughout this scene I facilitated the group process, making observations, reflecting on what sounded like significant statements and maintaining the psychodramatic structure.

The group spontaneously enacted a scene in which Pinkney dropped her pink beads and Leo found them. Leo said they were beautiful and decided to keep them. Pinkney was sad. Ra Ra, who was Pinkney's sister, said she had sharp teeth and could roar. She wanted to protect her sister because their grandmother had just died. She saw Leo take the beads and decided to chase and attack him for taking them. The use of psychodrama can involve some element of risk so it is important that the director ensures a level of safety for the group. Thus I explained to Ra Ra how she could 'pretend' to attack Leo.

Ra Ra took the beads from Leo and returned them to Pinkney, who said to Leo, 'they mean so much to me that I needed them back'. I 'doubled'—talking as though I was speaking as Leo—and said, 'I'm sorry I didn't know they were yours'. Leo nodded and repeated the phrase. Ra Ra spoke about Pinkney, 'she's part of me and lives in me'. The tree said to Leo, 'you can live in me, the tree, with the others and you can have one of my apples'. Sylvia, the friend, said to Pinkney that she was sorry she had lost her beads to Leo. Leo said he was glad to have left the circus, which he said was like a prison. I, as director, noticed out loud that Leo had lost his roar and he said he lost it at the circus. When I asked him if he had regained it he expressed a loud roar. I asked how the snail was and we noticed he'd crawled away.

In order to have sufficient time to process this enactment I brought the 'story' to a close by asking if anyone wanted to add anything in role. As one student and her classroom support assistant had not been directly involved in the drama and had not 'doubled' it was important to acknowledge them as group members so they were not isolated from the rest of the group. It is important that the group is re-established in the circle in order to acknowledge it as a whole and to facilitate the sharing process. It is significant, I believe, that the one student who did not participate directly in the psychodrama action was the girl with a disability. I suspect at this stage she did not feel fully involved or sufficiently confident to take part, although she became more actively involved in later sessions.

The girl who played the tree said she felt a variety of emotions in role as the tree: hurt that she had graffiti on her trunk; sad that the beads had been stolen; pleased that they made friends with the lion from the circus. The girl who played Pinkney said she was really upset when she lost her beads but was glad when Leo returned them. The girl who played Ra Ra said how worried she felt as Pinkney's sister. She seemed to suggest that this was a big responsibility for her. The girl who played Leo said as the lion she didn't like doing tricks in the circus ring for people, except for the children. The boy who played the snail had no comment. He and the teacher who played the friend were both on the edge of the drama, observing the action whilst also within it.

Some of them commented that the drama reflected 'real life' and conflict between friends. We discussed how we resolve conflict. Time had run out and we concluded the session.

PROCESSING THE SESSION

I experienced this psychodrama as an enchanting scene. There was such a creative and spontaneous magic to this story, emphasised by the manner in which the group interacted with one another. Davis (2002) writes of the arts as a non-verbal language for expressing thoughts, feelings and the inner life. The arts, within a person-centred atmosphere, can allow us to explore our feelings, and express them in a safe way. I too felt creative and spontaneous and was encouraged by the power of the participants' imaginations. I was moved by them and in turn became more creative and trusting in my ability to facilitate the action.

There is something about children and young people of this age such that their spontaneous expression of feeling has a quality unfettered by 'conditions of worth' experienced in most aspects of our society. Axline, who developed her ideas around non-directive play therapy in the late 1940s, says such play 'grants the individual the permission to be himself [sic]' (1947: 15).

Leo's escape from the confines of the circus seems to be significant: an escape from the bars of a cage, a kind of prison; an animal being made to perform for the pleasure of others rather than realizing its true self. The lion has had to conform to the oppressive needs of the circus and its escape may be seen as an attempt to get closer to his actualising tendency. Through the experience of empathic understanding from others in the drama and myself as director, this has begun to change so that he, 'Leo', can adopt his own frame of reference. I chose to 'double' for Leo, to provide some empathy for his character, to help him elaborate, for his benefit and that of the group as a whole, enabling what may be unspoken to be articulated. A double also provides information for the group on the basis of which they may wish to respond. I doubled here because I noticed that Leo had not expressed intent to steal, but had shown delight and surprise at finding the pink beads. The person or character who has been 'doubled' may reject what the 'double' has said and it is the responsibility of the director to check out its validity for the person in role. Those in role are not able to 'double' as this can be confusing for the group.

We learned later in the group of the difficulties in the personal life of the girl who played Leo that may echo some of her characterisation in role. She talked about conflict in her relationship with her mother, citing an incident in which her views weren't valued. She was saddened she had not been 'heard'—a loss of voice paralleling her role as Leo. (This may raise questions of girls' experiences of feeling silenced in society (Littledale, 2001: 26; Sharpe, 1976: 139) so that their self-esteem becomes dependent on others.) Interestingly, she finds her voice in the role of a male character and maybe this provides her with more inherent power.

Through the use of symbol and metaphor these young people were able to be in touch with and negotiate strong emotions without being directly confronted by them.

I am also interested in the experience of the one boy in the group session. He seemed quiet and shy. He usually sat close to one of the facilitators. My co-facilitator told me that he is often the subject of bullying in the school particularly at break times. I believe that this group became his sanctuary from bullying as well as a place where he was listened to and valued. He did not ally himself with the other two boys in the group—when they were present—and appeared more comfortable with the girls. The other two boys' attendance was more sporadic although when they did come contributed to the group in a creative and imaginative manner. They were sometimes not in school due to truancy or suspensions, or stated they simply preferred to be outside playing football.

Being a quiet, gentle boy meant the remaining male participant did not conform to the masculine stereotype within school and thus perhaps became an obvious target for bullying from other boys. There is enormous pressure on boys and girls to conform to the prevailing norms of masculinity and femininity. For a boy to be gentle can be seen by other boys as an expression of femininity and thus a cause for rejection. Interestingly, in a report written by Lofas and Burke (2001), it is indicated that boys envy girls their access to emotional expression. Hopefully this group provided a space for boys to express without censure.

Feedback from one of the boys at the conclusion of the group was that he had had 'fun' and believed there should be more such groups. I am also aware that as a 'naughty' boy he had kudos in the group and was mostly valued by the female participants. However I also wonder if playground gender politics made it harder to be seen as a member of this group; 'touchy/feely' subjects possibly seen as 'girls stuff'.

I never saw anyone tease or be intentionally unkind to the quiet boy within the group. Whenever we chose the soft toys he chose the parrot, a bright, stripy creature with few words but clearly visible by its colouring. He was consistent in this choice of symbol and would sometimes take 'him' (he called him male) out of my 'soft toys bag' and sit with him on his knee, even when we were not specifically using them for a group activity. I feel he was making himself visible through this character and sometimes would talk through him. His description of flying through the jungle may be representative of his need to remove himself from the regular pain of being diminished in the school recreation area.

Undertaking an auxiliary role, which is when someone takes on the supporting role of an object or person like the snail in this case, can be as powerful as playing the main or protagonist role. Here we can imagine that being a 'beautiful' snail and owning those qualities for himself may have had a regenerative effect on this young person. Holmes (1998: 142–3) says an auxiliary may derive great benefit simply by playing a new role, providing us with the opportunity to try out different roles and qualities from those we normally adopt or possess. This in turn may change his self-concept, and open up the possibility of experiencing his authentic self.

The story, introduced by the girl in role of Ra Ra, became the group's story whilst enabling group expression of its meaning. They began to find a language for their feelings and, furthermore, listened to each other express their emotional world through the drama and through discussions, developing also their empathic and listening skills. By identifying themselves or aspects of themselves in the animal or object, the students were able to explore a fantasy world of their creative imaginings.

Rogers (1983: 20) suggests that significant learning takes place when we utilise both sides of the brain: the intuitive, creative right side, as well as the cognitive, logical left side. Whereas in a school setting the emphasis is usually on the left, logical side of the brain; through the use of psychodrama the children were afforded the opportunity in school to also develop the right side of their brains.

THE IMPACT ON THESE STUDENTS OF BEING IN A PERSON-CENTRED GROUP WITHIN A SCHOOL SETTING

The process of being in a person-centred group was possibly therapeutic for the participants even though the primary concern of the research was how to foster emotional literacy within a school setting. In feedback from the students at the end of the group, a number of them appeared to value the opportunity to express 'feelings and emotions and things'. As a person-centred practitioner, I believe human beings have vast resources for self-directed behaviour and that belief underpinned my approach in working with this group of young people.

Collaborative power was also an essential ingredient of the group process, and this sharing of power is, I believe, quite different to most students' usual experiences in mainstream schooling, which are based on traditional power relations. The person-centred practitioner Peggy Natiello writes about the contrast between authoritarian and collaborative power (Natiello, 2001: 59–73). The emotional literacy group enabled, validated and provided for a sense of community. It also allowed these young students to explore their personal identity and personal boundaries within a system in which there is usually little possibility for emotional expression. Proctor (2005: 22) says that 'the experience of powerlessness is one of the most significant causal factors contributing to the experience of psychological distress.' I believe that being in a relationship in which a child can feel genuinely accepted and respected enables the child to develop the capacity for constructive self-direction.

THE DEVELOPMENT OF EMOTIONAL LITERACY: AN EVALUATION

The emphasis on creativity and expression of the students' emotional world afforded the students an alternative medium for learning in the school context. It provided legitimacy to those feelings which stand alongside their academic development, but which children, used to a narrow emphasis on intellectual capabilities, will only occasionally have the opportunity to address in school (Weare, 2004: 31; Antidote, 2003: 7; Goleman, 1996: xi).

The valuing of the participants by the adults in the group was a key part of this process. This 'spilled over' into other areas within the school and the teacher/co-facilitator described to me an incident in which her changed relationship with one of the young boys—who was absent for this session—was assisted by his attendance in the group. She also noticed increased interest by other teaching staff in the nature of the group and by the management group led by the head teacher. Later on I was also invited by this school to facilitate training with members of the teaching staff around themes of emotional literacy and in developing communication skills between teachers and students. I felt this was an important development as I believe emotional literacy needs to be seen as a whole-school approach; part of a school's ethos about the relationship between teachers and students, an understanding of how children learn, and further, how this links to local and national educational policy. It needs to be part of the agenda of the management structure and Antidote (2003), the campaign for emotional literacy, suggests it needs to be part of a 'whole school strategy'. If we don't concern ourselves with the emotional needs of children and young people in schools they are likely to feel alienated from a system that insists on academic success without a recognition of or respect for their emerging selves.

The teacher and I have co-facilitated two further emotional literacy groups in this school and whilst I am no longer involved, the teacher plans to continue this venture. The plan was that the project remains a live and vital part of this school's life.

CONCLUSION

The person-centred approach with its emphasis on dialogue, contact and connectedness has the potential to engage children and young people in a manner that supports and validates them. Combined with a creative medium, in this case psychodrama, the arts' potential to transform enabled the students in this group to explore, express and create in a relatively safe and affirming environment. Both psychodrama and the person-centred approach have a positive worldview and see the innate capacity of human beings to fulfil their potential. Whilst there are difficulties sometimes in combining the two approaches, not least in the use of the term 'director', I believe the combination, for this group, enabled participants' creative expression of feelings, thoughts and choices.

REFERENCES

Antidote (2003) *The Emotional Literacy Handbook: Promoting whole-school strategies.* London: David Fulton.

Axline, V (1947) *Play Therapy.* New York: Ballantine Books.

Bannister, A (2002) Setting the scene. In A Bannister & A Huntington (Eds) *Communicating with Children and Adolescents* (pp. 19–32). London: Jessica Kingsley.

Biancardi, J (2003) Idiosyncrasy through the core conditions and beyond. In S Keys (Ed) *Idiosyncratic Person-Centred Therapy* (pp. 139–49). Ross-on-Wye: PCCS Books.

Davis, S (2002) Psychological contact through person-centered expressive arts. In G Wyatt & P Sanders (Eds) *Rogers' Therapeutic Conditions: Evolution, theory and practice. Vol 4: Contact and perception* (pp. 204–20). Ross-on-Wye: PCCS Books.

Goleman, D (1996) *Emotional Intelligence: Why it can matter more than IQ.* London: Bloomsbury.

Holmes, P (1998) The auxiliary ego. In M Karp, P Holmes & K Bradshaw Tauvon (Eds) *The Handbook of Psychodrama* (pp. 129–44). London/New York: Routledge.

Kirschenbaum, H & Henderson, VL (Eds) (1990) *The Carl Rogers Reader.* London: Constable.

Littledale, N (2001) Mother blaming: Gender and psychodrama. *British Journal of Psychodrama and Sociodrama, 16* (2), 23–34.

Lofas, P & Burke, E (Eds) (2001) *Act Up: Speak out.* Hull and East Riding NHS Trust and Hull City Council, Specialist Health Promotion Service.

Natiello, P (2001) *The Person-Centred Approach: A passionate presence.* Ross-on-Wye: PCCS Books.

Office for Standards in Education (2004) *Healthy Minds: Promoting emotional health and well-being in schools.* <www.ofsted.gov.uk/publications>.

Proctor, G (2005) Working in forensic services in a person-centred way. *Person-Centred and Experiential Psychologies, 4* (1), 20–30.

Rogers, CR (1970) *Encounter Groups.* New York/Evanston/London: Allen Lane, Penguin.

Rogers, CR (1983) *Freedom to Learn for the 80s.* Columbus, OH: Charles E Merrill.

Sharpe, S (1976) *Just like a Girl: How girls learn to be women.* London: Pelican.

Weare, K (2004) *Developing the Emotionally Literate School.* London: Paul Chapman Publishing.

Wilkins, P (1994) The person-centred approach to psychodrama. *British Journal of Psychodrama & Sociodrama, 9* (2), 37–48.

CHAPTER 8

WIDENING PARTICIPATION
A COUNSELLING SERVICE IN
A SIXTH FORM COLLEGE

SUZANNE KEYS

Working as a counsellor with young people in an environment rich in diversity has taught me a lot, energised me, exhausted me and challenged my ideas of what being a counsellor means and whether even the term 'counsellor' is still relevant. It is certainly true that, despite Eminem's popular song lyrics suggesting that Stan could do with some counselling, it is still seen as a rather 'uncool' thing to do and as a sign of weakness. The counsellor needs to be able to empathise with those views and respond in a meaningful and accessible way. She needs to find different ways of being and acting without losing a sense of her identity and the particular role she has to play in the broader educational and political agenda of widening young people's participation in learning.

WIDENING PARTICIPATION IN LEARNING

Newham Sixth Form College (NewVIc) was set up 11 years ago in one of the most deprived boroughs in the UK where the take-up rate in post-16 education was well under 50%. It had a threefold agenda: to widen educational choices available to local 16-19 year olds, to increase the number of students staying on, and to increase achievement. It now has 2100 full-time students, 700 doing A-level courses, 500 at entry, foundation and intermediate level and the rest doing advanced vocational courses. Its exam pass rates are slightly higher than the national average, despite the fact that its entry requirements are lower than the national average. Most of the young people leaving college to go on to higher education or jobs have travelled a huge distance not only academically but in terms of their personal development. Some of the students have had to struggle with very difficult socio-economic circumstances and feelings of low self-esteem after having 'failed' in their previous education.

A shortened version of this article first appeared in the *AUCC Journal*, November 2003, which is the professional journal of the Association for University and College Counselling, a Division of the British Association for Counselling and Psychotherapy. My thanks to BACP for giving their permission to reproduce the article.

There is a considerable body of research evidence, which highlights the dangers of accumulated deprivation and disadvantage. The life chances of black young people are affected by a range of variables leading to their high representation in statistics around children looked after, homelessness, the juvenile justice system and unemployment. (Barn, 2001: 84)

The ethnicity of the local community is reflected in the make-up of the students attending the college and the counselling service: over 50% from South Asian backgrounds (Bangladeshi, Pakistani and Indian), 33% from Black African and Caribbean backgrounds, and approximately 10% from White British backgrounds. A large proportion of students are from Muslim communities. The other distinguishing factor about the learning community at NewVIc is its inclusiveness of young people with physical and learning disabilities as part of the mainstream as well as a discrete provision for approximately 20 students. This is a vital part of the learning environment for all students.

According to Sid Hughes, principal of the college, the counsellor was employed 'because of the area in which the college is located and the background of our young people and the relatively unstable nature of some aspects of their lives. The college needed to support them, otherwise learning would not have been successful.' The counselling service works as part of a learning support network with the tutorial system at its heart. The college is student-centred, aiming to make learning as accessible as possible to each individual student.

WIDENING PARTICIPATION IN THE COUNSELLING SERVICE

Widening participation in the counselling service is about the accessibility of the counselling service to such a diverse range of students as well as the 'width' of the counsellor and her willingness and ability to participate in a meaningful relationship with the individual young person. The following are the key points I have discovered in both these areas.

ACCESSIBLE SERVICE

- *Publicity*: colour, font, content, size, language, images.

- *Location and accommodation*: discreet, welcoming, physically accessible including being set up for students with visual impairments and using wheelchairs at all times.

- *Availability*: an open door policy so that students can drop-in and check out the room and counsellor. I often get groups of young men doing this. They comprise only a third of the students who make appointments so it is important to provide other means of access.

- *Proactivity*: the importance of thinking ahead, including diversity in all areas of planning and thinking. Recent changes in legislation emphasise this: Race Relations

(Amendment) Act 2000 and Disability Discrimination Act Part 4. Both underline the legal duty of educational establishments to be anticipatory (<www.homeoffice. gov.uk>, <www.drc-gb.org>). Being proactive as a service also means being aware of what may be less visible, for example, a homophobic atmosphere which might stop students coming out or accessing counselling.

- *Monitoring and evaluating*: keeping a check on who is using the service and what the student population as a whole thinks about counselling. For example, I have asked a question in a survey about whether the ethnicity and gender of the counsellor would affect a student's access to the counselling service. Interestingly for most respondents it was not a barrier.

ACCESSIBLE COUNSELLOR

I have found myself personally and professionally 'widening' in the following areas since starting work at NewVIc.

- *Flex-ability*: being able to be open to whatever happens during the day, which is often unpredictable. This includes being open to crisis appointments with staff and/or students, having short sessions, one-off appointments, students not turning up without notice, seeing students with friends. (See also Leach, 2003.)

- *Response-ability*: realising my duty to be fluid in my responding, to move from relating at depth to providing information, to speaking to social services, to writing a letter, within 45 minutes. The ability to participate in an authentic relationship, to engage actively and to be aware of my power has been of vital importance to disempowered young people who may never have experienced a caring, non-judgemental adult who listens to them. I have been forced to rely on my idiosyncrasy as a counsellor in order to fully meet the young people who come to me (Keys, 2003).

- *Resourcefulness*: not only having the resources to respond to a range of students but also to sustain hope in the face of often desperate circumstances young people find themselves in. Many of the issues students bring are about staying alive and this is also an issue for the counsellor—maintaining hope in humanity and the potential and capacity of the person to grow and develop despite what may seem like overwhelmingly destructive circumstances (Keys, 2002). I have been forced to acknowledge the importance of resourcing myself regularly physically, socially, emotionally and spiritually in order to sustain an open and flexible presence to the students I see.

- *Humility*: 'the ability to assess accurately and acknowledge one's own strengths and weaknesses' (BACP, Ethical Framework, 2002). It is important to know how wide you can go without over-stretching.

- *Empathy*: being able to hear and see the uniqueness of the individual in all their differences without making assumptions about their race, culture, religion or sexual orientation. Whether empathy is enough or whether you need specific training to work cross-culturally is an ongoing debate. According to the literature

(Eleftheriadou,1994; Lago & Thompson,1996; Palmer, 2002) two key features in effective cross-cultural counselling, which transcend therapeutic orientations are the importance of empathy and the quality of relationship.

> In a way, cross-cultural work highlights the issue of how, as therapists, we are not experts in the client's issues. Indeed, with the continual movement towards pluralistic societies we have an ethical duty towards our clients to be as open as we can and accept that we all have differing worldviews. (Eleftheriadou, 1994: 80)

- *Connect-ability*: recognising that the counsellor is part of a bigger picture, not only within the institution but also the local community. Counselling is not an activity which takes place in isolation, alienated from the outside world. A comprehensive referral list as well as personal contact and involvement with outreach from local services such as, in my case, the Newham Asian Women's Project, are essential.

- *Politicisation*: young people cannot be seen as divorced from their environment and the counsellor's role may include advocacy and being a social change agent (Lee, 1999: 31) as well as a human rights agent (Keys, 2000: 197). This is unavoidable working in a context of widening participation.

> Awareness of the social and political context is essential for therapists to consider the socially positioned individual, and to address the interaction of the individual with their environment and to avoid pathologising the individual. In particular the social causes of distress need to be considered and understood. For therapists to consider this issue with each client, it is essential that they have already explored their own structural positions with regard to power and oppression and the effect of these positions on themselves and others in relationships. (Proctor, 2002: 140)

This goes to the heart of the work of a counsellor in a diverse environment. It is about self-awareness as well as being aware of the client as part of a bigger picture, which impacts not only their world but also the counselling relationship. Moreover, the counsellor is part of the society she lives in and it is incumbent on her to take what she knows from the counselling room into the wider world. The world of the counselling room cannot afford to be separated from the so-called wider world: it is both a microcosm of that world as well as part of the macrocosm.

REFERENCES

Barn, R (2001) *Black Youth on the Margins. A research review.* York: York Publishing Services Ltd.

British Association for Counselling and Psychotherapy (2002) *Ethical Framework for Good Practice in Counselling and Psychotherapy.* Rugby: BACP.

Eleftheriadou, Z (1994) *Transcultural Counselling.* London: Central Book Publishing Ltd.

Keys, S (2000) The person-centred counsellor as an agent of human rights. In T Merry (Ed) (2000) *Person-Centred Practice: The BAPCA reader* (pp. 193–200). Ross-on-Wye: PCCS Books.

Keys, S (2002) Staying alive. Paper presented to the Carl Rogers Symposium in La Jolla, CA.

Keys, S (Ed) (2003) *Idiosyncratic Person-Centred Therapy: From the personal to the universal.* Ross-on-Wye: PCCS Books.

Lago, C & Thompson, J (1996) *Race, Culture and Counselling.* Buckingham: Open University Press.

Leach, G (2003) Raising the profile of your service, using the AUCC annual survey. *AUCC Journal, 3,* 18–24.

Lee, CC (1999) Mental health professionals as agents of social change. *RACE Multi-Cultural Journal, 19,* 30–2.

Palmer, S (Ed) (2002) *Multicultural Counselling. A reader.* London: Sage.

Proctor, G (2002) *The Dynamics of Power in Counselling and Psychotherapy. Ethics, politics and practice.* Ross-on-Wye: PCCS Books.

CHAPTER 9

THE BUZZ
A PERSON-CENTRED
PUPIL REFERRAL UNIT

TRACEY WALSHAW

My connection with the Buzz has over the years taken many shapes. My first encounter with the child workers was about five years ago when two of them came on the PCCS Certificate in Working with Children and Young People. Two things really struck me about them in the group: one was how different they looked from the rest of the students, (jeaned, pierced and relaxed), and the other was the aliveness with which they talked about their work with the children at the project. It made me really interested in the unit and the philosophies of this small, but apparently successful, pupil referral unit. What captivated me was the respect and warmth they had for themselves and their co-workers and the buoyancy which that seemed to give them when they were working with their client group. I have deep respect not only for the work they do with children and parents but how they have managed to provide and work within person-centred principles for themselves as a unit within such a challenging remit. I find this wider application of the person-centred approach interesting as so often child practitioners are good at providing the conditions for clients but they somehow get lost for the workers in an organisational setting. I have often wondered about the influence of this on the direct work and the seepage that might occur when organisations seem to have incongruence between what they offer their clients and their workers. How we are supported as practitioners is fundamental ballast for working with such a demanding client group. So I thought it would be enlightening to go to the Buzz and find out more about their work. The Buzz team consists of one head teacher, two teachers, and seven mentors. They would be seen by mainstream standards to be highly staffed as on average they work with twelve children.

The following is based on the conversations I had on this visit. First I have included the Buzz 'Vision Statement' and extracts from their 'Approach to Change and Social Inclusion for Excluded Pupils and their Families/Carers'. Both of these documents show how a person-centred perspective is central to the organisational structure and ethos.

THE BUZZ VISION STATEMENT

The Buzz unit's core purpose is to work therapeutically with pupils who have been excluded from mainstream education so as to prepare them for re-integration. In order to achieve this, the unit aims to create an environment in which pupils will experience emotional, social, behavioural and academic growth. The mechanism for this holistic change is based on the Buzz staff team providing a quality of therapeutic relationship between pupils, staff, families and carers to encourage engagement and commitment to the process of learning and change. As a team we have a set of shared values based upon respect, empathy and genuineness, which we believe create the necessary conditions for growth, learning and change. We are a team that provides a range of strengths to make social inclusion a reality for the pupils and their families/carers through:

* *Valuing the experiences of team members who have experienced exclusion themselves and who have a non-judgemental approach to the pupils' family/carer systems.*

* *Selecting, as team members, adults who are sensitive, emotionally literate and able to build positive relationships to create an educational provision that the pupils and their carers can trust, where all can experience success and start to re-engage with education.*

* *Providing a curriculum that raises attainment by responding to individual's needs, by providing opportunities for pupils to understand, to take responsibility and to make informed choices.*

* *Providing daily contact with the family/carer system so that adults at home can be challenged and supported to help the child's successful return to a new school.*

* *Employing adults who are committed to the concept of social inclusion and who understand that self-acceptance and self-awareness are central to change within each of us.*

* *Working and learning as an effective, compassionate team by modelling the approach for ourselves as individuals and with each other, by making mistakes, having fun and believing that every human being wants to fulfil their potential, given the right conditions.*

THE BUZZ APPROACH TO CHANGE AND SOCIAL INCLUSION FOR EXCLUDED PUPILS AND THEIR FAMILIES/CARERS (EXTRACTS)

We work closely with the family/carers individually and in groups to find a more positive way forward for the pupil to be successful at the next school.

Although there is a framework for managing the behaviour of the excluded pupils through a sanction and reward system there is great emphasis on understanding the child's experience and improving the behaviour. Staff spend a lot of time trying to understand the children's feelings and their views of the world which gives both the adults and children insights into the reasons behind behaviour and a focus to work on whilst the pupil is at the Buzz.

The staff at the Buzz are trained in counselling skills using a Rogerian approach, trained to listen to children and adults and to provide the key features in building trusting relationships, being genuine, being accepting and being empathic. They are sensitive and responsive to the emotional experience of the children and their families/carers. They believe that the quality of the relationship that the staff can build with the children is the crucial determinant in the process of change. Real change comes from within the child and their family/carers once they feel safe and accepted and are then able to trust and be honest about their experiences. This can be a very intense, exhausting, confusing and challenging process as staff deal with the demands of the pupils and their lives. Staff have to be able to understand their own emotional history, their own realities and their own responses to events as it is only through their self-awareness and their personal growth that they can facilitate growth and change in others. This is an ongoing process which staff are challenged with on a daily basis; there is a system for supervision for all staff and ongoing training for personal and professional development.

The team have an attitude that communicates hope and a sense of belief in the children and their families/carers and a sense of trust in the regenerative capacities of children and adults to overcome difficulties. In turn the children and their families/carers develop a sense of belief in themselves and show their potential by finding solutions that are meaningful for them. The Buzz staff team have helped many children through their difficulties, children who have been excluded from the education system and are at great risk of further future difficulties. Work is done by utilising the children and their family/carer's inner resources in increasing choices they have for emotional responses, how they cope with their anxiety and anger, how they can accept help, how to wait their turn, how to share attention and resources, how to make friends, how to negotiate conflict. Children make progress with their academic achievements before they go on to a new school where they can feel socially included again. They also work with the school system and school staff.

THE CHILDREN AT THE BUZZ

The Buzz focuses on inclusion for excluded children, providing education for young children who have been deemed unmanageable in mainstream primary school. They work with children who have experienced the social and emotional effects within their family units of poverty, drug addiction, domestic violence, living in disadvantaged neighbourhoods, parental and child involvement in gangs, parents involved in criminal activity, absentee parents (often because they are in prison or pending sentencing) and children with Anti-Social Behaviour Orders and special educational needs. To be here children have to have been excluded permanently from mainstream education but they still follow the mainstream curriculum because they know that for reintegration into mainstream education a pattern/routine that is familiar aids success. They are helping children develop realistic ways of coping with the standardised education structures. So they tend to follow the mainstream curriculum as closely as they can.

Some of the children have been in the unit a long time, others are part time and others come and go. The longest anyone has been here is three years. Integrating the new children into the unit and established peer groups can prove challenging. The Buzz encourages a sense that everyone is responsible for helping the new person with a sense of group identity. They work with emotional intelligence acknowledging jealousy as a normal emotion, acknowledging that this is a legitimate feeling and integrating it into the child's feeling response repertoire.

When a child enters the Buzz their needs are assessed and a tailor-made programme drawn up for them, based on individual personalised learning needs. Relationship building is crucial for the success of assessment and creating a programme that is empathic to the child's needs. Often children are quite nervous about coming to the Buzz because they have had a very bad experience at another school. The child and the parent/carer's previous experience with school has usually been negative. Often parents/carers have been constantly given the message 'your child is out of control!' The Buzz feels it's important that the initial contact is with someone who can be empathic, understanding, congruent and respectful. Nurturing affirmation, as opposed to 'all right you've done that and now you can do this', seems to pervade the building. Equally this does not make the staff a soft option as congruence gives respectful boundaries to what is acceptable or not. They work hard as a team at seeing through the behaviour to the personhood of the child. In empathically touching this personhood they can help to unravel the sometimes inappropriate responses the child has. They, as a team, ascribe to the belief that you have to understand the present to help the child have choice in the future.

The unit very rarely excludes children as the staff are aware that a child who is excluded from the Buzz hasn't got much of a chance anywhere else. So they often give them chance after chance. The team works with the social, economic and emotional context each child brings with them. Sometimes there are rules at home that are at odds with the Buzz's rules. They are in a completely different social context. The children have to work out quite quickly the skill of code switching i.e. changing their behaviour to fit their current social context.

Often the children have received a lot of criticism, so trying to find creative ways to give feedback is crucial. The mentors are excellent at finding the positive. They constantly challenge the self-concept the child comes with of 'I'm a bad boy' or 'I'm a naughty girl' or 'I can never do anything right'. The unit were surprised to find a lot of the children are very worried about their work and have higher standards for themselves than the team have for them. They often get really uptight and physically screw their work up thinking it's rubbish, so they never get anywhere. A lot of them can't accept that if they make one mark in the wrong place on the paper then their work isn't trashed. It's almost as if their work has to be perfect, as they are so imperfect.

Building strong, trusting, empathic and congruent relationships with the children is fundamental to this unit. What works for one child does not always work for another, finding out who they are and what they respond to is vital. The staff believe that behaviour is about children trying to get their individual needs met. It is a response to their anxiety, often a reaction to the issues going on at home. The child's behaviours are trying to meet his or her needs. The child knows exactly what he needs and he tries to get it through existing coping mechanisms. Often these coping mechanisms have become distorted and redundant and thus no longer meet their needs. So the staff work with the child identifying what their needs are and how they can develop more useful mechanisms. It's the basic philosophy that the client, in this instance the child, is the expert.

> Head teacher: *What kind of happens in other places is the child might be labelled by things like 'Oh, the child's manipulative, attention seeking', but the person-centred approach would be about him getting some need met without the labelling. We as a team ask what this behaviour means to this child by being empathic with the child. We find that when the children feel understood and accepted then their behaviour may change. We can look in on things because we have assumptions and certainly as an adult with children I do it but I'm looking at it from an adult's perspective. Only when I understand from the child perspective it will make absolutely perfect sense.*

> Tracey: *So in person-centred work you try and understand what it means to that child even if it makes no sense to you. In growing up sometimes the wires get crossed, children are not born evil or bad, something happens and that sometimes defines why they are behaving in a certain way. If you can really try and understand them and not be blaming then they have got a chance to realign themselves.*

PARENTS/CARERS AND MENTORS

Working alongside the parents/carers and being empathic to all the subsystems in the family structure is fundamental. Many of the parents/carers themselves are young and come from parts of society that are seen as unsavoury, troublesome or unattractive. The unit works closely with the families, not excluding them, as has often been their experience from other social agencies. The mentors are crucial in facilitating close personal links. They are physically on the doorstep every morning and evening picking the children up, genuinely interested in them. In being responsive the staff nurture both child and adult.

The head teacher told me that the work the mentors do with children and families is amazing. They are skilled and competent although some schools seem to want them to be more conformist in their appearance. My guess is that it is the very humanness and diversity across this team that allows the first process of accessibility. It is not only professionals but also families who judge by appearance.

> Learning Mentor: *I just think what's different about this place is for the first time we are meeting the parent on a different level, saying we know your child has all these problems we are here to help them and you. We report back every day, saying this is what's happened, these are the good things, these are the not so good things. This is often a totally different experience than at mainstream school. Sometimes at school the parents seem to hear the child is their problem. The Buzz emphasizes that if this child has a problem we are all in this together. In fairness to mainstream schools the child has often been an enormous*

problem; consequently parents are summoned to school to talk about their child always as a problem. They must get pretty fed up of that and especially if they haven't the resources to do anything about it.

Tracey: *You're saying a defensive response from the parent often feels a reasonable one when you are empathic with them in entering their frame of reference. The consequence of being non-empathic and judgemental with parents is a poor relationship developing between them and the schools.*

Behavioural Support Teacher: *Some parents don't want their children to come to the Buzz because they think it is special or retarded or whatever their concept is, peculiar or odd. In reality most parents want their children to go to a 'normal school' and do well. The fact that their children have already not done well is what we, the Buzz staff, have to counterbalance.*

Head teacher: *We encourage them to visit and talk to us and consequently more often than not they then want their child to have a place here. There's something very valuable about this environment of conveying hope to the parents for their child here. It's hard sometimes to sustain hope in the adults and this is one of our strengths that is pivotal to the success of the child's learning. Often these parents feel their children are written off. There is often a shift in the parents because of their link with the Buzz and/or a shift in the child. Well, either can come first. Parents then begin to trust their own judgements and the Buzz staff as well. This is fundamental in referring the child back to mainstream or another school that may be more appropriate for the child's special needs. The parents are much more open and ready to consider it. That's the potency of being honest and congruent, not alienating the parents and trying to understand what their lives are really like.*

COMMUNICATION AND ADVOCACY

Mentors accompany parents to the psychiatrist, the psychologist and meetings with other health professionals. Sometimes they speak for the parent/carer and sometimes with them. Translating and bridging these gaps takes time, interest and creativity by the staff. Often parents are relieved that they have found their voice in sometimes alien and judgemental forums. Sometimes, for example, the doctor's surgery telephones staff to inform mentors that a mother has not brought their child to an appointment for head scans or X-rays, which the child needs. The staff response is not to judge the mother but to be empathic, respectful and creative in helping her respond to the request. This can be time consuming for the service. It feels like organic advocacy. There is a gentleness about how the staff respond to the parents, which, because it embodies the core conditions, also paradoxically has firmness. It's like the staff acknowledge they cannot be like a bull in a china shop here! They appear to me to be some of the best listeners to the background as well as foreground sounds.

Head teacher: *Some of these children are very powerful in their family, playing family members off against each other. We check up on this through the relationship the mentors have with the family. There is often contact with parents and learning mentors when our children are picked up in the morning and returned home after school. This helps everybody know what's going on; communications and clarity are really important. Sustaining two connected systems, the family and the education system are together in a child's life. Once these systems split the child does not know where or how to align themselves. The more consistent these two systems are, the healthier the working relationship and the more the best interests of the child are served.*

The Buzz staff respect that families try to respond with the resources they have and sometimes they are not enough. Issues of class, wealth and environment exist here. If you are trying to work with an unruly child who can be controlled in a specific environment and then at home is exposed to gangs, drugs and crime in his/her community, placing the blame on the families is unhelpful and irresponsible, although an all too familiar response from society. Often these families speak a different social, political and economic language to the professionals they come into contact with.

TEAMWORK

Head teacher: *I know that every child will connect with somebody on the team. There is one child here that's still hasn't made the least connection with anyone, but he has been the slowest and the most distant child I've seen come here. I'd say he's made some loose connections with a couple of the team but not as strong as other children have made. I think that's the strength of our team because different kids respond to different people and different ways of being and that's the beauty of having a wide variety of people on the team. The kids have so many needs and also a lot of them come from a place where their opportunities are very limited. Coming here offers them opportunities and experiences that they would usually not experience till late adulthood if indeed at all. Like going to places, doing things, hearing musicians. It's not just about sitting with kids working out anger. It includes working with the reality of their lives, and about trying to build up their life experiences to open their minds to the fact that the estate you grow up in isn't just what the world is. That there's so much more out there for you, stuff you can do, for me that's one of the most amazing things.*

Learning Mentor: *We try to look after each other. If you're stuck with a kid who's going off their head and you've been with them for 40 minutes we may offer the team member a break, tag team in effect. We look out for each other—it's accepting that help and saying 'Yeah I do need to have a break from this child rather than gritting your teeth to get through it. If you're not honest with yourself it's the child that loses out. The kids know your buttons, and they can press them all day long. It's for you to realise you might be the problem. For the kid's sake as well as my own I will take that tag the team have offered me. Internal monitoring of yourself so you don't repeat patterns of what you did as a child.*

79

And that's the power. Sometimes I find myself saying I want to be like that, to be a mentor I need to be like that when I'm watching [another mentor] but that's not me or my role. We are all different; we all have different strengths. I guess that's like a model for the children because they are all individuals and are allowed to be individuals but also they have got to fit in to part of the community. Every one of them is brilliant at something. They all respond when they come here.

This is just a taster of the facilitative and creative emotional work done with children in this unit. For me the Buzz is an example of just what can be achieved by working in a person-centred way in the wider organisational context with some of the children and families often considered as 'hard to reach' or given up on. I hope this chapter has done some justice in its representation of the respectful and facilitative work this staff team offer to children who have so often been written off. I wish to thank all the staff at the Buzz, they are indeed a bunch of the most dedicated and amazing folk I have met in educational settings. I will conclude with the inspiring personal requirements for Buzz mentors, whose work with children and their families is so life-affirming and transformative. It sums it up really in ordinary, straight, clear and non-jargonistic language, and indeed in 'true person-centred speak'.

QUALIFICATIONS OF THE BUZZ MENTORS

Some of the mentors have few if any formal qualifications but the qualifications that are important are:

Staff who are genuine, earthy, respectful and empathic. (All have a *counselling skills* qualification.)

Staff who have an ability to build *trusting relationships* with children and adults who are not used to trusting others.

Staff who can *sense* what others are experiencing and are then able to act on it.

Staff who can provide a positive male or female role model and be a *'significant other'* for a child.

Staff who are creative and *flexible.*

Staff who have a sense of *humour* and use initiative.

Staff who are calm, patient and *listen* well to others.

Staff who are *passionate about children* and committed to building children's confidence in themselves.

Staff who are able to support children who are *ashamed* of themselves and their educational achievements and help them achieve success.

Staff who have pride in the role of *education* for promoting equality and inclusion, bringing *hope* and a belief that this can be achieved for the pupils and their parents/carers.

CHAPTER 10

ADOPTION AND THE PERSON-CENTRED APPROACH
WORKING FOR THE CHILD

CATE KELLY

INTRODUCTION

The key task for professionals who are working with a child who is either being prepared for an adoption placement, or in an adoption placement (i.e. prior to the adoption order being made) is to try to ensure that the *conditions* are such that the placement will be successful. What I want to focus on in this chapter, from a person-centred perspective, is what I am going to call the actualisation of the adoption placement. What I mean by this is the tendency for all parties in the placement to strive, individually and in terms of inter-familial relationships, to make the placement the best it can be. In adoption language: to make a *successful placement*. I will propose my reasons for believing that in the world of adoption placements it is rarely possible to work with a child in isolation. I will address some of the complexities both for the child and her[1] adopters in the events which have preceded the placement and why I believe it is impossible to disregard the profound influence adoptive parents have in shaping the way members of the new family relate to each other. I see the latter as being pivotal to how a child may resolve issues from her past, as well as providing the circumstances in which openness and fluidity can facilitate the process of the placement, thus leading to the potential actualising of the adoption relationships for all members of the new family.

I am proposing, therefore, that in working with a child where something to do with adoption is the key issue, it is more pertinent that the focus of my work is not in *my* building a therapeutic relationship with the child but rather my facilitating a way in which the conditions and relationships within the family can be such that there is a move towards the actualising of those relationships. I will present two case studies, which illustrate the theme of 'working *for* the child'. I will present a person-centred perspective of the development of attachment relationships and will widen the application of person-centred theory to other aspects of adoption work, which affect the 'success' of a placement. This will include acknowledging other influences on the placement relationship: birth parents, foster carers, sharing information with adopters, and helping the child gain an understanding and make sense of her adoption story.

The views I express in this chapter, some of which may sound forceful to the reader, are based on the robust experience I have gained as an adoption practitioner and

---

1. I will use 'she' as a non-gender-specific way in which to refer to the child.

manager of an adoption team. I own these beliefs based on the knowledge I have acquired about what works in the highly complex area of adoption work.

WORKING IN ADOPTION IN THE STATUTORY SERVICES

Working, as I have for thirty-four years, within a statutory setting like a local authority provides a challenge for a practitioner whose preference is to work from a person-centred perspective. It feels like the delivery of service, bound by the weight of a rigid structure, sits uneasily with the person-centred approach (PCA), which values flexibility, fluidity and a process understanding of the way people learn about themselves and about change. In the UK, local authorities have statutory responsibility for the provision of services which protect children and which meet their needs as defined in the Children Act 1989. Working with children in adoption adds a further dimension to this in that it is rare to be able to work with a child without an awareness of how each member of the 'adoption triangle' impacts on the others. Child, adopter and birth parent relationships interweave in such a way that it unlikely that one could work productively with a child without a nuanced grasp of these intricacies. Furthermore, the weight of adoption law brings both licence and restriction for a worker who is formulating plans for a child with the principle, only recently enshrined in legislation (Adoption and Children Act 2002) *that the welfare of the child is paramount.* Whilst the views of all parties must be sought (child and birth parents), it is the welfare of the *child* which is paramount. In most cases a child would wish to live with a birth parent, no matter what has been the quality of past relationships. Likewise most birth parents, whose children are the subject of care proceedings under the Children Act 1989 where a plan for adoption is being considered by the Court, will wish to have their child returned to their care. Working in a person-centred way for the child may conflict with my ability to offer the core conditions, in the short term, to a birth parent and, in the longer term, to the child's adopter(s). Whilst the National Standards in Adoption (2003) require that each member of the adoption triangle now has their own individual worker, I consider that it is vital for the child's worker to have a sound grasp of the impact on the child of the influences on her psychological and emotional well-being from her birth parents as well as from her adopters. It is also important to carry an awareness of the impact on the child of relationships with other significant members of her birth family, as well as the influence of relationships with any foster carers with whom she has lived. I cannot address the latter here as it is sufficiently complex to warrant a chapter in its own right.

Most children who are placed for adoption need to move to a new family because the decision has been made through the court (via care proceedings under the Children Act 1989) that they cannot remain in their birth family and, under the Adoption and Children Act 2002, that they should be placed in an adoptive family. In most cases this will mean that the child has not developed secure attachment behaviours to their parents or carers. Conditions of worth have developed that are based on not being valued for the unique person she is. Physical abuse and sexual abuse may accompany the psychological trauma for the child who has not had her needs met. Because court proceedings are often protracted, even an infant removed from birth parents within the first twelve months of life may wait up to a further twelve months before being placed for adoption. The quality of care in a foster home can be variable and the child may or may not have been able to establish a secure attachment to foster carers.

In the area of adoption, most practitioners approach their work underpinned by the application of attachment theory. I continue to acknowledge the relevance of attachment theory in this area of work. However, I also find it useful to apply the principles of person-centred theory to adoption work. Therefore I will now give a brief outline of attachment theory before presenting a person-centred approach to understanding the development of attachment behaviours and emotions.

ATTACHMENT THEORY AND ITS IMPACT ON ADOPTION PRACTICE

It is a widely held belief that in order to grow and develop, a child needs to be raised in an atmosphere of love, acceptance and a sense of belonging (known in adoption language as 'being claimed') within a reciprocal attachment in which the child's needs are met. For the past fifty or so years John Bowlby's pioneering work, which led to the understanding of attachment, has been widely acknowledged. The work of many theorists corroborated his assertion that a secure attachment between a child and parent/parent figure is an essential prerequisite for the healthy development of the child in all areas of functioning, including emotional well-being (Karen, 1994). Ideas about attachment, separation and loss, the importance of the mother/infant bond, as well as the *quality* of that bond, led to recommendations, which continue to have a profound influence on all childcare practice within social work.

The complexities of the growth of attachment behaviours were also considered from a biological perspective of protective strategies which are life preserving. Through her research, Mary Ainsworth, a close colleague of Bowlby, contributed to psychological understanding of child development in a reliable quantifiable way. Ainsworth studied attachment patterns in diverse cultures and her system for classifying attachment patterns continues to be recognised and to be widely used in assessing the type of attachment pattern a child has to a parent/carer. Ainsworth identified three styles of attachment, which she labelled 'anxious-avoidant', 'secure' and 'ambivalent' (Ainsworth et al., 1978).

Whilst Bowlby and Ainsworth based their approach to attachment theory on the first two years of the infant's life, leading to a gloomy prospect for a child's future attachments if those early relationships had been insecure ones, Patricia Crittenden (2002) takes the view that attachment can be understood in terms of culture, maturation and context. Therefore, in different circumstances from those in which an insecure attachment was formed, it is possible for new, mutually satisfying relationships to be grown between a child and a significant adult/significant others. I find Crittenden's approach to be in tune with the PCA in that both concern process and circumstances rather than a stage model of understanding personality development. I believe that it has an application to adoption work in that prospective adoptive parents have to believe that if they provide the right nurturing environment for their child she will be able to build a secure attachment and to thrive in an environment where being valued leads to the fulfilment of potential.

Changes in adoption practice since the 1970s, fuelled to a great extent by *Children Who Wait* (Rowe & Lambert, 1973) led to a growing belief that it is possible for older children (i.e. not only young babies) to be successfully placed for adoption. However, a radical change in thinking was required for professionals to be able to persuade prospective adopters about this. Evidence was needed to show adopters that it was possible to become parents to an older child who had experienced early emotional trauma as a result of insecure or disrupted attachment, including negative experiences of being in the care system. Such a significant change could only be achieved if adopters were guided in understanding the concepts of regression in children and would be willing to follow professional advice about regression, re-nurturing and re-parenting. Regression refers to a child's behaviour being such that she is considered 'young for her years', for example, a five-year-old wanting to play with baby toys. Re-nurturing/re-parenting are interchangeable terms, which describe the adopter's ability to facilitate what the child seems to need, for example, not trying to stop a five-year-old playing with baby toys and understanding that she will stop doing so when *she* is ready.

In the years/decades following *Children Who Wait,* as studies of adoption disruptions were published, it became clear that bringing up children who had such early negative experiences was a multifaceted task, including a high level of re-parenting. The apt title of the BBC adoption series screened during 2002, *Love Is Not Enough,* reinforced the highly complex nature of becoming parents through adoption to an older child. This series focused on several adoptive families who learned through the experience of having a child/children placed with them that a lot *more* was required of them than if they had become parents through giving birth to a child. The influences on the child of negative experiences from the past (insecure or disrupted attachments, and the possibility of several moves whilst waiting in the local authority care system) meant that the child needed a far more complex set of parenting skills than simply that the parent *loves* the child.

A PERSON-CENTRED UNDERSTANDING OF ATTACHMENT BEHAVIOURS AND EMOTIONS

Since training as a person-centred counsellor ten years ago and in my subsequent practice as such, I have inevitably become compelled to understand the development of attachment behaviours from the perspective of person-centred theory. A simple way of describing, from a person-centred approach, the way in which a secure attachment develops could be as follows: if a healthy emotional relationship is to develop between an infant and his/her mother (parent figure) the two must be in psychological contact. The adult must have an empathic understanding of the child's needs and be highly motivated to respond to and meet those needs. The child must perceive the adult as genuine in their response. The adult must feel and demonstrate an unconditional acceptance of the child, a belief in the child's desire and capacity to reach their full potential (actualising tendency) and the adult must be fully engaged in the relationship in a way in which the infant feels she is loved and valued.

Rogers, in outlining his theory of the development of the personality, described how conditions of worth or introjected values arise out of the infant's need for love:

> the infant ... comes to be guided in his behaviour not to the degree by which an experience maintains or enhances the organism, but by the likelihood of receiving maternal love. (Rogers, 1959: 225)

Rogers took the view that beginning, growing and maintaining attachment behaviours is an interactional business, based on relationships.

Vera Fahlberg is a highly regarded expert in the field of adoption. She devised the arousal/relaxation and positive attachment cycles (1991) detailed below as an easy way to help adoptive parents and adoption workers to understand what is happening to an infant during the interaction with a parent/carer. In both diagrams one can see interactions which can be described from the perspectives of both attachment and person-centred theories. The first diagram relates to the infant's initiation of interaction whilst the second describes a cycle initiated by a parent or carer. The baby initiates a signal to an adult because there is a need to be met (e.g. the baby is hungry or uncomfortable, or needs comfort). The baby trusts their visceral experience and signals the need to another. Where the need is met (food offered, nappy changed, a cuddle received, etc.) there is congruence: the baby feels good/satisfied and the repetition of the cycle leads to conditions of worth, which make the infant feel valued (a secure attachment). The infant who was in a high state of arousal can relax because their need has been met and the repetition of this cycle leads to the child developing trust in her adult. Where the need is not met the

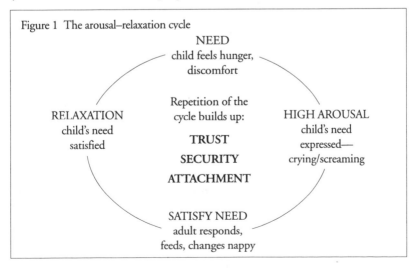

Figure 1 The arousal–relaxation cycle

NEED
child feels hunger, discomfort

Repetition of the cycle builds up:
TRUST
SECURITY
ATTACHMENT

RELAXATION
child's need satisfied

HIGH AROUSAL
child's need expressed—crying/screaming

SATISFY NEED
adult responds, feeds, changes nappy

feeling may be confusion/incongruence. Repetitions of this cycle would result in conditions of worth which would build a view for the infant that she is not valued (an insecure attachment).

The second diagram is a representation of the way a parent/carer will *initiate* enjoyable contact with the child, which is based on emotional interaction rather than physical need, and, in doing so, reinforces to the child her sense of worth. Of this Fahlberg notes: 'there is some evidence that these sorts of social interactions between adult and child contribute more to the bonds between them than do interactions that occur around meeting the child's physical needs' (1991: 29). For me this has echoes of Rogers when, in describing the organism as 'self-preserving and social' (cited in Tudor et al., 2004: 25) he alludes to the fact that, although in the early months of development the child's needs may primarily be physical, they are inextricably interwoven with emotions and relationship.

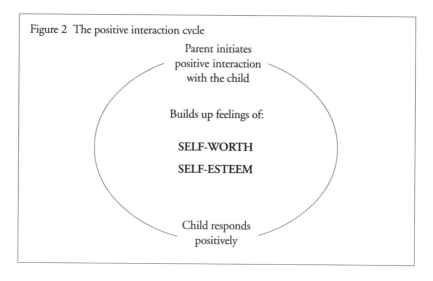

Figure 2 The positive interaction cycle

Parent initiates
positive interaction
with the child

Builds up feelings of:

SELF-WORTH

SELF-ESTEEM

Child responds
positively

In person-centred terms, the infant's and growing child's 'outer reality' (the physical and emotional environment in which they live) and 'inner reality' (the visceral experience and the emotional sense they make of that experience) will be shaped by the quality of 'parenting' responses they receive. For an infant who does not have a response to his call for comfort, for emotional interaction, and does not have his needs met, or receives an inconsistent response, over time, the impact will lead to the acquisition of conditions of worth which result in the child feeling negative about herself or not valued. As *'the organism behaves as an organised whole, responding to its own moving perceptual field'* (Barrett-Lennard, 1998: 75, based on Rogers 1951: 483–7, Propositions I–III) the dynamic interaction between infant/parent gives the infant repeated opportunities, through organismic experiencing, to consider, reconsider and to re-evaluate their conditions of worth. The concept of the 'self' changes, based on and reinforced by these interactions. An attachment pattern develops, which may be secure or insecure.

WORKING HOLISTICALLY FOR THE ADOPTION PLACEMENT AND CONSIDERING SOME OF THE FACTORS RELEVANT TO SUCCESS

A child brings with her into her new adoptive family the impact of her previous attachment relationships. If she has had a number of different carers—birth parents, other birth relatives and any foster carers—she will carry with her the memory of all these previously acquired conditions of worth. She may or may not have a clear understanding of why she cannot live with her birth family and why she is moving to a new family. Alternatively she may have strong memories of her birth parents and may not have resolved issues of loss concerning her situation. It is vitally important for a child to have a grasp of her circumstances and ways of talking to her about adoption must be adapted in line with her development and capacity to understand her 'story'. It is my experience that to assist the child with this a 'Life Story Book' is essential. This will provide her with an accurate written and photographic account of the reasons why she was not able to remain in her birth family, as much information as is known about birth family members, the places she has lived and the significant people within those places, the reasons why and the processes by which important decisions were made, and the circumstances in which she moved to her adoptive family.

Careful planning for the child's future, accurate preparation of assessment reports on the child (i.e. really knowing the child's history, including development and attachment history as well as having a true picture of the child's needs) are vital for the success of a placement. If the child has not been accurately described adopters cannot make an informed choice about whether they want to commit to the placement. Their subsequent ability to love and to 'claim' the child may be affected by how she presents day to day in comparison with the verbal and written descriptions they received about her, as the latter will have shaped their hopes/expectations.

The adopters have huge influences from past experiences and events in their lives. As well as their own individual conditions of worth about themselves as individuals and their self-concept as adoptive parents, they will also have been affected by the adoption application and assessment process. The latter can often be lengthy and very stressful and may come after years of disappointment of trying to have a child through birth. During this time they may have felt themselves to be in a vulnerable and powerless state. Members of their wider families may have varied views on their decision to adopt. Adopters will have their own unique perspective about the child's birth family and on the relative contributions of nature and nurture in the way they will raise their child. Having been approved as adopters they may have to wait for an extended period before a child is placed with them.

Birth parents will also exert an influence on the placement. It may be overt if there is direct or indirect contact, or may have a psychological influence if the child is confused about aspects of her relationship with a birth parent. It may be necessary, in the interests of the child, to work with birth parents or other birth relatives who may be suffering trauma and grief over the loss of their child through the court system. I believe this is an enormous challenge for a person-centred practitioner to be able to validate the complex feelings of birth parents/relatives yet still encourage them to share information about their child's past, or to participate in ongoing indirect contact with the child, which can be of enormous benefit for the child's feeling of self-worth.

THE ACTUALISATION OF THE PLACEMENT

In order for an adoption placement to be successful there is a huge responsibility on the adoptive parents who need to provide their child with the core conditions: to love, understand, value and respect her, as well relating to her in a way which she feels to be genuine. Given the complexity of the influences detailed in the previous section this begs the question of who will offer the conditions to these new parents, who will have a complex array of feelings themselves, so that they can actualise in their status as adoptive parents.

I aim to show that it is possible to work effectively *for* a child in an adoption placement rather than directly *with* her. I see the person-centred perspective in this as follows: that I offer the core conditions to the adoptive parents in valuing their capacity to facilitate the child's process and I trust the tendency in all parties to actualise in such a way that will bring them together and enable strong family relationships to grow. I would not underestimate the complexities of taking such an approach. I believe that the possibility of successful outcome relies hugely on the contribution of the adopters and on a supportive 'therapeutic' relationship between adopters and the worker. Not all adopters would be able or willing to work in this way. Nor would all practitioners.

At the time of adoption placement, the task of primary importance for both child and adopters is the formation of mutually rewarding relationships: a secure attachment. Variables include the child's age, the child's first attachment experience (including relevant trauma/abuse), and the quality of the attachments with all carers in any subsequent moves the child may have had. Given the already confused state of attachment in cases where a child is struggling to attach to her new parent(s) and where the prospective adopter(s) may be similarly struggling, it is probably not appropriate to offer therapeutic help to the child outside of her family context. I have had many experiences of guiding/ supporting adopters in undertaking 'therapeutic work' with their child in such circumstances and will describe two to illustrate the point. These case studies illustrate the actualising tendency in two very young children and their innate ability to be their own expert about what they need. When the conditions were provided in which their needs could be met and new conditions of worth could grow, Becky and Danny both moved towards an internal locus of evaluation and a state of congruence between organismic self and self-concept. The studies also confirm to me the importance of approaching work in this way with a reinforcement to adoptive parents in the belief that the child has the capacity to be self-directing in terms of knowing what she needs in order to heal. My professional experience leads me to fully agree with Peter Schmid (2005) when he describes the client as 'an active self-healer'. I had a well-established relationship with both sets of adoptive parents, founded on working with them during the training, assessment, approval and matching processes, during which I believe they had built confidence in me as a competent professional and as a person. Details in the case studies have been anonymised to protect identity.

BECKY

Becky had her second birthday about a month before she moved to her new mum and dad. She had a troubled start to her life, a premature delivery to a birth mother who had a history of substance abuse and whose older children had spent time in local authority care. When she was only a few months old, professionals became aware that Becky had sustained a number of non-accidental injuries for which there was no explanation. The standard of her care was generally poor and she lived in frequent physical discomfort, accompanied by pain and fear. Her emotional needs were not met. Becky's self-concept would have been based on conditions of worth reinforced by negative messages to her. Becky was removed from her birth mother via a court order and placed in a foster home in which there were two older, fostered children. The behaviour of these children indicated their own emotional challenges. Becky was a very fretful baby who was said to 'scream for hours'. The foster mother (who called herself 'mum' to Becky) stated that the only way she could settle Becky was to allow her to lie on her chest for hours at a time. Settling Becky became a family priority, no doubt to the detriment of the needs of other family members. As the months passed the foster carer was not able to establish firm boundaries for Becky.[2] There was no doubt that an attachment developed but it was based on an overdependency with Becky receiving the conditions of worth: 'You are loveable when you need me. You will not be loveable if you try to move towards some level of independence.'

The prospective adopters were a childless couple. The usual two-week period to introduce Becky to her adopters started well, but soon moved into tensions as it became clear how difficult the foster mother was going to find letting Becky go. I observed that it was proving far too complex for Becky to understand the concepts of having a mum (her foster carer), a 'new' mum (her adoptive mum) and also a birth mum. Within a short time of the move to her new family Becky was displaying many behaviours for which her prospective adopters needed some guidance. She also had the usually expected difficulties in settling to sleep at night without one of her parents sitting with her and she needed an unusually high level of attention during the day. It was clear that she was confused, had low self-esteem and was not used to boundaries. Clearly it would be inappropriate to take Becky out of the family, her age being the main consideration and another being the need for her to establish a secure attachment to her adopters. I saw my role from a person-centred perspective as my supporting the adopters in providing Becky with the core conditions, to trust her tendency to actualise and to have a belief in her ability to be self-directing. Most of this work was done primarily through the adoptive

---

2. Boundaries here refer to a carer providing guidance and structure to a child in such a way that the child knows what is acceptable and what is non-acceptable behaviour.

mother who was at home full-time. The adoptive father was in full agreement with this approach. My support to the adoptive mother took the form of weekly or fortnightly visits, listening and commenting on the observations she had written about Becky's behaviour and her emotional state. I was able to help in the facilitation of the adoptive mother's process in her understanding of the relevant adoption issues, as they were affecting Becky.

Over the following months what emerged was a clear example of the power of the PCA: the adoptive mother demonstrated a remarkable capacity to provide for Becky the conditions necessary for the development of an adoption attachment as outlined in the fourth section of this chapter. Becky used a small doll, which she called 'the baby' to give expression to some of what she was experiencing. She also used a mirror and would stand in front of it, taking on an adult tone of voice and adult mannerisms to tell herself 'you are a very, very bad girl'. Becky craved incessant physical contact with her adoptive mother, wanting to lie close on her chest for long periods. Exhausting as this was for both adoptive parents they were resilient and resolute in helping Becky to develop new conditions of worth. I observed that by accepting and valuing Becky's process and by establishing firm boundaries, which provided safety, predictability and then trust, a secure attachment began to develop which allowed Becky to be able slowly to work through some of the introjected values from her past. She could begin to develop a new belief system based on new conditions of worth.

During the following six years I worked intermittently with the adopters on other issues with Becky, especially the recurring theme of her overfamiliarity with strangers. While some issues remain and may continue, although with lesser intensity, Becky is a well-adjusted child who is secure in her family. Taking her out of her new family to address her difficulties through therapy could have resulted in a delay in establishing a sense of security for her and in the provision of the conditions through which she could change her concept of self. This could have been detrimental to the stability of the placement as it may have invalidated the capacity of the adopters to offer their child what she needed.

DANNY

Danny was also two when he was placed with his adoptive family, a mum and dad with two birth children, aged four and six. Danny's birth mother was seventeen years old when he was born. She had a long history of substance abuse, and had a very poor relationship with her own mother who, in turn, had been raised with very negative parenting experiences. Danny's life with his birth mother was characterised by inconsistency—he did not have a secure attachment, therefore his organismic experiencing led to conditions of worth based on inconsistency and unpredictability. Danny never knew whether or not his mum would respond to his needs. At the age of twelve months Danny was removed from his birth mother via a court order and placed with a single, older foster carer. Danny was a strikingly attractive child, with dark curly hair, blue eyes and an olive complexion. Considered 'cute' by all friends and visitors to the foster home, Danny was an indulged child who was given a sense of being more important than others. He was overdependent on his foster mother, who called herself 'Nanny'. At the start of the period of introducing Danny to his new family it soon became clear that 'Nanny' was not going to easily let him go. Whenever he had spent time with his new adopters, Nanny would say to him, 'Did you miss me?' On the day of his move to his new family, when she said goodbye she clung on to him so closely that he became very distressed. Danny was a confused little boy.

During the first evening at his adoptive home, Danny sobbed inconsolably; such that the older children said to their mum and dad, 'We must take him back to Nanny'. The following day, in discussions with the adopters, I invited them to remember what it felt like when each of them had lost a close relative through death. This helped them to access some of the feelings of bereavement and loss that Danny was experiencing. As with Becky's case, it would have been inappropriate to take Danny away from his adopters in order to provide him with the help he needed. 'Therapeutic' intervention took the form of my working with the adopters to value Danny when he expressed his feelings and to stay with him on his journey of loss and confusion. Although initially reluctant to accept my suggestion that there should be controlled contact between Danny and 'Nanny', this contact happened several times. At first 'Nanny' visited Danny in his new home; subsequent visits happened on neutral ground outside of the family home. There were times when it was very difficult for the prospective adopters to watch Danny's distress at the confused messages he received from his former foster carer. Tempted though they were to stop contact altogether, they realised that Danny's behaviour showed that he continued to have a need for 'Nanny'.

As the months progressed, it was clear that Danny was establishing an attachment to his new family. His adoptive parents intuitively took a very different approach from his foster carer, valuing Danny for his intrinsic worth rather than for the way he had been viewed in former relationships for his 'cute' appeal. They established firm boundaries so that Danny knew what was expected in his new family. Gradually, Danny's self-concept changed and he became more congruent. Approximately nine months after placement, when the adoptive father was putting Danny to bed one night, Danny said to his dad, 'I don't need my Nanny any more'. By staying with Danny in his journey to establish new conditions of worth and by trusting his tendency to actualise, Danny's parents were able to help him to let go of a previous relationship for which he no longer had an emotional need.

This case also illustrates a wider person-centred approach to the actualising of the placement through a collaboration of effort between adopters and adoption worker, acknowledging the inappropriateness of undertaking individual work with the child in these circumstances.

SUMMARY

Thirty-four years in adoption work has taught me that the complexity of this area of work cannot be underestimated. It often brought me challenges when trying to work from a perspective underpinned by the PCA and I am not sure that these can always be resolved. I believe that, in following the legislative principle in the Adoption and Children Act 2002, *the welfare of the child is paramount*, there may be times when it is impossible to resolve the conflict between what may be needed for individual members of the adoption triangle to be able to actualise, because the child's needs *must* come first. For instance, in most cases it is inevitable that there will be loss for a birth parent who has either relinquished a child for adoption or has had a child removed from their care via the court system. Despite this I can see that there is a place for a person-centred approach in the area of facilitating a successful adoption placement and that, when it is not appropriate to undertake individual work with a child, it is possible to work *for* the child through the medium of her adoptive parents. As well as a brief reference to attachment theory I have shown that there is a person-centred perspective which can aid our understanding of some of the intricacies of adoption work. It seems that this way of being and working can retain humanity at the core of what we do, respecting and valuing each person who is involved.

REFERENCES

Adoption and Children Act (2002) Available from <www.opsi.gov.uk/acts/acts2002/20020038.htm>.

Ainsworth, MDS (1967) *Infancy in Uganda: Infant care and the growth of love.* Baltimore: The John Hopkins University Press.

Ainsworth, MDS et al. (1978) *Patterns of Attachment: A psychological study of the strange situation.* Hillsdale, NJ: Erlbaum.

Barrett-Lennard, GT (1998) *Carl Rogers' Helping System: Journey and substance.* London: Sage.

Bowlby, J (1970) *Child Care and the Growth of Love* (2nd edn). Harmondsworth: Pelican.

Children Act (1989) Available from <www.opsi.gov.uk/acts/acts1989/Ukpga_19890041_en_1.htm>.

Claussen, AH & Crittenden, PM (2000) Maternal sensitivity. In AH Claussen & PM Crittenden (Eds) *The Organisation of Attachment Relationships. Maturation, culture and context* (pp. 115–22). Cambridge: Cambridge University Press.

Crittenden, PM (2000) Introduction. In PM Crittenden & AH Claussen (Eds) *The Organisation of Attachment Relationships. Maturation, culture and context* (pp. 1–10). Cambridge: Cambridge University Press.

Embleton Tudor, L, Keemar, K, Tudor, K, Valentine, J & Worrall, M (2004) *The Person-Centred Approach: A contemporary introduction.* Basingstoke: Palgrave Macmillan.

Fahlberg, VI (1991) *A Child's Journey through Placement.* London: BAAF.

Karen, R (1994) *Becoming Attached.* Oxford: Oxford University Press.

National Standards in Adoption (2003) Available from <www.dh.gov.uk/en/Publicationsandstatistics/Publications/PublicationsPolicyAndGuidance/DH_4018543>.

Rogers, CR (1959) A theory of therapy, personality and interpersonal relationships, as developed in the client-centred framework. In S Koch (Ed) *Psychology: A study of a science. Vol 3: Formulations of the person and the social context* (pp. 184–256). New York: McGraw-Hill.

Rowe, J & Lambert, L (1973) *Children Who Wait*. London: BAAF.

Schmid, PF (2005) Facilitative responsiveness: Non-directiveness from anthropological, epistemological and ethical perspectives. In BE Levitt (Ed) *Embracing Non-directivity: Reassessing person-centered theory and practice in the 21st century* (pp. 75–95). Ross-on-Wye: PCCS Books.

CHAPTER 11

CHILD-CENTRED NEGOTIATION
CHILDREN PARTICIPATING IN COLLECTIVE
DECISION-MAKING

JULIE WEST

INTRODUCTION

It is difficult for some children to simply just grow up. It was for me. Actually, I don't remember much of my childhood. I do remember I found adolescence something to endure. At school academic work was a struggle and I had very low self-esteem. My parents did the very best they could given their upbringings, knowledge and experiences, but still I found I had to find my own way to deal with the troubles and upsets of my life. I write of this because I believe it plays a major role in my attitude to children and young people. Don't get me wrong, there were no major incidents in my childhood, but I can empathise with the insecurities and difficulties that come with just being a child. I also recognise that children are capable of far more than many people give them credit for. Having access to even one supportive, attentive and respectful adult, children can flourish and shine even in otherwise stark surroundings. They, like me, can grow beyond the limits of their immediate environments and positively contribute to their communities and society as a whole.

I've always worked with children, concerned primarily with play and supporting adults to be respectful, resourceful contributors in children's lives. I have worked in the private, voluntary and public sectors, being employed and freelancing in a number of development and therapeutic roles. I have taken a year out and am approaching more freelance work in the areas of play therapy, training and children's consultation. The majority of examples discussed in this chapter on child-centred negotiation outside the therapy room come from my employment as a children's empowerment worker, involving five- to thirteen-year-olds in decision-making processes that concerned them, ensuring that when 'those in power' made decisions those decisions were influenced by children's views, ideas and experiences.

I am genuine and passionate about my work with children. Throughout my career I experienced that play and my interactions as a playworker were beneficial to all children; these experiences were complemented by a series of academic courses. Without any real understanding of the different theoretical approaches I attended psychodynamic play therapy training. I gained a great deal from the practical teachings, but struggled a huge amount with the psychodynamic approach. I rejected the idea of interpreting what children were doing and putting my own meaning on it and finally settled with accepting that an interpretation was a best guess, given all of the information presented. As part of this course I had to attend personal therapy, it was here and through subsequent person-centred training that I recognised that my approach to living and working is person-centred. By this I mean that on the whole I try to be non-judgemental; I accept people as they are in the here and now and I am congruent, ultimately with myself and as appropriate with others. I wholeheartedly accept that each individual, child or adult has the answer to their own questions, if we are given the core conditions in which to explore ourselves, to nourish, love and accept ourselves, warts and all. All of the knowledge, experience and belief that derive from this person-centredness are the foundation and base of the work I describe in this chapter.

WHAT IS CHILD-CENTRED NEGOTIATION?

There is no denying it: by the very virtue of our size, our roles, our public authority, our finances and our political voice, we adults have enormous power over children and young people. So then if we have this power, why do we need to negotiate with them at all? Certainly it would be easier and quicker to just tell them what to do. In answer to this question, I used to write to officials in a wide range of organisations giving them the hard sell, the 'carrot' and the 'stick' about why they 'should' involve children and young people in collective decision-making processes. The simple answer is: it's the right thing to do. It is the moral, logical and empowering thing to do. It enables children and young people, who are crucial members of any community, to play an active role in their community, to learn new skills and gain new experiences. Including children in negotiating decisions that affect them is a means to actively show them that they are important and valued, and so are their views, ideas and experiences. This sets an important precedent and one that is currently high on the Labour Government's agenda.

In 2003, the UK Labour Government brought in the Green Paper 'Every Child Matters'. This sets out five aims for each child in Britain, one of which focuses on 'Make a positive contribution'. The paper requires organisations involved with providing services to children—from hospitals and schools to police and voluntary groups—to work together in new ways to protect children and young people from harm and help them achieve what they want in life. The aim is that children and young people will have far more say about issues that affect them as individuals and collectively. This is in line with the United Nations Conventions on the Rights of the Child, particularly Article 12, which states that all children have a right to be involved in decisions made about their lives.

For services providers, who increasingly 'have to' involve children in the planning, delivery and evaluation of services they use, there is a very practical dimension. Instead of adults having to second-guess what children think would make things better for them, we can ask them and find out their views. In my experience, many adults think children are both incapable of knowing what is best for themselves and their peers and unable to communicate that knowledge to decision-makers, rather believing that, if asked, every child would make unrealistic totally selfish suggestions without any realisation of the limitations of funding or the welfare of the whole community. In practice, as I have seen time and time again, when children are given an *empowering environment*, an environment which is creative and enticing for children and young people, where they are afforded *the time to explore* the practicalities and limitations of their ideas, the possibility for true negotiation can occur. At times compromise has been made and empathy has certainly occurred as different viewpoints are considered and explored. When these conditions are in place they have produced end results that children, young people and adults are happy with.

This chapter refers to the term 'child-centred negotiation' and not 'consultation' because, in my experience, many people have jumped on the 'consultation' bandwagon. I have seen and heard many more scenarios where service providers said they had consulted children and young people on decisions, where in fact they had simply presented a choice of their ideas to a conveniently gathered group of children and young people and asked for their preferences. This is consultation in its most basic form. Negotiating with children is not about listening to children and then just giving them what they want. It is also not about manipulating them into agreeing to what you want. It is not about taking children to a presentation to be the mouthpiece of adults' ideas, reworded so a child or young person could understand it. Child-centred negotiation in collective decision-making is about being honest and genuine; it's about empathising and respecting children's views. It's about helping them to find their voice, helping them to think about what they think and feel about issues that affect them. And it's also about saying what is possible and giving them a realistic framework within which they truly have some scope to negotiate on shared decisions and action. It is about believing in them and their ability to make reasoned decisions that enhance their lives and those around them. Empowering children and young people to be involved in and/or to question decisions made for or about them has to be done sensitively, as in my experience a large proportion of adults want juveniles to accept what they say and to do as they are told. Child-centred negotiation includes raising awareness of the risks involved in speaking up, in disagreeing or challenging decisions or actions. When I am honest with children and young people and help them to explore the possible consequences of voicing their opinions in different situations, I give up the power to them to determine their own actions, for them to be the decision-makers of their own actions. This is true empowerment and requires the transfer of my person-centred skills out of the therapy room and into any situation where I trust and believe in children and young people to be players in their own lives and not always the subordinates of controlling adults or passive or powerless in educational, cultural or social systems.

WHAT IS NEEDED TO BE AN EFFECTIVE CHILD-CENTRED NEGOTIATOR?

The quality which is the most important in order to be an effective child-centred negotiator is a fundamental belief that *children can negotiate*. Without this I don't think anyone can be an effective negotiator with children. This is because the truth will leak out and even in subtle ways children will be undermined; their views misinterpreted as you seek to have your belief realised. It takes longer to negotiate than it does to direct, enforce or persuade. So *time to work with children* to establish trusting and respectful relationships is also vital. As well as time to build trust, time is needed to work creatively with children to engage them in negotiation. You need *creativity* to provide opportunities for children to gain the skills, knowledge and understanding to make informed decisions. How often has someone asked you to fill in a questionnaire and how many times have you declined, yet if you had the time and the inclination how much more likely would you have been to participate if you had been invited to contribute using a medium that attracted and/or intrigued you? In situations where children have freedom to participate I have experienced that the amount of creativity in the approach has influenced children's participation take-up rates. Alongside creativity comes *knowledge of child development*, to pitch activities at approximately the right level so that children are interested and challenged without being under- or overstretched. You also need *flexibility* to adjust, adapt or scrap activities and/or plans that are not working for the children and young people.

All of the above has to be communicated to the children, so an ability to express your own and the group's intentions in a variety of ways in order that people at all levels will understand and appreciate the importance of the work children and young people are involved in is a valuable attribute to obtain. There have been numerous times where my patience and perseverance to stick with things have been tested as the negotiation process evolved. This has been more relevant to the work with the adults involved when they wanted to give up on the children when results were slow to appear. An ability to be congruent and to share one's own feelings will benefit the group and the negotiation process. An example of this is when I was really struggling with a group as we were trying to make a collective decision from their suggestions. I told the group I was struggling with how to do things so it was fair and so that everyone would agree with the decision and asked for ideas from children and workers about how to progress. I role-modelled 'it's OK not to have all the answers and to ask for help'. We agreed on items not to take forward and left a shortlist for children to go away and think about and decide on their reasons for choosing their preferred option.

Last, but by no means least, an understanding of what issues face the children in the group you are working with, whether that be poverty or privilege, will support you to be respectful and to empathise with where they might be coming from. Additionally, individual children will have their own personal circumstances and this will affect them and their contributions to the group. An ability to accept individual difference, and to support children to contribute this if they so wish, is a major part of being an effective person-centred practitioner and negotiator with children.

These tools and attributes also enable me to negotiate with other adults to bring them on board. There is huge potential to influence other professionals as I model an often alternative way of being with children. The positive effects and results of working in a person-centred way are proof to many colleagues that, when we as adults are trusting enough to let down our guard and open up to the children, then these tools enable us to 'hand over the reins' to the vulnerable and the insecure—and see success.

THE CHALLENGES OF NEGOTIATING WITH CHILDREN

It takes longer and can cost more to negotiate than it does to dictate. Working creatively is simply more demanding than asking a series of questions or completing a paper questionnaire. Working with a multi-agency group entails dealing with different and often conflicting agendas and perspectives on 'how' to work with children. A child-centred playwork approach is not mainstream and can be a challenge for many teachers, managers and politicians. But it can also be stimulating and refreshing.

In fact, on the whole the most difficult challenges I have encountered were with the adults involved. Either they resisted getting involved in the first place—they didn't believe that children and young people could play an active role in decision-making— or they resisted committing the time and putting children's voices high enough on their agenda. And if a teacher or worker has been made to bring a group of children to an event which involves a great deal of negotiation, his or her own attitude and style will come into play. This is where the skills, commitment and person-centredness of the facilitator come to the forefront. As these adults saw that the children could productively participate in decision-making processes and as service providers realised some of the benefits of negotiating with children and young people, most of the 'reluctant' or 'unbelieving' adults got over these hurdles and their participation in the whole process became easier. I found that forming multi-agency steering groups and creating our own aims and objectives together brought about a greater sense of ownership and commitment to the process of involving children and young people in joint decision-making processes, which went a long way to minimising these difficulties before they arose. They were used to refocus the group as and when needed.

BENEFITS OF CHILD-CENTRED NEGOTIATION
FOR SERVICES AND SOCIETY

When children and young people are involved in decision-making processes service providers do not have to second-guess what is best for children and they do not have to think of all the ideas to improve or develop services themselves. This can also make services sustainable as attendance can increase when children and young people's suggestions are implemented; when children see that their needs are being met. I have found that children and young people's behaviour is more co-operative and less disruptive when they are involved in decision-making because of a sense of ownership when activities and/or delivery style are reflective of their likes and dislikes.

As part of the government's 'Every Child Matters' Green Paper, service providers are required to involve children and young people in decisions that affect their lives, and this includes being consulted on the services they use. As part of the UK government inspection of services, via Ofsted, this key aim of 'making a positive contribution' is measured. Therefore, effectively involving children and young people in planning, monitoring, delivering and evaluating services will ensure higher Ofsted results. Achieving a good Ofsted inspection amongst other benefits has the potential to attract additional or extended funding and to attract more purchasers (in this case, children and their parents) to choose your service over others.

For society as a whole, when children and young people are included in decisions that affect their lives they become valued contributors to their communities. When children and young people are valued and engaged in the social and political agenda at an earlier stage they may be more likely to vote as soon as they come of age and continue to influence their local communities and potentially to influence decisions on a regional and national level.

If children and young people are engaged in the solution and are not just seen as 'the problem', whole communities are brought together rather than children and young people being excluded, which has happened for so long. This point is crucial. Through child-centred negotiation, lines of communication are opened up and this is critical for healthy communities. In the consultation, empowerment and negotiation work I have facilitated, the children have worked alongside adults to identify common problems and explore practical solutions. We invited relevant adults in to help and through a variety of sources took the children's issues to adult forums and, when appropriate, brought the groups together to address shared concerns. True and effective child-centred negotiation is two-way: by the adults letting down their guard, a wealth of different rules and agendas become available to them, bringing in much needed fresh ideas, perspectives and a mutual respect for each other's contribution. Also, when all parties really know each other, finding common goals are far easier and therefore efforts are concentrated and results are more likely to be achieved. When achievable goals are agreed and reached this provides stimulus for the negotiation process to continue.

CHILD-CENTRED NEGOTIATION IN PRACTICE

Here I give two descriptions of how I have given some of my adult power over to children and negotiated with them on issues where I wanted their contributions and *they wanted to participate.* I emphasise that last point because I think voluntary involvement is key. This principle is one I apply whether I am working with a child in play therapy or I'm facilitating at a children's forum. For me, this permissiveness is part of my person-centred approach.

99

CASE STUDY

I was approached to include children and young people in a piece of community consultation for a Neighbourhood Regeneration Strategy (NRS). The government had set out NRS themes for local community consultation. It was my job to think creatively about how to engage the children in the issues of employment, housing, education, health, crime, transport and leisure. Play is the child's natural medium for communication, so for each of the issues I thought of a play medium that might stimulate interest in the children and enable them to share their views in a way that was beyond simply asking them a handful of questions.

To begin with, I got together a group of seven- to ten-year-old children in the regeneration area and told them that adults were going to make some decisions about how to improve their estate and they wanted to know what ideas the children had. The children were told why their views were being sought and what was likely to happen to their responses. They were all given the choice to participate or not. I gave some explanations about what was being proposed to them, and on coloured cards with pictures and some simple wording I presented the issues and the play ideas to the group. Those who chose to take part in the consultation then decided which of the issues they wanted to address and in what order. Their rationale was recorded on flip-chart paper and they identified a simple ranking system to put the issues in order of importance to themselves. After all of this discussion the children were invited to put forward any issues they were concerned about that were not already covered. These were added to the list and/or incorporated into the issues as appropriate and agreed by everyone.

The initial order of priority was set so we knew what issue we would explore on my next visit. Then it was highlighted that there would be opportunities to review what we thought and for the children to have time to think and reflect upon what they had said and to change their minds if necessary. We would also carry out further negotiation about the order of issues and play mediums to be used as other children joined and/or left the consultation group. I told the children that I would keep a record of what they said to me; what they choose to share of their experiences of living, going to school and playing on their estate and surrounding area. As a person-centred facilitator, once the group decided on that session's theme, they were free to bring to the group whatever was relevant to them; I listened, reflected back and sought clarification to ensure that I had understood what they were sharing, thus reducing my own interpretations. For their record, each child made a passport and they could collect stamps at each session representing their contributions. I have to admit that with the passports I also had the explicit aim of trying to engage them for the series of consultations and for them not just to participate in the odd one, although beyond the accumulation of stamps there were no additional incentives however many sessions children took part in.

Throughout the project, I engaged the children in different ways to explore these apparent adult themes. For example, on the issue of employment, the introductory card I made asked: What sorts of jobs do people do around here? What job do you want to do when you are an adult? The play medium was either role-play and/or the creation of a job centre. The job centre had real posters and job advertisements, newspapers' job pages, job cards from private employment agencies with spaces for children or me (under their instruction) to complete the title, salary and skills needed. The children could also engage in role-play and puppetry with occupation puppets.

When I have had to consult children and young people about issues that have been set by adults, as opposed to them setting their own agenda, I often experienced real internal and external tensions. When I felt confined by my consultation/empowerment role and when I felt that my person-centred approach could be compromised I had to centre myself and be congruent and empathic. I reviewed the situation and in that congruence and with empathy, I was able to make decisions about what was the most appropriate action to take. So with the role-play and puppetry I clearly manipulate a play situation to serve certain ends. I was there to find out the children's career aspirations and wider views about their experiences of growing up in the area. Although I set up a job centre and occupation puppets because they fitted my agenda, the play also fitted into Garvey's (1991: 4) widely accepted definition of play. The children appeared to enjoy the play; they had no goals in their play despite my having some; they chose to participate; they actively took on roles and spoke for the puppets; and they were purposeful in their activity. I negotiated with the children about what they wanted to do and they agreed or they complied; it's very difficult to ascertain for sure. But I am with them in the moment and I accept that if I ask them if they want to do this or that or something else, and they say that they want this, I respect that decision.

While the children played I listened to their spontaneous talk. Even though I had negotiated with them that in this session they agreed to work on the issue of jobs, at times it appeared that their play dictated something else. Whether I had the same interpretation of the issue as the children cannot be fully known, so trying to enforce my interpretation would not be person-centred and it would deny the children self-expression. Enforcing a strict parameter to the session content would have also denied me the opportunity to gain a reading on their understanding of the project of negotiation, to get in tune with them; not just have them dance to my tune. Instead, I offered the core conditions of empathy, respect and congruence. I empathised with the children's understanding that now it was their play time and they wanted to divert into their own agenda. I respected that they were entitled to this, especially since finding out their agenda was part of my agenda. Part of the 'respect' condition is respecting that they may have a different way of doing things. Given that I'd spent much time helping them to understand what the issues were that I wanted their views on and telling them how much I would value their contributions, it would have been inappropriate to stop their play or to redirect it to meet my own needs. Moreover, I assessed the situation and could see that the children were not compartmentalising the Neighbourhood Renewal Strategy issues. From all the years of personal counselling and training, I have learnt that processes don't happen in isolation. When a child makes the doctor puppet tell a firefighter, 'Wait or come back another day, I'm just too busy to see anyone else today', one should listen to what she says about her perspective or understanding of the health service (that often people have to wait a long time for the service they need and that health professionals are overworked). I made note of the children's comments and added them to my findings when we moved on to the consultation session which specifically explores health issues. I don't know if my interpretation was correct; I don't know if it was a psychodynamic interpretation or an assumption or what. What I know is that as a person-centred adult working as a Children's Empowerment Worker it was my job to ensure that children had a voice in decisions that affected them. That they were listened to and what was said was taken note of and brought to the attention of decision-makers. Wherever possible I worked creatively with children so that their own words, drawings and actions spoke for themselves. However, sometimes I had to present the children's views and experiences in ways that adults not literate in understanding children's perspectives could derive some useful meaning and thus children's views, ideas and experiences could influence their decision-making.

This whole piece of consultation and negotiation with children was beautiful to be part of. It was real and meaningful and enjoyable at the same time for us all; the children's frequent and responsive participation was an indication that they also gained from the experience. The children's contributions were collated and presented at a whole community consultation event. Everyone was able to see that there were many shared concerns and possible solutions. These were incorporated into the neighbourhood strategy for improvements to the area. A programme of feedback sessions was organised so that the children knew how their contributions were used. It was also explained why some of their ideas could not be acted on. When negotiating with children it is important not to leave this feedback time off the program; without it they are less likely to want to enter into further negotiation, as they would not be able to see any results and/or benefits of their involvement.

OUTLINE FOR A CHILD-CENTRED FORUM

A forum is a gathering of individuals who work together on shared aims and devise objectives about how they hope to achieve agreed goals. They often involve a range of people to support them to bring about positive changes. When I have set up and run Children's Forums I have used much child-centred negotiation to really get to the children's true thoughts. This is fundamental to the effective working of any Children's Forum that aims to give children and young people a real voice on issues that affect their lives. To ensure that the participants are representative of the target group, high importance is given to the selection process. Here are practical details about how I put child-centred negotiation into practice. Once the target group has been identified by the multi-agency working group, I make arrangements to visit all these children in their separate groups. Mostly this has happened in schools, but after-school childcare providers and specialist activity clubs (e.g. 'Young Carers' and support groups for children with disabilities) have also been points at which selection has occurred. I tell the children who I am, why I am there and what I would like to achieve with their help. I emphasise how important they are and that lots of adults value what they have to say about things that are important to them. To explain why I'd like their involvement, I set out the broad political background by asking them questions about who makes the important decisions in the country. I then bring this right down to their own lives by asking how big decisions are made locally.

In order to make the session more participatory and fun I introduce several games to help the children express their thoughts about common issues. For example, I ask them to imagine a line across the room: one end represents 'never', the middle represents 'sometimes' and the other end represents 'always'. I ask a series of questions and invite the children to move to the place on the line that represents their view. Example questions are 'Do you feel safe when you play outside?', 'My parents/carers listen to me' and 'Can children and young people make good decisions?' After each question I ask for contributions about why they had stood in that particular place. On the safety type questions where a child has said they always feel safe I ask 'What sorts of things make you feel safe?' When they share their thoughts I point out to the group that sometimes they might know something that others don't and that the forum is about sharing ideas, about listening and learning and working together. I make a point of emphasising the importance of their own opinion counting even if it is different from their friends. So after the children have got used to thinking for themselves I ask another question. This time I invite those who are in the same area of the line and therefore have similar viewpoints to work together and negotiate and decide on three responses to feed back to the whole group. This negotiation between the smaller groups has always been a difficult challenge for the children; trying to decide which of all of their responses will be chosen and who will speak for the group. With some help each group gives feedback and they experience first-hand and through my explanation 'that making a collective decisions takes more time and skills'.

This type of activity gives the children a little taster of what they might experience in a forum. It is then expanded upon using more discussion about what skills or sort of person would be good at a forum. This is followed by another interactive exercise. I explain that there are too many children in their big group and ask them to think of all the ways we could decide who should attend. They are given some time to think about it and to talk to their neighbours before they start calling out all the possible ways. These have included: names out of a hat; first three boys and girls out of a hat; members of the school/club council; voting for the child you think would be best; names out of a hat but not school/club council members as they go to everything. After all options are exhausted the hardest part of the child-centred negotiation is to get the group to decide on the method for choosing who attends the forum. It seems essential to me that in order for the children to have a sense of ownership of the forum they need to decide who should attend. This has played a large part in the wider involvement and success of the forum, where children have fed back information from the forum to the wider community through the use of class-/club-based activities. The wider consultation and contributions have engaged a much broader group of views, ideas and experiences, which has made the forum much more representative and in turn a stronger force for change and influence, especially amongst opponents who do not acknowledge that children can make valuable contributions to their communities.

The children who attend the forums and those that link into them via feedback sessions and wider consultation exercises all experience being involved in child-centred negotiation. All participation is voluntary so they not only learn that they can be valued contributors to their community, but also gain the autonomy that comes with realizing the power of their developing social and communication skills. The gains of child-centred negotiation are thus long term; they go well beyond the immediate goals of the forum.

CONCLUSION

When I work with the children and young people I find that offering person-centred principles gives me the freedom to be flexible and to be honest about the difficulty of the tasks. Carl Rogers talks about the attitude and orientation of the counsellor saying,

> It is common to find client-centered therapy spoken of as simply a method or technique to be used by the counsellor ... It may more accurately be said that the counsellor who is effective in client-centered therapy holds a coherent and developing set of attitudes deeply imbedded in his personal organisation, a system of attitudes which is implemented by techniques and methods consistent with it. (Rogers, 1951: 19)

I have provided examples of how I put my person-centredness into practice in an environment other than that of the therapy room. Once you possess this way of being and these skills you take them with you to every interaction. Being congruent, one doesn't always have to be like the off-duty police officer responding to incidents as if s/he were at work. As human beings we are fallible. With my work with children and young people if this fallibility and vulnerability is present in our encounters I name it and accept responsibility for this part. This can begin a new round of negotiation, with children and young people hopefully knowing that they are accepted exactly as they are, as I am by them, fallible and good enough.

REFERENCES

Every Child Matters (2003) <www.everychildmatters.gov.uk/publications>.

Garvey C (1991) *Play* (2nd edn). London: Fontana.

Rogers, CR (1951) *Client-Centered Therapy.* London: Constable.

United Nations Conventions on the Rights of the Child (1989) available from the Office of the High Commission for Human Rights, <www.unhchr.ch/html/menu3/b/k2crc.htm>.

CHAPTER 12

RENT BOYS

ASHLEY FLETCHER

When I was 14, as a young gay man hiding my sexuality from my family and a hostile world, I was isolated and alone. I had no advice, information, support or relationships that enriched me. I was in the closet. Once I went to a public toilet about which I had heard rumours that men met for sex. I hoped to meet people like me. I did and I had sex and to my surprise, at the end, the man I had sex with gave me five pounds.

Thirty years later, as an out gay man, blessed with all the things absent in my teenage years, I met a man in his thirties in a train station who had made his interest clear. I went with him, and we had sex. Afterwards, to my surprise, he demanded money, declaring himself to be 'working'—a euphemism for selling sex. The antinomian world of marginalised sexuality can appear, at times, seamless.

I have been working as a person-centred therapist for the last four years for a leading HIV charity in the North West of England. For the last 20 years, HIV and sexual health have been the focus of my work with clients both in the statutory and the voluntary sector. As a young gay man beginning a career in the 1980s, the era of AIDS, it seemed the logical area of work for one driven by a high sense of community responsibility. It has felt like a fairly consistent path from there to here. It felt like a logical extension of earlier career decisions to train as a person-centred counsellor so that I could work at a more creative depth with my clients. In fact, the connection between my understanding of the person-centred approach and theory and the intuitive way I have always worked becomes more and more apparent to me, even though throughout most of my career I have been unaware of the theory or the words associated with it.

In August this year, I was admitted as an emergency to the local hospital with a suspected heart attack—mercifully, it turned out to be much less serious, but, for a while, I was incapacitated, vulnerable and feared the worst. Whilst prostrate on the bed, wired up and with an oxygen mask covering my face thinking of little other than my own crisis, I was taken aback when the male nurse taking care of me suddenly said, 'I know you …'. 'Do you?' I feebly replied, unable to recall any context in which this could have been the case. 'Yes,' he said with a real look of fondness in his eye, 'you used to work at the Health Shop in Nottingham didn't you?'

I did. Fifteen years before, I worked on an innovative project trying to make contact with, gain the trust of, and support a range of then 'marginalised' communities. My nurse was a gay man who apparently had come to see me while coming to terms with his sexuality at the age of 16: 'I used to come and see you when I was "coming out"; it made the world of difference to me, and I'm doing the things that I do now largely thanks to the support I got from you.' I was gobsmacked, not just that I was recognised after such a long time, but that I really could have made such an impact on someone. But I was additionally very grateful, and had an immense sense of pride. It is rare that we are privileged enough to gain a glimpse of, or have reflected to us, the significance of our role, on any level, in the lives of those around us.

The experience took me back and got me thinking. In many ways my values and approach feel as if they have stayed on an even keel, but clearly I have evolved since then, at least as much as the degree to which times have changed.

The Health Shop was not a wholefood store or a vendor of animal-testing-free cosmetics. It was an NHS initiative, the product of a long and hard campaign by my then boss to get Public Health to respond appropriately to the needs of those traditionally shut out from mainstream services. The Health Shop was set up as a base from which to address the then unmet needs of a range of client groups considered 'hard to reach'. Its philosophy was essentially that no one is hard to reach if you actually reach out and provide a space where disenfranchised groups feel they can develop a sense of ownership.

Karen, my boss and the project's founder, had been amongst the pioneers of street-based services to women involved in the sex industry—walking the beats ... talking ... and distributing condoms; a radical thing to do at a time when possession of more than a few condoms was considered evidence of prostitution. Karen, as a result, had been detained on more than one occasion. The Health Authority had gone along with the idea behind the Health Shop as traditional methods of health promotion and service provision were clearly failing to engage with communities that were both being reviled and blamed for the spread of AIDS, and at the same time seen as key to successfully address the epidemic.

Experienced staff were recruited; their personal experiences counting as much as their professional experience of enabling communication and dialogue. I was employed as Gay Men's Outreach Worker, one of the first such appointments outside of London. While Section 28 of the 1986 Local Government Act institutionalised the refusal to 'reach out' by banning the public funding of the 'promotion' of homosexuality, significant resources were being made available for other work with the gay communities.

The health funding agenda was clear—to work with Men who have Sex with Men (MSM)—to get them to use condoms, practise safer sex, and stop the spread of the epidemic. In the agenda there was no expression of concern for any intrinsic value to these men's wider well-being or other priorities and interests. It was a public health agenda, not a 'gay' one, despite the apparent crossover of interests. The area remained a political minefield. Even our alleged allies in the Labour Party had shortly before laid the blame for their 1987 electoral defeat on the unpopularity on the doorstep of their support for (minimal) gay rights. The de rigeur term 'MSM' itself, while supposedly coined to encompass differing identities, was a de facto denial that such identities could be held with any real sense of pride, ownership or power.

As a gay man, a gay rights and an AIDS activist, I relished the opportunity to use my knowledge of my community, my experience, and my empathic sense of connection to work in a way I felt to be appropriate. Although sex between men was still illegal under the age of 21 my work that took me to youth groups and into the clubs and bars with workshops and information stalls, distributing condoms and encouraging gay men to come in to discuss and explore issues going on for them was not so controversial. More complex was the brief to work with young men involved in the sex industry: rent boys or male prostitutes. This is where the Health Shop came in.

Always at the back of our funders' minds was the potential for scandal, and in many ways, if the truth about the nuts and bolts of the work had been fully understood, then 'promoting deviant sex on the rates' may well have emerged as a tabloid headline. We see the potential for that all around us now, particularly with help and support for asylum seekers and immigrant communities. In those days homosexuality and corruption of youth were number one tabloid obsessions—these were the days of the first gay kiss on Eastenders—the controllers of our purse strings were fully aware of the risks they were taking. We were uncompromising—NHS leaflets with the words 'fuck' and 'cum' on them. We argued there were no half measures, we must talk in the language of our clients, or yield to the defeat we would deserve. To their credit, after raised eyebrows, we were trusted to do what we knew best. The needed cooperation of the Vice Squad was effectively obtained by not challenging their belief that our job was to get this 'filth' off their streets. With that objective in mind, they were happy for us to get on with it.

The energy expended on fighting our corner was far from draining. We knew we were cutting edge, but as gay men we were used to controversy and conflict; our activist instincts were a source of pride, not just for us, but for the communities that formed our constituency.

In such an environment then it is no surprise that the first barrier to overcome when initiating contact with the rent boys was their mistrust of any interest in them that was not with an eye to purchasing their services. They had good reason to be suspicious. All the young men we worked with were under nineteen, their encounter to date with most adults had resulted in pathologising and punishment. Most had been expelled from, or abused, in their families. Most had been arrested, or detained, and were in care or under supervision. Most had had some form of judgement made about their mental health, and their sexuality was seen as either symptomatic of these other problems (e.g. they were going through a phase, or were too young to know, or were reacting to abuse or neglect …), or the cause of them.

However these boys' sexuality had been defined, it had always been defined by others—by their families they were seen as deviant or uncontrollable, by the courts as irresponsible or incapable, by the police as criminal, and by health authorities and politicians generally, as vectors of infection.

No one would doubt the importance of protecting young people from the possibility of abuse, but what society has yet to own up to is that the most systematic abuse in the lives of young gay people (amongst others) is the institutionalised denial of their right to have a sexuality and to make decisions on the basis of their needs and desires. This remains the case, with the fantasy role of the anonymous abusing predatory paedophile dwarfing the vastly larger reality that most abuse takes place within the family. A family that, on the one hand, is revolted by and denies the reality of young people's sexuality, and yet on the other has a disturbing history of successfully exploiting it.

We appreciated from the start, that to inform and support begins not with 'interventions' or lecturing, but with presence and listening. If anything was glaringly missing from the lives of these young men it was anyone who actually listened to what was important to them. To get a sense of the utter lack of support these boys experienced, one need only consider some of the key differences between male and female street workers in Nottingham at that time, which we discovered early on. The rent boys lost their market quickly the older they got, whilst the women in many cases continued to work into their forties and beyond; the boys were more peer-led and influenced and lacked the 'management' that pimps provided (which, again paradoxically, provided a security role to many of the women); women worked distinct areas where their role was clear and widely understood, while the boys worked around 'public sex' environments—toilets, parks—where other men were also having sex for free whilst trying to conceal that activity from public awareness. Moreover, the women were often themselves powerful managers and in control of their own lives, whilst many of the boys were in some form of statutory care or supervision. All of this meant that generally the boys were younger and less experienced, more isolated and often with some external agency already trying to exercise some level of unwelcome control or supervision over their activities.

For all of these reasons, unknown people on their patch were viewed either as getting in the way, taking up valuable time, or judging and up to something. We spent much of our early sessions trying to fall in and out of conversations and quickly felt that leading with 'our' 'health' agenda would merely add to the weight of judgements people already felt subjected to. It didn't take long for people to take note of us and acknowledge our presence, most often initially by offering some sort of business, which allowed us to start chatting at least about what they did. Problems with their work and issues important to them didn't take long to surface. HIV was invariably low as an agenda item compared to queer bashing, being cold and concerns about police, parents, drugs, homelessness, their care home, hoping they meet the right punters, etc. The condom-loss-leader was always a welcome facility, as many punters insisted on it. Armed with these, we were at the very least 'minimally facilitative'!

It wasn't long before we managed to build enough of a relationship to get some of the boys to pop into our base at the Health Shop now and then for a break, a rest, or to watch some pornography. We had with great effort and controversy managed to get hold of very explicit hard-core German and American 'safer' sex films that proved very popular and roused more curiosity about what we were up to. The beginning of the epidemic had been marred by the frequent confiscation of even the most conservative safer sexual images. There was nothing modest in the images we were using, but to soften the tone would have been both patronising and uninteresting to these young men who, like it or not, were far from being naïve or inexperienced.

At no point did we advance any agendas not raised by the boys themselves. We knew that some of them were very young. Our key contacts, and key opinion formers in their networks, were around 15 or 16 years of age, but they would talk of younger boys who would be too shy to come and talk to us directly. Whatever we may have felt around their vulnerability and our possible desire to be rescuers, being genuinely non-judgemental and respectful and friendly in our approach enabled a dialogue that nobody else had succeeded in engaging them in.

Our work put us in a very ambiguous position. We were aware of the provisions of the Children Act that could have (and in some ways it could be argued should have) compelled us to bring in other people, inform of illegal activities and play a more policing/protective role. That would however, in my view, have been counter-productive, if not simply a betrayal of trust. One line of 'I'm just going to call your social worker', or 'You should report that man to the police' and we would have lost everybody. It would have put an end to contact and dialogue, abandoning the chance to build trusting relationships that at least enabled the prospect of help, support and safety. We were walking a tightrope by prioritising these young men, and the agendas they wanted us to work with.

The harsh reality was that this activity went on and would continue to go on whether we were there to observe it or not. The opportunity to be 'present' was a privilege available to no one else, and we were not going to squander it. What we were doing was understood by our peers, other professionals in our social care field, and by the purse holder, but maybe no one wanted to consider it in too much depth ... certainly not on a public level. Some boys we worked with had come to see us on a nudging prompt from a social worker or health worker who knew we would work at great depth and were better able to influence than they were. This was both liberating and very scary; we knew we were working beyond officially sanctioned boundaries, and knew we were right to do so in order to be effective, but at times there was the fear of being 'caught' and accused of being inappropriate. My own introjects had long distanced me from younger people and children in particular. Mindful of the social hysteria around young peoples' sexuality, and the popular, ignorant (or malicious) equation of homosexuality with paedophilia and abuse, there was always the danger that 'external' eyes would judge us according to these prejudices.

It was a genuine dialogue. What we heard allowed us to be more and more useful to the boys we met, who in turn confided and shared with us more and more. We produced small wallet-sized 'bust cards' that contained condoms and lube, safer sex advice and all the emergency and help numbers they would need; information on how to avoid, and how to handle arrest, including telephone numbers to sympathetic solicitors we had managed to persuade to come on board (these we made available to all outreach clients, not just the rent boys).

We would see some boys on a weekly basis, more we would see only from time to time, and others would always come in together. For us this was not a number-crunching exercise but an exercise at working in depth. As our clients felt valued, and trusted more and more in their own locus of evaluation, so trust, openness, sharing and relationship grew. We would try to enable networking that could provide safety through information/skill sharing, knowledge of punters and risk in different areas and the chance for emotional support. As time went on, the boys themselves would take out our materials and distribute them; not just to other rent boys but to their clients as well, sometimes getting them to come in if they felt that they were not sufficiently clued up to cope with sex or risk.

As I write a lot of this I realise it's actually the first time I have thought about it for a long time. And as I write, I can feel how open I could be to all sorts of judgements about my irresponsibility or negligence, of how I should have done this or done that. In retrospect, I see the fineness of the line more clearly than I did then. But my reality as a young gay man in the early eighties was that my very existence and right to claim my place in society was in itself a fine line, brinkmanship between hostility and tolerance— itself an immaculate form of oppression. The lives of the young people I worked with impacted on me greatly, in them I could not but help see my own struggles reflected, and maybe it was my personal conviction of my usefulness and knowledge, and my intense sense of pride in serving my community that helped obscure the fineness of that line. But, what I know for sure is, at that time at least, it worked. The trust we gained I believe helped the young men to grow in confidence and feelings of self-worth. Involving them in the design and planning of aspects of the work we were doing enhanced and enriched this process, making our work both more relevant and effective. One of the most popular things we did were some workshops—and a lot of one-to-one work— around 'tricks of the trade' that we had learned from Dutch colleagues, the working women, and the anecdotes of some of our clients themselves. They included how to pull a punter safely; being witnessed and letting the punter see that it had been; how to fake getting shagged; how to put a condom on someone without them knowing it (for reluctant punters); how to keep one's identity while working, and distancing oneself from smells and feelings about punters that might get in the way; and how to separate sex with clients from sex with friends or lovers.

If there is one remarkable observation I have made about young people it is that they are really quite unremarkable in comparison to adults around them. More remarkable is how adults often forget or are unable to empathise with the anguish and dilemmas of growing up, and deny competence and capacity in young people. Whatever struggles, dilemmas and problems many of our clients dealt with, they were always aware when they weren't being listened to, when a gesture of concern was not genuine, when they were not being taken seriously, respected, or when they were being patronised. They often spotted when they were being judged, or when their judgements on themselves were being exploited or used against them. Clearly, the young people we worked with were aware of the double standards, the prejudice and the injustice that surrounded them on both a petty and a profound level.

They were unremarkable in that these were capacities, intuitions, aspirations, values, hopes and fears that they shared with everyone else, not as a separate species of human by virtue of their youth. It is a key article of faith for me that people who value themselves, who feel they have worth and that they have a future are more likely to take care of themselves and those around them. Trust and time to open up gave the space that the boys needed to explore the impact of their lives and activities on themselves from their own viewpoint, in their own context and not based on the evaluation of others. This was the key enabler for some who wished to change their activities or perhaps deal with some of the dynamics that led them to where they were. Not wishy-washy tea and sympathy, but self-awareness and choices.

Success is always a difficult thing to really assess in outreach work. Is it numbers? How does one measure change? How long does change last? And, ultimately, did a change owe anything to outreach or was it always going to happen? The numbers we worked with were really quite small, maybe no more than about 15 or 16 young men over three years. This was still more than other similar projects and it exceeded our expectations. That we remained in contact on an ongoing basis over time with those we made contact with, and that these boys themselves had been brought to us by existing contacts and then introduced new people to us, both clients and other street workers, demonstrated to us that a real relationship of trust and respect had been established.

In hindsight I realise that key to what we achieved was the effective provision of the core conditions of person-centredness:

1. Our clients were in a state of incongruence, battling against external introjects around their activity, identity, their youth, and the vagaries of an adult-imposed, at times prurient, care system, struggling for identity and a functioning self-concept against a deluge of imposed conditions of worth. Despite this, there was psychological contact borne out of a tremendous desire to be heard and understood.

2. We were in a state of congruence, aware and conscious of our role and purpose, centred in ourselves and capable of responding to the impact and resonance the work had on us.

3. We were always respectful, believing and accepting.

4. We worked empathically to see the world of our clients through their eyes and always attempting to respond appropriately to their expressed need.

5. We were honest with them, congruently feeding back what we thought and felt, genuine about who we were and our identities, and clear about what we could and could not be or do.

6. The reality of our relationships meant that these core conditions, which I believe were present, were experienced as being present by our clients.

It is with genuine conviction that I believe at our worst, we were minimally facilitative in our role with them, providing a real environment enabling growth, process and change.

The project's benefits met our wider objectives too. We were for the most part able to provide health screening and safe sex support and advice to our regulars, and through these contacts were also able to do such work with some of the most vulnerable people on the rent scene, including an 11-year-old boy in care whose activities were unknown to his carers.

At the time, we knew we were working in a new field and relying more on gut instinct and intuition to augment and make available the other knowledge and skills that we possessed. At that time I had heard of the person-centred approach, but had no understanding of it in any depth. Though we used counselling skills in the work that we did, we were not counsellors in a therapeutic sense. With the hindsight and knowledge gained on my path to becoming a person-centred counsellor, I realise now that many of the ways we worked were fully consistent with my current understanding of person-centred theory.

I see that my 'person-centredness' is not an external add-on to my skills base, or the learning of a previously 'alien' doctrinal specialism, but rather a development and enhancement of my 'self': a honing of my way of viewing and relating to the world around me and to others. Our starting point was one of unconditional positive regard. Respect for the boys and what they brought to us. Belief that what they told us, however contradictory the detail might at times be, was what they needed to bring to us in that moment. We discovered quickly that they were not 'hard to reach', it was that no one had simply tried to reach out to them in a manner by which they wanted to be reached. This had always been our instinct and we felt our success bore this out. The boys' desire to communicate was strong and the quality of 'psychological contact' correspondingly high.

Their differing identities were not a source of confusion. It didn't matter to us the labels or descriptions they adopted. Some may have called themselves rent boys, prostitutes, gay, bisexual, cottagers, paid, unpaid; it only mattered that on encountering us they were believed and not judged. To an extent, the empathic nature of our relationships reflected our own experience of growing up in the 'closet', and trying to be our best in the face of the hostility and rejection that homophobia inflicts on young gay or questioning minds. What gay men have in common is not just same-sex attraction, a superficial common denominator, but the scarring of exclusion and heterosexism.

I have always seen gay men holding three key things in common. I offer a crude outline here.

1. The realisation that, at some point, our adolescence had been stolen from us. No encouragement personally or culturally had been given to explore the unfolding flower of sexual development or relationships, in fact, the opposite.

2. The ever-increasing awareness of the conditionality of the love and care offered to us and the punitive consequences of failing to meet those conditions. Our families were never really a safe place to be.

3. The acceptance that ultimately to triumph in adversity and emerge with an identity intact—to 'come out'—is finally to take the risk of rejection, violence and abandonment in the face of society's barely concealed hatred of us.

Despite much progress in recent times, this remains the common experience and shared journey—though engaged in alone.

Our ability to help and facilitate the 'rent' boys' exploration of this personal journey took us to real relational depth and was, in my experience of the work, a powerful facilitator of growth and development. Our being able to reflect congruently, and appropriately, the personal impact and resonance of the experience and lives they shared was a powerful aid to our communication.

Though I would not have used these words at the time (or even understood them had they been used to me), the personal process of the boys' locus of evaluation shifting from the myriad tyrannies of externally imposed conditions of worth, whether benignly or naïvely applied, or punitively explicit, was the key and maturing factor or outcome of our work and relationships.

CHAPTER 13

WORKING WITH LESBIAN, GAY AND BISEXUAL YOUNG PEOPLE

LISA ANTHONY

INTRODUCTION

I am thirty-eight years old, I work as a person-centred counsellor with lesbian, gay and bisexual (LGB) young people, I am a mother, a partner and I am a lesbian. In this chapter I explore some of the issues specific to my work with young people who are LGB, or who are questioning or exploring their sexuality. My aim in doing this is to raise the profile of some of the issues, which I believe are essential for every counsellor to consider in working to ensure that LGB clients are not discriminated against when accessing counselling services.

I have found it difficult to write this chapter; there are so many things I want to say. I hope it is useful and personally meaningful. I have tried to share something of the joy, inspiration and challenge I experience in my work and to communicate something of the beauty and strength I see in the young people I work with. I hope that what I have written will contribute to the changing of attitudes and prejudices that LGB people of all ages experience every day.

The young people I work with are important to me. Members of a minority community, they experience homophobia often and everywhere and as such they are vulnerable. Because they are lesbian, gay or bisexual, the young people I work with sometimes get bullied, harassed, judged, laughed at, rejected, or attacked. Because these things happen, the young people I work with may feel lonely, different, isolated, scared, 'abnormal', worried, anxious, depressed, lacking in confidence. Because they are people, the young people I work with may struggle with issues of identity, relationships, family, self-worth, intimacy, loving and being loved.

Hearing over and over again the struggles encountered by these LGB young people makes me angry. Hearing how young people find their way through, each in their own unique way, inspires me. The privilege of being allowed in to someone's inner experience of their world, their joy and their pain, their successes and failures, their growing and their stuck places, their hope and despair, is a gift that touches me in ways I don't have words for.

STANDING FIRM IN THE PERSON-CENTRED APPROACH

I have been working as a person-centred counsellor for many years now, having discovered in the person-centred approach a theory that explained my intuitive understanding and experience of myself and people around me. I have a strong connection with nature, with the continuous cycle of seasons, of the growth that encompasses death, loss and letting go. On discovering the work of Carl Rogers I was struck by the concept of the actualising tendency: 'the tendency of the organism towards maturation, as maturation is defined for each species … It moves in the direction of greater independence or self-responsibility (1951: 488).

This defines my own experience of myself and of seeing people striving towards growth and development. The more I look for it the more I find it, this striving towards wholeness and full potential that makes each of us both unique and intimately connected with all other life. I *feel* it to be true and the empirical evidence I collect, in my work, my personal relationships and my connection with the natural world confirms this for me time and again.

Knowing and trusting this actualising tendency grounds my work and I find Rogers' six conditions to be both necessary and sufficient. I find that when I am congruently able to be deeply empathic and actively valuing of another person, when I am able to communicate these feelings to the other and when the other is willing to be in a relationship with me, then there is the freedom and possibility for growth and change to occur (for both of us). When I have felt stuck in my work with a client, and found myself wanting to be able to 'do' something or help in some way, I have always, on reflection, found that one of these conditions is missing or impaired at that time. I do not claim that the person-centred approach is *the* answer. It is a way I can be and in my experience it has been facilitative of growth and change in myself and in others.

BEING A LESBIAN COUNSELLOR TO LGB YOUNG PEOPLE

As a young person I was in heterosexual relationships and suppressed my sexuality fairly thoroughly, occasionally wondering if bisexual was a better description for me than heterosexual but unable to confirm this as I only had relationships with men. I 'fitted in' with the norm of heterosexuality and when I did struggle with feelings of belonging I didn't connect this with my sexuality. Coming out as lesbian, aged twenty-nine, I felt released and more wholly myself and I am still grieving the loss of my lesbian youth. Although I sometimes see clients who wish they were 'straight', wish they could 'fit in better' with their peers, I envy them their self-awareness and their discovery of themselves and their LGB community.

Finding myself has brought its challenges too. I walked straight into judgement and discrimination. I had never had to verbally disclose my sexual orientation and was shocked by how hard I found this. I am often asked if I am married, a question which assumes heterosexuality and draws attention to a form of acknowledgment which is unavailable to me. Suddenly I had to learn how to challenge such assumptions. Disclosure is not straightforward and all LGB people are faced with situations where we have to choose if, when and how we wish to disclose or be open about our sexuality. In our service for young LGB clients the issue is addressed in our leaflets and I make reference to sexual orientation openly at our initial meeting. For the young people who see me, knowing I am a lesbian helps them feel able to be open about their experiences. They often assume that I will identify with them and not be shocked or judgemental. When I then reveal in fact that I came out later in my life, it does not seem to matter. Indeed I find that although our experiences are different, candidly acknowledging this communicates something of my acceptance, willingness and ability to understand the client's experience.

My experience of working with young LGB clients in other settings has felt different. If a client is not aware of my sexuality there may be a period of checking me out and dropping hints around their sexuality to test my response. I do not come out as a matter of course in all of the settings where I work with clients but I listen carefully to the client's use of language in describing themselves and their relationships. I am careful that my language is inclusive and I am not afraid to ask directly if I sense that a client is being careful in their descriptions. For some young clients it is a relief to find that they can be open about their sexuality and to acknowledge this without making it an 'issue' is helpful. A recent article by Hodgson (2007) offers useful suggestions around use of language and highlights the importance of exploring these issues for all counsellors who may work with LGB people.

Often I hear LGB clients describing feelings of isolation and of being different and alone, even amongst family and friends:

> [It felt] like I woke up and all my people have moved away, and I don't know where they've gone.[1]

This loneliness I hear has a quality, a depth that I had not encountered in working with heterosexual clients, or perhaps not understood prior to coming out. Some young clients have no place in their life where they feel 'the same', fit in or share this fundamental part of themselves. So even if you have good family relationships, however much you love them, however great they are, they still seem so profoundly different from you. Every place you look there are images of heterosexual couples and relationships and any portrayal of LGB people is commented on as different, or feels token. For this young person then, meeting another LGB person, an adult who is openly and confidently LGB, can have huge significance. As a gay (my preferred term) adult in a young person's life I may be one of few adult role models they have.

---

1. The words in italics are taken (with permission) from client feedback. Much of this comes from one client, who agreed to give me feedback, both verbally and in writing, specifically for the purpose of this chapter. The client has read and agreed to the use of the feedback as it appears here. I want to say thank you to the client here, for their participation in this process.

Adult role models are significant to young people and whilst there are ever more LGB adults in the media and LGB characters in film, television and books, it can be reassuring to know an LGB adult personally.

When I was younger I didn't know anyone else who was gay, I didn't know any gay adults.

As a counsellor I can feel scared about this. I don't want to be anybody's role model, I have enough trouble being me! Yet I cannot deny the importance for a young LGB client of having an LGB adult to talk to. I hold onto my trust in the person-centred approach when this happens, remembering that I don't need or want to be an expert of any kind, I don't have to know any answers, my wish is to be as closely with the client, in their frame of reference, as I can be and to maintain my trust in them and their actualising process. Having realistic expectations of myself frees me to be more fully with the client and allows me to be self-accepting, to know my own vulnerability and my own continuing journey as a gay woman.

I think it's good that Lisa's gay; I've seen other counsellors and felt like they just didn't get me in the way Lisa does. It's like I was a dalek seeking help from cybermen and it wasn't working but now I've found another dalek, well, she helps.

THE SAME WORLD BUT DIFFERENT

My work with young people who are LGB has led me to new places in exploring my understanding of what it means to be empathic. Empathy is a journey into the unique world of the other, finding a deep understanding of the simple and the subtle experience and feelings of this other person who is different from me and yet the same. I can only find my way to this understanding through a genuine curiosity and a willingness to see the world from a different perspective.

She helps out, saying 'so is this how you feel?' or 'do you mean this?' and most of the time she's spot on.

I don't get it right all of the time and I don't need to. My intention is to deepen my own understanding, to get closer to the client's experience and frame of reference and this can be helpful for the client in identifying and understanding themselves and their feelings more clearly.

With LGB young people empathy raises some particular challenges for me. It is not as simple a process as it sounds above. Can I hold separate my own experiences, especially when they are similar to those of the client, and hear the uniqueness of the other? Can I hear similar experiences from a number of clients and hold each one individually? I need to be able to do both of these things and I need to be able to communicate this understanding to the client. For the heterosexual counsellor the reverse may be the case. The challenge in being empathic may arise from lacking similar experiences or contact with a culture and community which may be different from their own.

Another challenge to my ability to be empathic comes from sometimes working with clients who know other clients or who talk about the same people or events. The LGB community I work in is relatively small, and this overlap of LGB clients happens with more frequency than with other clients that I see. When it does occur I have to make full use of my ability to hold clear boundaries and to enter as fully as possible into each client's unique experience, unclouded by what I have heard elsewhere. Sometimes it may be appropriate for a client to work with a different counsellor, sometimes this is not possible and I therefore make careful use of supervision to check out and monitor my boundaries. As well as being a challenge this can also be a helpful experience. There may be overlapping and conflicting boundaries in clients' social and relationship networks; this is a fact of life in a small community and may be significant in the issues a client is working on. Working hard to develop my capacity to hold and maintain complex boundaries has helped me understand how problematic and challenging boundary management can be for the client.

Heterosexism, the constant and implicit promotion of heterosexuality as normal, preferable and better than homosexuality, is rife in all of our everyday life experience. What seems important is that I understand the prevalence and subtlety of heterosexism and homophobia and that I am open to recognising and understanding the unique ways in which it may affect each client. The subtle yet pervasive messages that heterosexuality is compulsory and the only acceptable option for relationships were messages I internalised deeply. It was only after years of personal development work that I was able to explore my sexuality to any degree and my coming out was sudden, when I fell in love with my partner. My knowledge and experience of LGB culture has grown significantly since I have come out; my own experiences of the homophobia of others has given me an insight and understanding that was very much intellectual and impersonal before. The more I talk with other LGB people, watch gay films, read gay literature, read the gay press, the more depth and breadth I gain in my understanding of homophobia and its impact and this helps me be more fully empathic with these experiences and feelings when a client brings them to counselling. I had done some of this work, to broaden my understanding, before coming out. I know now that what I thought was a broad understanding was actually very limited and superficial. I noticed and would challenge direct discrimination and homophobia, I used inclusive language most of the time but I was generally blind to the heterosexism that I now see all around me. Maybe some of this was a consequence of my own suppression of my sexuality but I also think it is hard to keep 'noticing the wallpaper' in a room you spend your whole life in.

INTERNALISED HOMOPHOBIA AND POSITIVE AFFIRMATION

She won't shout, judge or send me to my room.

Since coming out and having my own first-hand experiences of homophobia, I have developed my understanding of acceptance, realising how, in the past, I was sometimes passive in my acceptance of others. I had no difficulty with someone's sexuality being different from my own, but I lacked empathy and knowledge of the life experiences of LGB people and I had internalised homophobic attitudes, which I both felt and communicated. An example of this was my assumption that my coming out was a decision which precluded me from having more children. It was only over time that I became more aware of and considered the options I had around parenting and having more children with my partner. Feeling and communicating acceptance is a much more active process for me now. I continue to pay attention to my use of language, I watch for and challenge the homophobia I find in myself. To watch for and acknowledge our own internalised homophobia and heterosexism is essential to continuing development and to work with clients (Davies & Aykroyd, 2002). Developing my acceptance and valuing has also meant understanding and finding out more about the diversity of the LGB experience, lifestyle and identity, and being able to not just accept but celebrate what this brings into my life. I find inspiration in the opportunity to have deeply personal relationships with clients, who have often held onto and protected their identity in the face of discrimination and a lack of positive images and role models. It feels easy to actively accept and value these clients. If I hope that clients will be able to share the deepest parts of themselves with me it is imperative that I have visited these deep places in myself. It is by doing this that I can hope to be a worthy companion on the client's own journey of self-understanding and actualisation.

Self-acceptance, the necessity of being comfortable with my own sexuality, is of paramount importance. How many of us have ever had significant opportunities to explore and discover our own sense of our sexuality? It is an area much avoided. Although it's now more present in social and personal education in schools than it ever has been, heterosexuality is still promoted as the 'norm' and in most counsellor training the development of the self in relation to sexuality is rarely mentioned, or is at best token.[2] I don't think every LGB client needs an LGB counsellor—I do not presume to know what clients need—but I do believe strongly that whether sexuality is an issue or not, it is essential that the counsellor be comfortable and self-aware in relation to their own sexuality and actively accepting of difference in the client.

---

2. This gap in counselling training needs addressing and I recommend the work of Davies and Neal (see references) and the Pink Therapy website (www.pinktherapy.com) as good places to start.

ANGER AND OPENNESS

When with a client I sometimes experience strong feelings, from my own frame of reference, in response to the client. It may be appropriate for me to share these feelings or it may be better for me to hold these feelings and deal with them later. It probably wouldn't benefit the client if I launch into a tirade of anger about homophobia, yet it may be very important and helpful for me to express anger about such issues at times. My anger may get in the way of my empathy but it may also be experienced by the client as permission to feel their own anger and as a challenge to stop blaming themselves for what homophobia does to them. In each moment-by-moment encounter with a client I have to decide how to respond. I sometimes get it wrong and I trust each relationship to be stronger than one mistake.

My openness communicates something of my willingness to be a real person with a young LGB client, not an authority figure like many other adults. Being close to the feelings of the young client can also touch off in me the feeling of loss that I described earlier. I had internalised the norm of compulsory, assumed heterosexuality and I wish this had been different, although I see advantages that came from this too. My being visibly heterosexual brought approval, which helped me develop (conditional) confidence and self-esteem. By the time I came out, I was more solid in my self-acceptance and therefore less shaken by the negative responses of others than I may have been previously. I also wonder whether the people I knew felt less able to voice judgement or criticism to an adult than they might to a young person. I value my increasing congruence and self-knowing, even when there is a price to pay in relation to external validation.

FROM THE PERSONAL TO THE POLITICAL

I see my work as simultaneously personal and political. When I work with a client I want to be with them in a personal and intimate way. I hope that the work we do together will contribute in some way to the client's own growth and healing. For me this work also has a spiritual element, in the connection it creates between two people. I believe actualisation in one person is beneficial to the actualisation of humanity and so for me, individual counselling contributes to changing the world.

Homophobic bullying is an issue that affects many LGB and straight young people. Whether occasional or persistent, most LGB young people will have some direct experience of homophobic bullying. From the use of the term 'gay' to describe something as rubbish or pathetic to the verbal taunts and physical violence that many young LGB people experience. It is a form of abuse that is persistent, pervasive and profoundly damaging. It is also an issue that often goes unchallenged in the young person's world. Though some schools address homophobic bullying in their anti-bullying policy, there are many more schools that do not. Teachers often feel unable and unsure about how to challenge this kind of bullying, yet until this changes I will continue to see clients who have been traumatised by it, sometimes to the point of attempting suicide. My work with young LGB people—providing a space where to be LGB is understood and valued—is a political act, which communicates to clients and to the wider community that these forms of discrimination are unacceptable.

The other clients I see are those who are 'questioning', that is those who feel unsure about their sexual orientation and have confused or ambivalent feelings about it. With these clients I invariably meet someone who is struggling to find a clear sense of who they are and unable to find a label to 'fit'. It seems to me unsurprising and wholly appropriate that young people are wrestling with these issues, exploring their sense of identity, their place in a peer group and trying out different experiences of relationship. That this becomes problematic for some is, in my experience, always related to the conditions of worth internalised from the messages about who and how they should be. These young people don't need to have counselling to resolve their questions; they need the world to be a place where they can freely and with acceptance discover an identity for themselves. Often the young people I see feel attracted to people of both sexes, and might sit most comfortably with a bisexual identity. Young people who are bisexual can find that they are not accepted by those who identify as lesbian or gay. There can be intolerance of bisexuality. It may be seen as a 'cop-out' or easy option and judged as a refusal to accept and come out as lesbian or gay. More recently I hear young people talking about it being fashionable to be gay and sometimes feeling cynical or suspicious of those who are questioning, fearing that they are trying to 'jump on the gay bandwagon', in order to appear interesting. The conditionality of acceptance can come from all sides.

THE WHOLE PERSON

I have focused on how my work with LGB young people is different from or raises different issues from my work with other clients. This is only one part of my experience. Taking into account all of the issues I have written about above, I do not work with LGB clients any differently than I work with any other client. For me being a person-centred counsellor is something I either am or I am not. The core conditions are enough or they are not; if I do not trust and believe in the client's capacity for self-direction and actualisation then I am not a person-centred counsellor. It is how the core conditions exist and are communicated that varies in each relationship I have with a client. Each relationship is unique and co-created and for me this is the beauty of the person-centred approach. So I am the same and different in each counselling relationship.

LGB young people come to counselling for the same variety of reasons that any client comes for counselling. Being LGB, and the experiences this may bring, may not be an explicit feature of the work we do together. Being LGB is an integral part of identity, is unique in each experience and, as such, needs to be understood and accepted. It may have an impact on the issues the client brings to counselling, it may not. My job as a person-centred counsellor is to stay *with* the client, not to make connections for them.

Something I do know is, most of the time, when I come out after seeing Lisa, I feel more confident, bigger somehow, but lighter—if a small weight has been lifted.

CONCLUSION

I hope I have communicated something of my learning and understanding of some of the issues relevant to working with young lesbian, gay, bisexual and questioning clients. I believe that every client who walks through the door of a counselling room deserves to feel valued, that being lesbian, gay, or bisexual matters and deserves acknowledgment. Heterosexuality is affirmed all the time, every day. As counsellors we have an ethical responsibility to work in a non-discriminatory way as far as possible. This means taking time to examine and reflect on our counselling practice in supervision and elsewhere. Accepting that we all make assumptions and hold prejudices enables us to identify, own and challenge them. There is no 'right way' to develop equality in our practice; what matters is an attitude of curiosity and valuing and an intention to learn and celebrate more about the rich diversity available to us in all of our relationships. Books, newspapers, films and television can be ways of expanding our knowledge and experience of difference, and there are many training courses and workshops on offer, which address the issue of inclusive practice for LGB clients. For me, working in a person-centred way necessitates a genuine desire to deeply know and experience the client and their world. That is my baseline for working with any client. In learning of their humanity I acknowledge and develop my own.

REFERENCES

Bridget, J & Hodgson, A (2007) Closeted and vulnerable. *Counselling Children and Young People* December, 2–9.

Davies, D (1998) The six necessary and sufficient conditions applied to working with lesbian, gay and bisexual clients, *The Person-Centred Journal, 5* (2), 111–24.

Davies, D & Aykroyd, M (2002) Sexual orientation and psychological contact. In G Wyatt & P Sanders (Eds) (2002) *Rogers' Therapeutic Conditions: Evolution, theory and practice. Vol 4: Contact and Perception* (pp. 221–33). Ross-on-Wye: PCCS Books.

Davies, D & Neal, C (Eds) (1996) *Pink Therapy: Guide for counsellors working with lesbian, gay and bisexual clients.* Buckingham: Open University Press.

Davies, D & Neal, C (Eds) (2000) *Therapeutic Perspectives on Working with Lesbian, Gay and Bisexual Clients.* Buckingham: Open University Press.

Hodgson, A (2007) Lesbian, gay and bisexual young people: Counsellor notebook. *Counselling Children and Young People*, December, 10–12.

Rogers, CR (1951) *Client-Centered Therapy.* Boston: Houghton Mifflin.

CHAPTER 14

EXPLORING ISSUES OF BEREAVEMENT AND LOSS WITH CHILDREN AND YOUNG PEOPLE
A PERSON-CENTRED PERSPECTIVE

SEAMUS NASH

The aim of this chapter is to explore, from a person-centred perspective, working with children and young people who are experiencing bereavement issues. This chapter outlines how I practise as a person-centred psychotherapist in a hospice. In particular it is concerned with describing the provision of a 'listening and accepting' space for any child or young person to 'be' in.

WORK AT THE HOSPICE

I work at a hospice located in Yorkshire where I am part of a team comprised of four: two counsellors and two psychotherapists. My work is with children and young people aged between five and seventeen. I work individually, with small groups of children and with whole families. I also co-facilitate some group work with colleagues and volunteers. We work within the pre- and post-bereavement spheres with both adults and children.

At this point it may be helpful to the reader to clarify terms from my reading of the literature: *loss* is referred to as being deprived or ceasing to have something or someone to which one is attached. Loss can be physical, for example, the loss of eyesight, or relational, losing a relationship through divorce. *Symbolic loss* is often more intangible, usually involving the loss of a spiritual or even psychological attachment, for example, losing one's hopes or dreams. *Bereavement* is the state of having suffered a significant loss and *grief* is the subjective reaction to loss. *Mourning* may be defined as the conscious and unconscious intrapsychic processes a person utilises to attempt to cope with grief and loss. *Complex, complicated or pathological grief* is the serious reaction to loss that usually leads to 'severe mental health problems', and finally *anticipatory grief* is usually experienced by the client, family and friends during life-threatening or life-limiting illness.

The team was established primarily in response to a growing need to assist, emotionally and psychologically, families and friends of patients using hospice services. Rather than use one theory of bereavement, for example Kübler-Ross (1970) or Worden (1983), we first and foremost focus on the 'patient' or 'client' as a *person*. We offer ourselves in a warm, open and non-controlling way. For the team, counselling and therapy are just one response to the client. We also attempt to offer a range of responses from information sharing, facilitating family conferences, education and bereavement support groups. Our philosophy is one of non-medicalising and non-pathologising of clients and their grieving processes.

THE THERAPIST'S OWN EXPERIENCE AND INTEGRATION ON BEREAVEMENT AND LOSS

I can only take the client as far as I have travelled myself. If I am unwilling to look at areas in my life and relationships that need attending to and nurturing, how can I assist another along their journey? What I do not deal with in my life will remain there until I do. I have been no stranger to personal therapy and have experienced many losses and bereavements in my life. These experiences have had a profound effect upon me and in turn upon those close to me because of my handling of them. I am an identical twin and my brother died shortly after his birth. Through intense personal therapy *and* personal development I am in a position to say that I feel I have some degree of understanding of, and have worked through, the impact of my own losses and I now know I have grieved. It has become apparent in my practice and indeed in dialogues with my colleagues that if we, as counsellors, psychotherapists or helpers, do not have insight and to some degree, integration or 'ontological friendliness' with our losses and bereavements, we will be therapeutically less potent in our facilitation of others to grieve and heal. It sounds simple, yet it is rarely simple to work on what is bothering or hurting me. In my experience all healing costs.

It is important to have at least an opinion, or theory, on the nature of bereavement and loss. I feel that this aids and informs practice. It is the dictum attributed to Carl Rogers: to learn all you can about counselling and psychotherapy but forget it when you enter the counselling room. I take this to mean that it is right and necessary to learn as much as I can, but it is the relating and the relationship with the client that is central. It is the encounter with the client as a human that matters and indeed heals. Yes, it is necessary to know what Freud (1917/2005) and Bowlby (1980) wrote. It is entirely relevant to study the research by Strobe and Schut (1999) and to know what exactly Parkes' (1972) and Kübler-Ross's (1970) positions are. However, as a practitioner, it is vital that I know, for my practice as much as for myself, my own understandings and internalisations regarding death, dying, bereavement, grieving and loss. For it is in my understanding that I construct and influence my practice. This chapter explores this idiosyncratic mixture of my experience informed by my learning and vice versa.

RESPONDING TO CHILDREN AND YOUNG PEOPLE

I believe that how we deal with our losses and how we grieve is modelled closely on how we have witnessed significant others in our own lives deal with their losses. In my work I have often been involved with children and young people who are struggling to come to terms with their losses and the extremely powerful emotions that are engendered by them. The young people report they feel blocked by parents' and guardians' inability to assist them to grieve. The picture is one of the parents' and guardians' avoidance of their own responses to these losses. The following are comments by young people who sadly confided:

> *I look after my brother, get him to school and keep him out of trouble. I cook, clean, do all the housework and see to the stables. Dad just cries and gets drunk. Nothing is changing for me.*

> *I'm coming here for my Mum.*

> *I've been told to come here by my teacher/social worker/youth worker/psychologist.*

It is my perception, based on my clinical experience, that attitudes to bereavement and grieving are changing and it appears to be getting more complicated for children and young people. There seems to be a reduction in rituals which the young can use for their benefit, no rite of passage or 'marking' ceremonies. Certainly in my clinical experience young people see their peers as able to distract them or 'to snap me out of it', as one young woman described. An illustration of this is Pauline,[1] a sixteen-year-old, still at school, who came to see me regarding the suicide of her boyfriend a few weeks previously. Pauline was six months pregnant. She poured out the most soul-wrenching pain: missing her boyfriend, the fact that their child would never know him, the shock and suddenness of his death and going through the many unanswered questions and searching that suicide often brings. Pauline's friends 'refused to talk' about the tragedy, often cutting her off in mid-sentence or blatantly changing the topic when it came up. Pauline felt 'she was mad' and her mother was worried that she was withdrawing further into herself and felt her daughter 'to be slipping away' from her. Through her therapy Pauline came to believe she was not mad, that her friends were trying to protect her and that 'maybe I'll just have to live with this pain, I don't think it'll ever go away'.

The fact that adults in the young people's lives seem ill-equipped to deal with their pain or appear unavailable to them is an observation based on my clinical casework. If I have an opinion or criticism, it is this: the professionals refer the adults to us, the adults drop their children off to us to 'fix' them. 'You are the experts, you get on with it, don't ask me to get involved!' was one such command. It is my experience that professionals such as social workers, educational psychologists, teachers, youth workers, school and community nurses and GPs often refer children and young people to our service for 'specialist bereavement counselling'. In dialoguing with them I have ascertained that the main referral reason is that they feel ill-equipped to deal with this 'type' of case and that referral to an agency who they see as a specialist in this area is usually most appropriate. There are few agencies available to support children and young people with these difficulties apart from the Children and Adolescent Mental Health Services (CAHMS) which are usually oversubscribed with long waiting lists.

---

1. All details of clients have been altered to ensure confidentiality.

THE IMPACT OF BEREAVEMENT AND LOSS ON CHILDREN AND YOUNG PEOPLE

Stokes (2004), whose work is published by the childhood bereavement charity 'Winston's Wish', promotes the following:

Realities for grieving children:
- All children and young people grieve.
- Grieving is a long-term process.
- Children and young people revisit their grief and frequently construct a changing relationship with the person who has died.
- Younger children will need help in retaining memories which facilitate a continuing bond with the deceased.
- Children express their grief differently than adults.
- There are clear developmental differences between children and young people in the understanding, experience and expression of grief.
- A child's grief process occurs within a family and community context and will be influenced by significant adults.

(based on Stokes, 2004: 18)

The team has witnessed children's and young people's grief manifest in the following dimensions:

- *Feelings:* sadness, anger, guilt, fear, self-reproach, anxiety.
- *Physical symptoms:* pains, aches, shortness of breath, lack of energy.
- *Existential:* meanings of life, purpose, point of living.
- *Spiritual:* meanings of pain and suffering, sense of meaning, hostility towards 'God'.
- *Cognitive:* constant thinking of the deceased, confusion, dissonance.
- *Behavioural:* sleeping problems, eating problems, crying, lack of social interaction, anti-social behaviours.
- *Relational and social dimension:* inability to create or sustain loving, meaningful relationships, problems at home, in the family or school.

(based on Stokes, 2004: 19)

The above manifestations of grief are particularly susceptible to parent/guardian's and significant others' projections and attitudes. As a team we are mindful of the primary clinical objectives identified by Winston's Wish and allow these objectives to inform our work:

126

1. *Support, information and education:* supporting the children, young people and families to understand death. We provide written information, face-to-face sessions, school work, consultancy and telephone assistance.

2. *Understanding and expressing grief:* encouraging the sharing of feelings and ways of coping. As a team we encourage the family to do this, and we facilitate both individually and with the whole family.

3. *Remembering:* talking about the person who has died. We offer a space to do this; we do special memory jars and boxes where the young person can store special memories.

4. *Communication:* encouraging all to talk openly: support and encourage the young person to do this one-to-one and if needed with their family/guardians.

5. *Meeting Others:* providing opportunities to meet other children, young people and families in a similar position. We facilitate, when numbers dictate, bereavement groups especially for children and young people.
(based on Stokes 2004: 33)

INVOLVING PARENTS AND GUARDIANS

The team has recognised that it does not provide the most effective service unless the parents or guardians are willing to be part of the therapeutic process. If the significant adults in each child's life will engage in the therapy we offer, our statistics show it to be more 'potent' or successful.

Parents must be offered a safe space in which to be able to hear their children's thoughts and feelings. The role of therapy and an explanation of 'how it works' must be clearly spelt out to all family members. The therapist must be able to offer and maintain respect for each individual and uphold each participant's dignity, so when critical moments arise movement can occur for all concerned.

I have found that when the parents/guardians are grieving they are often under the misguided impression that their children will somehow mirror/copy their grieving process and undertake the same coping mechanisms. Clearly this does not happen and sadly it can require therapy to illustrate this.

Below is a vignette which may help the reader understand my belief in encouraging other family members to participate in therapy to support the young person who is struggling with their grief.

THE WINE BOTTLE UNDER THE DECKING
A fourteen-year-old girl, Megan, referred herself to the team to talk about losing her mum to breast cancer three years previously. During the first session it became clear that there were issues at home around her dad's remarriage to her mum's closest friend. My client found this new set of circumstances unbearable at times and often felt very alone.

I offered my client a safe space, with her dad and stepmother present, where her voice could be heard. We had three family sessions which were very facilitative, especially to her dad. I believe by using family therapy he was able to empathise with his daughter and understand her pain, loneliness and frustration. In his drive to move on with his life he had somehow left his daughter behind.

In between the initial session with Megan and our first family session there had been a house party. Megan had taken a bottle of wine and hidden it under the decking in the back garden. Later that night she went outside and proceeded to get very drunk 'to block things out'. This incident, along with the therapy, had allowed Megan's dad to see how much she was suffering and just how far she was prepared to go to try and deal with her losses.

WORKING IN A PERSON-CENTRED MANNER

Joseph and Worsley (2005) write that the person-centred perspective to understanding the human condition is radical and revolutionary. It is founded on the premise 'that human beings have an inherent tendency towards growth, development and optimal functioning' (2005: i). This becomes an even more radical and revolutionary understanding when it is applied to children and young people. The idea of trusting in a child or young person to make suitable decisions about their life or even to have an opinion is revolutionary. The person-centred approach to counselling/psychotherapy gives power to the young person to voice their opinions and trusts in their directional capacities and choices. The basis of this approach to psychotherapy is that it is the client/child/young person who best understands their problems and who knows how ultimately to change their situation. The task of the therapist is to create the conditions which can assist this process.

In terms of psychotherapeutic praxis, working in a person-centred way means I seek to provide a space for working and being with a client where they are at the centre of this activity. In a sense then, the client and I mutually *co-create* this relationship. This space is characterised by certain conditions, characteristics and attitudes: empathic understanding and attunement, non-possessive warmth and a non-judgemental attitude, therapist genuineness, trusting in the client as resourceful and tending towards actualisation, therapist presence and attention to power (Rogers, 1957, 1959; Schmid, 2002). The dynamic of power within the therapeutic relationship must be considered, particularly with children and young people, whose perception is that they are the last to be consulted on issues.

I work from a base that is heavily informed by what some would call the 'classical' viewpoint. For a full explanation of this, see Merry (2002), Sanders (2006) and Wilkins (2003). I am also informed by the writings on person-centred theory offered by Schmid (2002, 2006). I am particularly influenced by Schmid's thoughts on psychotherapy as a 'dialogical' relationship. I perceive these two modes of being and understanding 'person-centred' as complementary. More importantly, my practice is based on Rogers (1951,

1957, 1959, 1961) who identified the ingredients that are necessary to provide a climate of trust and therapeutic potency.

When I practise, above all I try and be as non-directive in attitude and being as possible. I attempt to be human and warm, open to the young person, trying to enable them to relax and feel safe. What I have noticed is that to build the bridge of empathy, some talking at the beginning of a meeting is necessary. For example, asking how the week has gone or usually just joining in their banter. When the young person then starts to 'flow' I shut up and listen.

Dave Mearns often makes great sense to me and provides comfort and reassurance with illustrations from his own rich experiences. Here (2006a: 131) he describes a dialogue he had with Carl Rogers regarding a client:

> Rogers: Do you know what you are doing with him [the patient]?
> Mearns: Not a bloody clue, Carl.
> Rogers: That's alright then.

This example illustrates for me the philosophy and practice of the person-centred approach to counselling and therapy. It is not about having a treatment plan or agenda for the client; nor is it is about 'doing' anything 'to' the client. It is, as Mearns went on to explain, '*trying to relate with the client in a way that gives him space enough to do almost anything*' (ibid., my italics). It is about empowerment and genuinely prizing the *whole* person. This is what I attempt to do.

To paraphrase a saying translated from Gaelic which I feel affirms my way of being and working; 'I am drawn to the life the client carries'. For me, the essence of classical person-centred praxis is centred on the belief that I do not know better than the client. The client knows what hurts, what needs fixing, what requires changing and how they can do this. Children and young people have convinced me that this is so. It is, as Mearns suggested, a struggle for integrity and authenticity and of 'showing your work' (Mearns, 2007: 124, 2006a). A person-centred therapeutic relationship is thus necessarily *co*-created (Mearns, 2006b).

My practice may best be illustrated with the following vignettes:

MEETING
Kevin is twelve. His mum died of breast cancer and he has an older sibling with whom he is close. Kevin's father was worried that his son might be showing instances that he was not coping with his mum's death. Kevin had just started high school and there had been a number of incidents when he 'lost his rag quite badly', screaming and shouting at other pupils in response to 'trivial' things, like 'falling out and arguing with a friend over nothing'. I spoke to Kevin on the phone and he was reluctant to meet, however, he knew his dad was worried and agreed to see me, with his dad, 'to see what counselling was like'. On greeting Kevin and his dad for the first session, he was lively and jokey, with a natural curiosity. Kevin asked what music I liked and did I have any children. I replied to both questions. Eventually, after a silence, this happened:

Kevin: *What do you do then?*

Seamus: *I'm a therapist.*

Kevin: *I know, but what do you* do?

Seamus: *I work here at the hospice with children and adults who have had someone close to them die. What I do is I try and listen to how they feel about that and try and help them.*

Kevin: *In what way?*

Seamus: *Lots of ways, I try and listen when they talk. I think I try and help them to talk by giving them the time and the space to do that. I am with them when they are sad [Kevin lets a tear roll down his cheek], just like now, with you.*

Kevin: *But, I don't want to talk about it now.*

Seamus: *You don't want to talk about it right now. That is OK too, Kevin. [Pause, to allow for reflection. After a while I said ...] Look, we can leave it here for now if you like. If you want we can see each other next week and see how it goes.*

Kevin: *Ok, then, I'll see you next week.*

THE DEATH RATTLE

I lifted the phone one morning to a colleague who with great urgency told me I was needed on the inpatient unit. A patient was close to death and her daughter was distraught. (A natural and understandable reaction, I thought.) I proceeded to the patient's room. There I met Jennifer, aged thirteen, with her dad. Jennifer was sitting holding her mum's hand, and the awful sound of 'Cheyne Stoke' breathing resounded within the tiny room. I introduced myself and explained I had come at the nursing staff's request.

Jennifer: *I asked the nurses for you to come ... I'm upset by how my Mum is breathing ... and ... (bursts into tears)*

Seamus: *I can see that you are upset, this is extremely difficult, and it can be very scary (I attempted to reduce my size and meet her at eye level).*

Jennifer: *Why is Mum breathing like this? (through sobs and tears)*

Seamus: *Well, when people get to where your mum is now, their breathing gets very laboured ... very noisy ... she is not in pain with it, but it tells us that she is close to death.*

Jennifer: *I understand ... but I don't like it. This is my Mum. (crying)*

Dad: *We have been through this, I have explained this but maybe she will hear it better from someone else.*

Seamus: *Maybe ... This is very, very difficult for you Jennifer and I know that I am a stranger but I am wondering if you may want a little time out. We can go over to the Family Care Centre (FCC) and maybe have a drink and if you feel like it we can talk.*

Jennifer: *Yes, OK.*

We left the room through the sliding doors and went into the garden. Jennifer was still crying and I felt it was important that she knew she wasn't alone, but I wasn't taking any lead. I followed her as we slowly walked over to the FCC. As we walked I felt that there was a sense of rhythm between us and it was within this rhythm that Jennifer started to talk. Jennifer spoke of her immediate fear of losing her mum and then her fears of what would come in the next few days without her.

Our 'time out' was not more that 15 minutes but it was enough for Jennifer to 'get out' what she couldn't say in front of her parents and it allowed her to return to her mum.

Jennifer's mother died an hour and a half later with Jennifer and her dad present.

GRANDMA'S JUMPER

Nicole, aged thirteen, was referred by her mother. Nicole's grandmother, with whom she had been extremely close, had died six months earlier, after a fight against cancer. The end itself was very sudden.

I found Nicole very articulate and thoughtful. She could clearly explain what she wanted to talk about.

The first issue she wanted to talk about was her guilt. On Nicole's last visit to her grandmother, she had been told to go out and play, which she did. When she returned from play her grandmother had died. Nicole carried a lot of guilt about not being present at the death and needed to talk where she could be heard and not rescued, where she could explain how she felt without any guilt being imposed or anyone trying to 'make it better'.

The second issue was her fear of her own behaviour. For the past six months Nicole had been wearing her grandmother's jumper. It still had the wonderful smell of her grandmother so during her waking hours she wore it and at night she folded it neatly and put it on her pillow. The overwhelming sense I took from our sessions was Nicole's need to have her direct questions answered. 'Do you think I am mad?' 'Is my behaviour a sign of madness?' My response was very honest on both counts: 'No'.

I felt it was important to give a direct answer to Nicole. If I had not responded as I did I believe Nicole would have heard any other reply as a medicalising of her behaviour. We went on to spend time discussing how she missed her grandmother and how the jumper was the only thing Nicole felt she had left, letting go of the jumper had been too much. I believe that by spending time empathising with her loss and really holding and prizing her 'mad' behaviour for what is was—part of her grief—Nicole was able to move on and let go of her guilt and fear.

MEMORY JAR

Gemma was ten years old and was not settling in at school; she was behind in her lessons and was experiencing bullying.

When Gemma was referred by the education psychologist the areas of concern were that she was failing at school and it was felt that she was suffering now from a bereavement that occurred many years past. In fact when Gemma was three her father had been murdered yet Gemma was only told that he 'had died'. The truth came into her reality when she inadvertently discovered information that went into detail surrounding her father's death.

Our work mainly consisted of Gemma struggling to know what was reality and what was fantasy as she was having a lot of dreams that made her question everything surrounding her father. I saw that my role was to provide a space for her to cry and speak of her frustrations. As therapy progressed Gemma felt a need to have something concrete to hold onto, something that connected her to her dad. In the end we decided on creating a memory jar. A memory jar filled with coloured salt. Each colour constitutes a 'memory' that the child or young person holds as special to remind them of the person who has died. To make it we filled a washed-out baby food jar full of salt, poured out the salt and divided it into five equal parts: Gemma had five special memories that she wanted to keep. Each portion of salt had a coloured chalk rubbed into it and each one was poured into the jar. We had a moment of silence as each memory was thought of and placed within the jar. Only Gemma knew what each colour represented. At the end the lid was placed on. I believe that the jar has allowed Gemma to reconnect with her father in a way that is now her reality. The memories in the jar are real to her and that is enough.

In summary I attempt as much as possible to:

- hold a firm belief in the client's capacity to self-actualise and in both the formative and actualising tendencies.
- be a 'journeyman' with the client, not an expert. The client is the expert on their own life and material; I walk with them.
- be caring and to offer non-possessive warmth, to really '*be*' this.
- provide a safe, unique space, free from judgement and agendas, goals or outcomes, which is particularly important for a child or young person.
- stay with the client by careful, deep, attuned empathic reflection.
- check regularly as to my understanding of the client.

THE MEDICALISATION OF BEREAVEMENT AND GRIEF: A PERSON-CENTRED THEORETICAL RESPONSE

The team's work is made difficult by other professionals and families assuming we are the experts, with assured outcomes. Often I feel 'set up' as the expert—the scapegoat. Working with children is difficult and, at times, 'dangerous', because as professionals we want to get it right, we do not want to make it worse. But ultimately, it is difficult because adults get in the way—if we really trusted children and young people things would be different. I really believe that. Reflecting on this chapter I am convinced that professionals and the public feel that bereavement and grief are professional issues, which can be solved only by specialist help. Bereavement, grief and loss are becoming steadily medicalised and professionalised, steadily more 'complicated' or 'pathological'. The medical model is so ingrained in our society that, for many, it has become the only parameter within which to think. However, clinical supervision and comradeship, both vital, keep me potent and vibrant.

Maybe it is time to explore and to formulate more fully a person-centred understanding of bereavement and loss: an approach which does not pathologise. There are problems with the whole notion of psychopathology and its related concepts from a person-centred perspective (Sanders, 2006: 47). In the *Diagnostic and Statistical Manual of Mental Disorders-IV (DSM-IV)*, the manual of psychiatry and psychology (American Psychiatric Association, 1994), there is no entry for simple grief. 'Simple' or uncomplicated grief is considered routine and workable. Clients are not considered at risk of sliding into serious mental health problems. In *DSM-IV*, complex, complicated or 'pathological' grief is considered under post-traumatic stress. If clients do show signs of 'complex' grief professionals become concerned about how to 'deal' with the client. Assistance is usually based on a medical model of intervention. Something in the organism is broken, the expert fixes it.

Mander (2005), writing from a psychodynamic perspective, is a typical example of how counsellors and psychotherapists who work from a 'deficiency'-based model might work or 'treat' loss and bereavement issues. Bereavement and loss issues are viewed as atypical, derangement, a mental illness or reality avoidance. Within a person-centred model, it is entirely the opposite. The experiences of grief, loss and bereavement are natural, scary, difficult and life-defining. Fear and devastation can be worked through and the therapy need not be an endlessly protracted affair.

Person-centred counselling and psychotherapy offer a way of thinking about all bereavement and loss as part of a process. Perhaps the actualisation process is interrupted, or a stalling in living, a 'freeze-frame effect' takes place. Our modality is about trusting the client's resources, ultimately, yet also being available, willing and able to provide supportive relationships to children, young people and their families.

Jürgen Kirz's (2006) work on self-actualisation may hold one way forward. A 'psychopathology' based on actualisation/self-actualisation is not labelling, it is based in potentiality and is hopeful, holistic, natural and dynamic. The client is met not as an engine to be fixed but as a complex, intricate and self-regulating organism who is ready to relate and explore if the conditions are favourable. The client self-heals in response to a warm, empathic and non-judgemental human relationship. The organism is made for self-healing; it is an inborn trait to self-regulate and to give meaning to our experiences. Another aspect is the individual and collective construction of meaning regarding loss and bereavement. The person-centred practitioner takes his lead from the client as it is their meanings and understandings that are important, not the therapist's. Finally, a person-centred approach takes as its beginning the 'person' of the client—so rather than fit the client into a preconceived model or theory, the practitioner takes as their starting point the phenomenal world of the client, what it is they are thinking, feeling, experiencing and how they respond to these stimuli. The client's distress is thus not medicalised.

The relevance of this to work with bereavement and loss and young people is that within the therapy relationship the young person leads and takes control. This is contrary to the philosophy prevailing in schools and society in general—that the young are wayward, feckless and need to be controlled. However, the therapist trusts that the young person can work through their issues in a safe manner. The therapist *trusts* the young person. This, then, does call into question the 'professional assessment'. If the young person does not want to come to therapy, they can make their own choice. This will threaten parents who are concerned that their child is not 'getting better' or who think that 'they need professional help, now!'

CONCLUSION

Children and young people are the 'forgotten mourners' according to Smith (1995). I keep this in mind when I practise. In summary, I feel that the following are important for me in my work with grieving children and young people:

- Listening.
- Honouring childhood and young adulthood by providing support, encouragement, non-judgemental caring and love.
- Empowering children and young people by hearing their voices and acknowledging what they say and considering strategies *with them.*
- Having the support of parents and guardians.

Mallon writes that 'making sense of the loss is the task the child (or young person) must face at whatever age they experience it' (1998: 43). I can journey with them, on their terms. I can facilitate this journey in a humane manner or I can pathologise and label this exploration. The choice is mine.

I wish to acknowledge the support and encouragement of my line manager and colleagues in assisting me with this chapter. To all the clients who brought their pain and allowed me to be with them on their journey, I am a better therapist for encountering you. Also to Rebecca. Thank you all.

REFERENCES

American Psychiatric Association (1994) *Diagnostic and Statistical Manual of Mental Disorders* (4th edn). Washington, DC: American Psychiatric Association.
Bowlby, J (1980) *Attachment and Loss, Vol 3: Loss, sadness and depression.* London: Hogarth Press.
Freud, S (1917/2005) *Mourning and Melancholia.* London: Penguin.
Joseph, S & Worsley, R (2005) *Person-Centred Psychopathology: A positive psychology of mental health.* Ross-on-Wye: PCCS Books.
Kriz, J (2006) *Self-actualisation.* Herstellung und Verlag: Norderstedt.
Kübler-Ross, E (1970) *On Death and Dying.* London: Tavistock Publications.
Mallon, B (1998) *Helping Children to Manage Loss.* London: Jessica Kingsley.
Mander, G (2005) Bereavement talk. *Therapy Today,* November, *16* (9), 42–5.

Mearns, D (2006a) Psychotherapy: The politics of liberation or collaboration? A career critically reviewed. In G Proctor, M Cooper, P Sanders & B Malcolm (Eds) *Politicizing the Person-Centred Approach: An agenda for social change* (pp. 127–42). Ross-on-Wye: PCCS Books.

Mearns, D (2006b) Being-with and being-counter: Relational depth: The challenge of fully meeting the client. *Person Centered and Experiential Psychotherapies, 5* (4), 255–65.

Mearns, D (2007) *Working at Relational Depth in Counselling and Psychotherapy.* London: Sage.

Merry, T (2002) *Learning and Being in Person-Centred Counselling.* Ross-on-Wye: PCCS Books.

Parkes, CM (1972) *Bereavement: Studies of grief in adult life.* London: Pelican.

Rogers, CR (1951) *Client-Centered Therapy.* London: Constable.

Rogers, CR (1957) The necessary and sufficient conditions of therapeutic personality change. *Journal of Consulting Psychology, 21,* 95–103.

Rogers, CR (1959) A theory of therapy, personality and interpersonal relationships, as developed in the client-centred framework. In S Koch (Ed) *Psychology: A study of science. Vol 3: Formulations of the person and the social context* (pp. 184–256). New York: McGraw-Hill.

Rogers, CR (1961) *On Becoming a Person.* London: Constable.

Sanders, P (2006) *The Person-Centred Counselling Primer.* Ross-on-Wye: PCCS Books.

Schmid, PF (2002) *The characteristics of a person-centered approach to therapy and counseling: Criteria for identity and coherence.* Carl Rogers Symposium, University of California, San Diego, La Jolla, CA, 27th July, 2002.

Schmid, PF (2006) The challenge of the Other: Towards dialogical person-centered psychotherapy and counseling. *Person-Centered and Experiential Psychotherapies, Special Issue 5* (4) 240–54.

Smith, S (1995) *The Forgotten Mourners: Guidelines for working with bereaved children.* London: Jessica Kingsley.

Stokes, JA (2004) *Then, Now and Always: Supporting children as they journey through grief: A guide for practitioners.* Cheltenham: Winston's Wish.

Strobe, MS & Schut, H (1999) The dual process model of coping with bereavement: Rationale and description. *Death Studies, 23,* 197–224.

Worden, W (1983) *Grief Counselling and Grief Therapy* London: Tavistock Publications.

Chapter 15

THE WISDOM OF LITTLE PEOPLE
A REFLECTION ON FORTY YEARS
OF PERSONAL AND
PROFESSIONAL LEARNING

Sheila C. Youngson

I want to be clear from the start about why I have chosen to use the words 'little people' instead of the more familiar 'children and young people', despite knowing that this could be provocative or misunderstood by some readers. For me it is a political statement, and by drawing attention to the language that we use I make some attempt to redress the power imbalances so often inherent in how we think and talk about little people. Too often in my professional life I have experienced little people being ignored, disenfranchised, disempowered, and oppressed, often by the very organisations, services and systems that purport to be offering support and protection and care. In these contexts the words 'child', 'childish', and 'childlike' are used in a denigratory sense. I use the word 'people' to emphasise and underline that little people have equal rights as individuals in this world. The word 'little' describes only the number of years they have lived, not their experiences which, in many cases, are immense. My clients know that I refer to them as little people, and they say this makes them feel respected.

I hold the fundamental belief that the best teachers in my professional life have been little people, and their families/carers. They will always know themselves better than I. What I can and do offer is who I am, my willingness to be of help, and what I know.

Intertwined with my fundamental belief in the wisdom of little people there is a second fundamental belief: that the person-centred approach works. For nearly twenty years I have been a person-centred companion to little people as they struggle to make sense of their experiences and their lives. They say they have been listened to, and understood, and helped to get on with what they need to do.

These fundamental beliefs have taken shape and hold over many years, and it is that journey, from then to now, that I wish to share here: the why and how I have come to be a person-centred therapist, primarily with little people, and what they have taught me. This is a personal story, and not meant to be an elaborated synthesis of theory and practice. I have included moments from these forty years that may seem odd or even out of place, but they came to mind in the reflective process and are about me, and who I am. Moments of closeness to others; moments of laughter; moments of recognising the surreal that is frequently embedded in organisational structures; times of pain and upset; times when I recognised the personal journey before me. In a chapter of this length there is only space to describe critical moments, and snapshots from those forty years. I hope the reader can make the links and follow the road.

SHEILA C. YOUNGSON

I begin with memories of the time I spent in an orthopaedic hospital when I was a little person, following a sporting accident, because that seems to me to be the time when I first came to realise that others lived in different contexts, and ways, and relationships, and I had some choice in how I decided to live my life.

AN EVENING IN A HOSPITAL WARD

A moment in time, nearly forty years ago, and yet still tangible, available to my senses and memory, particularly if it is dark outside and I sit, as now, in a pool of diffuse light. (Reminiscent of old black and white movies, and starched uniforms and huge, and surely impractical headgear.) The ward was a large square space, open plan, with four rows of seven beds, all occupied by female little people. A converted sanatorium, with large glass windows, and a wall of glass doors out to a large paved area. At night, across the expanse of lawn, lights from the houses opposite could be seen. I had a classmate who lived over there, and I watched for her, going to and from school. During the day, this place was busy with activity and talk. I remember efficiency, usually accompanied by kindness. Camaraderie and dark humour from adolescent patients. It was difficult to engage in rebellion as our age would dictate we should, when encased in plaster, or attached to metal frames, but I remember our attempts. There was a daily ward round made by the Matron, preceded by a flurry of anxious nurse activity. All pillows had their open ends facing away from the door, and all bed wheels placed precisely in line. As we saw the Matron arrive in the nurses' station we would reverse our pillows and use our crutches to knock each other's wheels out of line.

At night it was never completely dark. Light could be seen through the portholes in the large double doors that led out to the long corridor. The nurses' station was outside these double doors, but had a sizeable glass window that looked into the ward, though screened at night. Faint light from that window gave hint to a reassuring presence through the long hours. It could be lonely then. Even with the sounds of others: creaks from bed springs, the rustle of plastic mattress covers, the stifled moan or whimper (stoicism was a requirement of acceptance and belonging). The unique sound and smell and taste and touch of such institutions—the startle squeak of patient trolleys, the nasal sting of antiseptic, the metallic tongue of medication, the restrictive entombment of limb or body, the faint and dissolving scent of the last meal cart.

One evening. Two days after my third and particularly painful surgery. My parents had visited and returned home to look after my brother. I was weary, so weary. The father of a girl in a bed opposite rose, picked up his chair, and came and sat beside me. He said nothing, and asked for nothing from me. He gave me companionship for a while, freely, unconditionally. Looking back, it was a most remarkable and extraordinary empathic understanding. He was close, but separate; very present but not intrusive; parent-like, but not usurping my father's role. It was absolutely right. After a while, he stood up, gave me a nod, and went back to his daughter.

137

Looking back over the years, and at the months I spent in hospital in my adolescence, I know that I gained much from my experience. I mean this, not in a 'must positively reframe this time' sense, but in reality, despite the pain, the fear, the uncertainty. I learnt how sheltered and narrow and privileged my life was. I witnessed an extraordinary range and variety of human experience and relationships, and how those relationships could be differently expressed. Perhaps most importantly of all, I began to learn that, despite the requirement of stoicism and the legacy of repressed Scottish Presbyterianism, my emotional life had a validity and a right to expression, and could be seen and understood by others. It would take many more years until that could be seen and understood and validated by me.

That was then, when I was a little person aged thirteen, July 1967.

ABERDEEN, GLASGOW, LONDON AND EDINBURGH

At eighteen I went to Aberdeen and completed a university degree in psychology. I lived in a hall of residence, then in a shared flat, then in a wonderful, rambling farmhouse some miles north of the city, overlooking the sea. I was there during that hottest and longest summer of 1976. It was a great time, experiencing communal living at its best, with four others. Those others had a much clearer understanding of the socio-political context of our lives, and three had lived and worked in a radical arts and education collective in Liverpool. In holidays and weekends I worked with them on inventive and startling (to me) play schemes for city children. I have a photograph of myself splattered with paint, wearing a hard hat, standing beside a large inflatable we had just built. I also remember a slightly fraught moment when we needed to get inside the nearly finished inflatable to re-do some internal roping, and the two of us on the outside, monitoring the air flow, realised that our friends, working in an enclosed space with industrial strength glue and electric drills, were becoming a little uncoordinated and overly amused.

From there, I worked for the next two years as a residential social worker, with young people who had committed offences or were deemed to be 'out of control' (whatever that means) in Glasgow, in a List-D school; and then in the east end of London, in an Assessment Centre. By the time I was twenty-five, I had moved far from my conservative upper-middle-class beliefs and politics, partly because of the people I had lived and worked with, but mostly because of the life stories I had been told by many little and bigger people, and the places they had shown me, and the experiences and feelings they had endured, and had the courage to share. Stories often told with considerable humour, sometimes of course as a defence against pain, but sometimes also as a chosen way of being in desperate times and places. The resilience of little people struck me then, and has remained with me to this day.

My beliefs and politics may have changed, but I was also aware that my privileged upbringing would always be part of me, both in terms of some seemingly 'in-built' attitudes, assumptions, and prejudices that I struggled, and struggle, to notice and question, and in terms of the education and resources, material and financial, that were available to me. My upbringing was also my history and remains embodied in my relationships with my family. Thus a perpetual struggle towards reaching some understanding and acceptance of who I was.

Where was I to go next professionally? Despite my personal learnings and development, I know (now) that I still had an arrogance and a degree of omnipotence. I thought I wanted to have more influence and flexibility (for whose benefit? is the real question) in my work, and thus I embarked on a self-funded postgraduate degree in clinical psychology at Edinburgh University. The choice of Edinburgh was a wise one as the course did not interview (it allocated places based on application forms) and therefore did not know how little I actually knew about clinical psychology, the profession I was about to enter.

A MAN WHO FOUND LOVE

Clinical psychology training in the late seventies/early eighties taught me a range of techniques, more or less broadly designed to effect behaviour change. These were done *to* people at worst, and *with* people, at best. There was very little emphasis on how *to be with* people, although I did not know that this was to be important to me at the time, or indeed for some time after.

My first job, post-qualification, was split. I worked in a large institution (several hundred residents) with both little and adult people with a learning disability, and in an adolescent mental health unit. My learning that I wish to highlight here took place in the former setting and involved an adult client.

I was called to one of the villas in the extensive grounds of the institution. ('Villa'— how we use language to pretend, to mask.) The staff were concerned about a resident, a man called John,[1] who had stopped caring for himself. He would not wash nor change his clothes. He would not communicate with anyone. He would hit himself in the face with his fists, and hit out at others if they tried to intervene, or communicate with him. I visited the villa, and observed the situation for a number of hours. The staff (and I) expected that I would devise a suitable behavioural programme for the staff to implement. It happened then that I had a three-week holiday from work. On my return, I revisited the villa to be told that John was a changed man. He was now taking great care of his appearance, had stopped hitting himself, and was more approachable and communicative. What had happened to promote this considerable change? He had fallen in love with a resident in another villa.

Somewhere deep inside of me I knew this was a critical learning point. However at that time the staff had moved on to new and different worries. And so I simply moved with the staff into discussions over the rights of people with a learning disability to have consensual sexual relationships. Yet I stored in my inner archives the realisation that the

---

1. In this chapter all client names have been changed and all potentially identifying characteristics altered.

one factor that moved a man from isolating despair and the wish to literally knock himself out was a meaningful and mutual relationship with another human being. A relationship where he loved, and was loved in return, where he was considered special and important, where he was seen and accepted for who he was. I acknowledged this on an academic 'head' level, and shrank away from the wider ramifications, that had to include a feeling-level realisation that the institution, the staff, and myself were not offering even a basic human and individual contact to John. We were in the business of containing, not relating.

My underlying critical comment here concerns how people with learning disabilities are treated generally within our society, and my avoidance. It would be inappropriate to be critical of staff teams in a situation where two staff members, one with no training, have responsibility for thirty-five residents. During the time I worked at that institution the nursing staff went on strike to complain about terms and conditions. It was agreed that villas had to have the minimal nursing cover during the strike period. The minimal standard was more than had been on any villa for years.

ON LEARNING FROM BEING HIT BY PLAYDOH

Four years later found me in a seaside town working in a child and adolescent multi-disciplinary mental health team. Here I met Rachel, aged five, who is directly responsible for my becoming a person-centred therapist, and hopefully, more of a person-centred person. Rachel will now be in her twenties—it would be good to be able to thank her for making my professional and personal life so much the richer.

Rachel had had the toughest time. One day she was left in the company of her beloved elder sister while the rest of the family went elsewhere for the day. Sometime during that day Rachel's sister collapsed and died, and Rachel was on her own with her sister for a number of hours. Rachel's family found the death of their daughter literally intolerable, and did not speak of her, whilst acting as if she was still alive and would return home at any minute. Faced with this silence Rachel too was silenced, and communicated her distress through pulling out her hair. Colleagues in the team began work with the family, and I offered Rachel time in the playroom with me.

On first meeting with Rachel I was struck by the self-containment of this solemn little person, with luxurious dark hair and many bald patches. On the day of our first session, she silently followed behind me as we climbed the stairs to the playroom, and stood in the centre of the room looking at the floor. When I had been told Rachel's story by the team's social worker, I had been very moved by the tale, and had thought hard about how to help. Now, I gently told Rachel what I knew about her circumstances and expressed my willingness to be of help. She looked at me briefly. I said that I guessed it might be very difficult to talk, and that therefore I had brought out from the cupboards various toys and paints and paper that she could use. She glanced briefly round the room. I moved towards the table where I had laid out the toys. Rachel picked up a tub of playdoh near her, and slowly climbed halfway up a small climbing frame. She opened the tub and fashioned a number of little balls of playdoh, and looked a me. I was at a bit of a loss, and after a few moments, I again talked about how the toys and art might be used. Rachel gently lobbed a ball of playdoh at me. Still at a loss, I picked up a puppet, and began to have a conversation with it, about being in the room with Rachel and wanting to help her. Rachel came down from the frame and sat opposite me at the table. She began to explore the toys, in silence. She appeared to be beginning to enact a story with some small figures. I made some guesses as to what might be going on. Rachel went back to the climbing frame, and threw another playdoh ball at me.

For a number of weekly sessions I (not we) struggled in this way, and I felt stuck. In the end, feeling helpless and of no help, I stopped trying to direct activity, acknowledging to myself that then this would mean that no work could be done. How very, very omnipotent that now sounds. Gradually Rachel moved into the space I had, at last, vacated, and began to use her choice of toys to tell her story and express her feelings. Slowly, I learnt to follow and not to lead. Sometimes I would step in with a question, or an interpretation, or link what she was doing to her own story, and each time she would return to the frame and throw the playdoh balls. For many weeks she would come in and make the playdoh balls first, and leave them on the frame, just in case. When she was finally convinced that I had understood her silent, but very active and powerful message (what extraordinary patience this little person had with such an obtuse grown-up), she pointedly put the tub of playdoh back on the shelf.

We worked together for about eight months. Rachel began to speak and to talk about her story, but mostly she used just one toy, a spaceship, and wove all her feelings into life on board. Slowly adventures into the known and the unknown became less unpredictable and less hazardous and dangerous. Fun and laughter began also to happen on board, and finally the spaceship turned for home. Rachel's hair grew back, and I heard the first of her very infectious giggles. At our last meeting, she had a sweatshirt printed with a message for me, which was very funny. I burst into laughter when I walked into the waiting room, and Rachel looked very pleased as well as knowledgeable. As she left the playroom for the last time, I said 'this is for you', and gave her a tub of playdoh. She gave me the last of her direct looks, and giggled. I watched from a window, a smile on my face and tears in my eyes, as she skipped and hopped down the path, holding her mother's hand.

Rachel taught me one of the most important lessons of my professional life. To know and to trust that little people will know what they need, and how to heal; to believe in their wisdom. And perhaps, if there is a clear and experienced sense that the therapist wants to understand and be of help, then little people will wait till we catch on and catch up.

I reflected a good deal on my work with Rachel, and what it meant in terms of my training and perceived role. I talked with colleagues, one of whom mentioned person-centred play therapy. I found a weekend introductory course in Newcastle, and went. Almost as soon as the day started I knew I had found my professional home. I enrolled on a diploma course in child-centred therapy. The politics and philosophy of the theory and practice 'fitted' with what I believed, although there was much to learn (and unlearn).

Here was an approach that addressed power issues, that was truly collaborative, and more. An approach that held that my clients were the experts in terms of making sense of their experiences and finding a path towards healing, and that this was true even when past relationshps and experiences had left them separated from their feelings, their selves. My task was to offer myself, to provide a real relationship that might provide an alternative experience. Here was a way I could be, without role and pretence. Here was the way I could be, in deep and meaningful and respectful contact with others, and be myself. It wasn't an easy way to be, but it felt real, it felt genuine. It still does.

SOME CHALLENGING YEARS AND
A NEED TO STOP FOR A WHILE

I moved inland and joined another child and adolescent mental health team at its inception. I remained there for the next twelve years. This was the time that the extent of child sexual abuse, often within the family, became known, and more and more little people who had experienced all forms of abuse were referred to the service. It seemed to me that the person-centred approach was the only appropriate way to work with these little and bigger people, through play therapy and counselling. Their bodies were traumatised; their minds confused; their feelings shattered and scattered; their wills ignored or subtly manipulated and corrupted. In attempting to offer therapeutic help I believed we must not recreate any sense that grown-ups would direct, dictate, decide, dismiss—as much power, control, choice, and self-determination needed to be given back. And so I spent increasing amounts of my time bearing the unbearable alongside these little people.

As the years went by, we also became involved in situations where the child abuse had been organised on a large scale, and in a few instances also involved ritual and satanic elements. My role expanded to include supervision of others, consultancy, teaching and training, and appearing as an expert witness in court. These were challenging times, and I was ever more grateful that I now had a way of being with little people in their deepest distress and anguish that was both validating and ultimately healing for them.

What I did not do was take care of myself. The person-centred approach requires me to be fully present in my encounters, to offer empathic following, to be open to experiencing. I heard too much horror, too many details of abuses, supported too many other professionals. The metaphor is that I forgot to remain on the bank, as close as possible to people in the swamp and reaching out, and instead I fell in. My vision narrowed, the darkness threatened to encompass me. I found the world unsafe, unpredictable, and potentially malign. Although the parallel to the experience of abused little people does not escape me now, I ignored it then. My body dictated that I stop, and after some minor surgery, I simply did not recover and was away from work for nine months. I could not recover until I looked inward. I found a good psychotherapist and together over a number of years, we helped me reconnect to a long suppressed little self. During this time I had an astonishing, somewhat spiritual experience of going back to the hospital where I had spent much of my adolescence, and finding, outside the operating theatres, a thirteen-year-old little me, lonely and cross at being left for so long. I came away with her inside again. I found a good homeopath and got back on my feet.

However, I knew that I needed to change direction, and take my now person-centred soul into new areas. I felt I had to leave a marker of where I had been before I could move on. Hopefully not in an arrogant or egotistical sense, but rather as self and other validation of the stresses of the work, and to register what I had learnt about supporting and encouraging coping and resilience in the workers. So I wrote and published just that, and then found I could look up and look forward and look ahead.

NEW DIRECTIONS

I went in three new directions, and as I write this, continue in all three. Firstly, I became a clinical tutor on a university clinical psychology training course, for three days each week. I had provided teaching sessions and clinical placements to the course for over ten years, and enjoyed the mutual benefit that came from working with people who knew more up-to-date academic psychology but had less experience of applying such knowledge. I also felt that there should be more emphasis on personal and professional development in clinical training, and the course was keen to promote that. Based on my personal experience, I wanted to help those starting out in the profession think about how they might take care of themselves. Finally, of course, I wanted to bring person-centred ideas and ways of working into clinical psychology training. The last ten, nearly eleven, years in this context have been good ones. There is mutual liking and respect in the core staff team, and acceptance of differing approaches and emphases to our work. There is a significant level of expertise, and no arrogant posturing. There is considerable humour. Personal and professional development is now one of the three core themes; and trainees leave the course with at least a rudimentary understanding of the theory and practice of the person-centred approach, and having had some of their misperceptions (was it ever thus?) of person-centred work challenged.

The second and third new directions involved my joining a department of clinical and health psychologists in a large acute hospital setting. In the first of these I took on the role of coordinator of supervision with the invitation to develop and expand the remit. With the profession finally stating that supervision was mandatory, this was an interesting challenge. I completed a diploma in person-centred case-work supervision over a year, which gave me space to think about and explore theory, practice, models, settings, content and process, and so on. This diploma course also gave me the invaluable experience of working with and learning from a cohort of people who were not clinical psychologists, and where there was a range of difference and diversity (in terms of age, gender, ethnicity, disability, class, and sexuality) that is rarely encountered in clinical psychology settings. I rewrote the department's supervision policy, and began to develop ways of organising, reviewing, monitoring, and evaluating the supervisory needs and requirements of the thirty-five clinical and health psychologists and counsellors employed by the Trust. This has given me the continuing experience of talking with a whole range of people at different stages of their careers, with a wealth of knowledge and experience. I have learnt and continue to learn about the broad sweep of clinical psychology involvement in a physical health setting: from individual work with patients (sic) and families; developing psychological knowledge and thinking in medical teams; teaching and training; supervision of other professionals; the usefulness of clinically relevant research that directly feeds back to teams and services and influences policy; the relevance of developing psycho-educational resources; and the efficacy of preventative measures and strategies that may mitigate against the emotional and psychosocial consequences of illness.

Writing that list, it's almost as if I have finally brought together my person-centred being and the best of clinical psychology, and found that not only can they co-exist, they can work together. I am pleased and surprised by this. For years it has felt that I was out on a limb, far from the main trunk, following the person-centred approach within a profession that promotes models that have the psychological therapist as agent and expert (e.g. cognitive behavioural, psychodynamic, solution focused, cognitive analytic therapies). These days clinical psychology training is beginning to re-emphasise the importance, but not centrality, of the therapeutic relationship, and collaborative inquiry; however core competencies continue to stress the development of skills in assessment, formulation, and the use of multiple techniques.

For me, I continue to be classically person-centred in my relationships with little and bigger people and their families and carers, and with my colleagues in supervision. I also recognise that I have other skills that are useful, and can be delivered within a person-centred framework that respects and values others, wants to hear and respond to the experience of others, wants to learn from others, and wants to share what is known. Two immediate examples are conducting qualitative research that involves talking with little people and their families/carers about their experience of being involved in treatment decisions; and working within a systemic model to further understand the complex team dynamics.

RELATING WITHIN A BUBBLE

My third and final new direction was to work with one paediatric medical team who cared for little people with a specific chronic illness, requiring many hospitalisations, surgery, invasive treatments, organ transplantation, and huge psychological adjustments to a life-threatening and life-limiting illness. In this context I frequently need to be with little people in medical settings. They can be in bed, attached to machines, about to see a doctor in an outpatient clinic. Gone is the fifty- or sixty-minute session time, gone is the regular weekly session, gone is the planned-ahead day, gone is the environment I can create, gone is the knowledge that we won't be interrupted, gone is confidentiality as many conversations or interactions are witnessed and overheard by others. There are further differences, contrasting to my previous years in a mental health setting. Here my colleagues in a medical setting do not have an extended training in aspects of psychological health, and therefore there is less of a shared language and understanding. This is not to say there is not a shared purpose.

My perception is that in this setting distress is not so easily accepted, be it our distress or that of our clients. An 'upbeat' atmosphere is the pervading culture, partly I think in response to our own, largely unacknowledged, sense of failure as we cannot cure this condition, we can only slow it down. Distress, despair, anguish must therefore be overridden, sidelined, hidden or short-lived, or we face our own impotence and mortality. When I first joined the team seven years ago, I think it was hoped that I would remove the distress, literally by taking the person away and bringing back a composed individual. Sometimes, of course, it is appropriate to find a quiet space and time to talk, to be, and that is what is wanted. However, it is also important to hold the belief in holistic care and understanding, where one's feelings and thoughts about being ill, or working with ill people, are heard, accepted, valued, respected. Where feelings and thoughts are part of what we do, who we are. Thus, I go to the outpatient clinic, or the ward, along with my colleagues, and our clients see the doctor, the nurse, the social worker, the dietician, the psychologist. This also seems to act against the sometimes perceived stigma of being seen by the psychologist with the implicit suggestion that someone 'is not coping'.

When I am on my own with a little person and we cannot have a private space, then we seem to be able to create a kind of bubble around us both, in which it seems only we exist, however briefly. I have pondered about how we create this. It is something about being and behaving differently to those around us, and this separates us. Around us there is bustle, busyness, noise. People are multitasking, having to react quickly, being called away. Doctors and nurses have to ask direct questions, elicit symptoms, make speedy physical interventions, request quick decisions. Frequently it seems they do not have enough time to do all that is needed. A little person and I are together in a different way. We talk quietly, and allow silences. We are calm, usually. We focus only on each other and what is happening between us. We ignore interruptions whilst letting them happen; thus we pause when the nurse comes to make a change to a machine, hold each other's gaze, and continue when she is gone. We have time, and there is no pressure. We want to be with each other, and my only aim is to hear and understand the world of the person with me.

Sometimes it feels that the little person has less time. There is a need and an imperative to talk and talk now. He or she has often been precipitated from being well, or feeling relatively well, to being diagnosed with a serious and chronic and life-changing illness. Often, after a brief acquaintance, and sometimes no prior meeting, we can be talking about deep and deeply felt feelings, including fears of death and dying, within a matter of minutes. It is almost as if my little clients recognise that they need help to touch and hold their feelings about all that is happening to them, in case those feelings get lost in the medical whirl and swirl. I am struck again by the courage and resilience of little people, and how helpful it is to a little person when an adult can hear the fears, the anger, the hopelessness, the uncertainty, the loneliness, the sadness, the loss, and join them in the darkest of places, have those hugest of conversations about life and death, and not be overwhelmed. They watch to see if I can manage, and move to a deeper level when they see that I can. I think and feel that it is not so lonely then, and there can be hope that this altered life can be accepted or accommodated, and sometimes a new perspective developed.

ANOTHER EVENING IN A HOSPITAL WARD

A few months ago a message came through from the ward—Akashi wanted to talk with me. I had briefly met with him, aged sixteen, some months before when I had introduced myself to him and his family and explained my role within the team. I went to the ward that evening. Akashi was in a single room, lit only by the bedside light. He wanted to talk about how it would be to die. Something he was facing as treatment options ran out. We talked together for about an hour. When I left the building, I stopped outside, leaned against a wall, and looked up at the towering building I had just left, and thought about what had happened. I was not tearful, although I could have been. I have written about the cost of this work, but that is not what I felt at that moment. When talking about the work that I do, I have said that often I feel privileged and humbled, but that was not what I felt either. I felt moved in the most powerful way, but not distressed. I felt that I had experienced the deepest and most profound sense of connection to another human being. Death, that great taboo, had been looked at, explored, and had lost its fearful hold, at least for a while. Life was likewise considered and evaluated, and what life might still give, and what suffering life might entail, was also given a voice. And all with such honesty, such clarity, such intrinsic courage. Such wisdom.

This is now, when I am an adult aged fifty-two, April 2007.

CONTRIBUTORS

Lisa Anthony
Lisa lives with her partner, daughter and interesting collection of pets in Stourbridge in the West Midlands. When not working as a person-centred counsellor, supervisor and trainer she is likely to be avoiding housework, drinking tea or singing in her local community choir. She is optimistic about life, people and relationships and is seldom disappointed.

Gill Clarke
I work as a person-centred therapist and supervisor in Manchester working with children and young people. I am married and have a disgracefully naughty cat! My life is filled with people and relationships that contribute to who I am and how I live my life. I love nothing more than to cook vast quantities of food and share this with family and friends.

Ashley Fletcher
Ashley has spent 20 years working in the NHS and Voluntary Sector managing community-based services, particularly around HIV, with gay and lesbian communities, and with refugees and asylum seekers. He has been a gay community and liberationist activist for over 25 years. He is currently Co-Director of Essence Counselling Collective (www.essencecounselling.org), a freelance person-centred counselling practice and training consultancy. He has been community trainer for 20 years and a qualified practicing psychotherapist since 2003. Ashley is also a member of the Directory of Pink Therapists.

Sue Hawkins
I currently work as an Educational Psychologist in Stockport, Cheshire and have a small therapy practice in South Manchester. I originally trained as a teacher and person-centred therapist and then went on to train and supervise other therapists. Despite experiencing something of a 'culture shock' in becoming a psychologist, I remain firmly rooted in the person-centred approach and challenging the medical model. More recently I have become interested in systems work and how the person-centred model can offer a challenge to the systems (school, family, work, etc.) that oppress people.

Richard House

Richard is Senior Lecturer in Psychotherapy and Counselling at Roehampton University, an NHS counsellor, a publishing editor, and an early years Steiner teacher. He writes regularly on child care and educational issues for *The Mother*, contributing regularly to a range of peer-reviewed psychotherapeutic journals. With Sue Palmer, he co-orchestrated the open letters on 'toxic childhood' and play to the *Daily Telegraph* in September 2006 and September 2007. His book *Therapy beyond Modernity* was published by Karnac Books in 2003. Correspondence: <richardahouse@hotmail.com>.

Cate Kelly

I worked for over thirty years for local authorities, specialising in adoption. Since 1999 I have worked as a person-centred counsellor in private practice. In March 2007 I obtained an Advanced Diploma in Client-Centred Play Therapy. I offer therapy to children, young people and adults individually or in groups. I am especially interested in the facilitative power of expressive work and the PCA. Married thirty years, I have three adult children and two young grandchildren who are lights in my life.

Suzanne Keys

Suzanne works as a counsellor in a sixth form college. She wrote a chapter with a young man: *Disability, multidimensionality and love: the politics of a counselling relationship in Further Education* in Politicizing the Person-Centred Approach (PCCS Books, 2006). She has published and edited writings on person-centred therapy and love, ethics, politics, prayer, human rights, gender and idiosyncratic practice. She lives in London with her partner and young son and is increasingly interested in taking time to experience different ways of being. She can be contacted by email on: suzanne@abcfilm.clara.co.uk.

Nadine Littledale

I am a person-centred practitioner, psychodramatist, trainer and supervisor. I have worked as a social worker and psychotherapist for 33 years working with children and adults in both government services and private practice. I am currently living in Brisbane, Australia and working in Children and Youth Mental Health Services. Life is offering my daughter and I lots of new opportunities that are both exciting and challenging.

Seamus Nash

I am a psychotherapist within a hospice in West Yorkshire. I am passionate about the person-centred approach, remain optimistic about people, the planet and life. I am currently a doctoral student researching practitioners' meanings of person-centredness at the University of Strathclyde. I believe my practice is informed by being both a father and a partner and that my family, children and young people have taught me much about the core conditions. I am also mad about music and guitars.

Sue Palmer

Sue is well known to teachers around the UK through her many books, TV programmes and presentations on literacy and her articles and columns in the educational press. She has also acted as a consultant to the Basic Skills Agency, the National Literacy Trust, the DfES and the BBC. Since publishing *Toxic Childhood: How modern life is damaging our children … and what we can do about it* in 2006, she has been involved in various campaigns around early years provision, play, and the commercialisation of childhood.

Tracey Walshaw

I am a passionate, idiosyncratic and humanly flawed person-centred practitioner, trainer and artist. Play and creativity are at the centre of my being and practice which is probably why I am so attracted to working with children and young people. As well as being an independent counsellor and supervisor, I am also a Director of PCCS Training Partnership in Manchester. I am currently training to be a sociodramatist which will help me take my person-centredness into the wider social and political context. She can be reached via: traceywalshaw@hotmail.com.

Julie West

Julie is a freelance play therapist and trainer in the North West region. She has worked for 24 years with children, young people and families in the private, voluntary and public sectors. Contributions for this book on Child-Centred Negotiation have come from experience as a Children's Empowerment Officer involving 5–13-year-olds in local decision-making processes. Person-centred training and therapy is central to her approach to work and everyday life.

Jo Woodhouse

Jo has a background in ecology, which she taught for 16 years, before training in counselling. More recently, training in person-centred play therapy has led to her working as a counsellor and play therapist with children in school. She also works as a supervisor and in private practice and is the village caretaker in the place where she lives. She sees her ongoing relationships, including those with natural places, plants and animals, as vital and sustaining for working in the person-centred approach.

Sheila Youngson

What a privilege to be invited to reflect on one's working life, as it nears its end! I thank the Editors for the opportunity. I also want to acknowledge three colleagues who made a significant difference to my journey, coming alongside for parts of the way: Jenni Biancardi, Gabrielle Syme, and Kevin Chandler. I'd be pleased to hear from any reader: <s.c.youngson@leeds.ac.uk>.

INDEX

FACILITATING YOUNG PEOPLE'S DEVELOPMENT

INTERNATIONAL PERSPECTIVES
ON PERSON-CENTRED
THEORY AND PRACTICE

EDITED BY
MICHAEL BEHR &
JEFFREY H.D. CORNELIUS-WHITE

ISBN 978 1 906254 00 1

Facilitating children's and adolescents' growth has been a challenge and major concern for person-centred work since the beginning of the approach in the 1940s. During the past decade, a shift in this domain has generated numerous new concepts, research and practice, making a considerable impact on both the professional tasks and training of educators, counsellors, and psychotherapists.

Fifteen original chapters and a foreword from Brian Thorne describe this development. The chapters reflect international perspectives emerging around the world today. Framed by two chapters from the editors, the book provides a comprehensive overview of state-of-the-art person-centred work with children, adolescents and parents, and identifies emerging themes in the field.

Editors

Michael Behr is Professor of Educational Psychology at the University of Education Schwäbisch Gmünd, Germany. His research topics are person-centred counselling, child and adolescent psychotherapy, young people's emotions, and parent–school relationships. He has authored several books about school development and person-centred work in education.

Jeffrey HD Cornelius-White, Psy.D., LPC is Dean's Fellow for Teaching and Learning, Associate Professor of Counseling, and former Director of School Counseling at Missouri State University. His work mainly concerns person-centred and social justice issues in counseling psychology and education.

Making and Breaking Children's Lives

Edited by Craig Newnes & Nick Radcliffe

ISBN 978 1 898059 70 7

Are we confident that current services to children and families do more good than harm? *Making and Breaking Children's Lives* examines how children are hurt in modern society and how our concept of 'childhood' serves to exclude children from participating meaningfully in decisions about their care. After paying lip-service to the effects of early abandonment and trauma, children's experiences are sanitised through medical diagnoses, and neatly treated with prescription drugs. Nowhere is this more evident than in the current trend to label children with ADHD. The authors' careful and critical examination of ADHD as a diagnosis and the damaging side-effects of drug therapies on developing children make for disturbing reading.

In this excellent book a plurality of voices return to one consistent theme— the importance of psychosocial context, which has become increasingly dismissed as irrelevant in the rush to label and prescribe. The final chapters describe inspiring examples of how services and communities can be developed which give both children and their families a chance to prosper— evidence that there is nothing remotely inevitable about the breaking of children's lives.

Sami Timimi writes:

… what's happening with child mental health services is negative. Perfectly healthy kids are being labelled and medicated and grow up believing there is something very wrong with them, and our professions are silent about this and silent about the adverse social circumstances that often accompany those who end up labelled.

Contents

Gerrilyn Smith, *Construction of Childhood;* Jonathan Calder, *Histories of Child Abuse*; Elina Baker and Craig Newnes, *The Discourse of Responsibility*; Freddy Brown, *ADHD and the Philosophy of Science*; Geraldine Brady, *ADHD Diagnosis and Identity*; Sami Timimi and Nick Radcliffe, *The Rise and Rise of ADHD*; Dorothy Rowe, *ADHD—Adults' fear of frightened children*; Arlene Vetere and Jan Cooper, *The Effects of Domestic Violence*; Grace Jackson, *Cybernetic Children*; Helen Rostill and Helen Myatt, *Constructing Meaning in the Lives of Looked After Children*; Katherine Weare, *The Holistic Approach*; Raj Bandak, *Empowering Vulnerable Children and Families*; Carl Harris, *The Family Well-Being Project*; Bliss W. Browne, *Imagine Chicago: Cultivating hope and imagination.*